Śaku

Acknowledgements

Grateful acknowledgement is made to the University of Chicago Press (Chicago) for permission to include *Ādi Parvan* (Chs. 62-69) from *The Mahābhārata* Vol. I, The Book of the Beginning, trans. by J.A.B. van Buitenen (1973); and to Columbia University Press (New York) for permission to reproduce *Śakuntalā and the Ring of Recollection*, the play by Kalidasa, from Barbara Stoler Miller (ed.) *Theater of Memory* (1984); and to the University of Pennsylvania (Department of Special Collections, Van Pelt Dietrich Library Center) for the Monier-Williams reproductions.

Śakuntalā

Texts, Readings, Histories

Romila Thapar

COLUMBIA UNIVERSITY PRESS

NEW YORK

Columbia University Press
Publishers Since 1893
New York Chichester, West Sussex

Library of Congress Cataloging-in-Publication Data

Thapar, Romila.
Sakuntala : texts, readings, histories / Romila Thapar.
p. cm.
Originally published: New Delhi : Kali for Women, 1999.
Includes bibliographical references.
ISBN 978-0-231-15654-7 (cloth : alk. paper)—ISBN 978-0-231-15655-4 (pbk. : alk. paper)—ISBN 978-0-231-52702-6 (ebook)
1. Kalidasa. Sakuntala. 2. Sakuntala (Hindu mythology) 3. Sakuntala (Hindu mythology) in literature. I. Title.

PK3796.S5T43 2010
891'.22—dc22 2010014597

∞
Columbia University Press books are printed on permanent and durable acid-free paper.
This book is printed on paper with recycled content.

Printed in the United States of America

c 10 9 8 7 6 5 4 3 2 1
p 10 9 8 7 6 5 4 3 2

Contents

Remembering Barbara Stoler Miller

Śakuntalā Patralekhan (Ravi Varma) *Shobha Deepak Singh*

Preface

THE genesis of this lengthy essay lies in a lecture I was asked to give during the tenth anniversary celebrations of the publishing house, Kali for Women, in 1995. Given the occasion, a theme with a gender orientation was thought to be appropriate. I had earlier toyed with a comparison of the two Śakuntalās—that of the epic and that of the Kālidāsa play, but not in any detail. I decided to revive this theme and although the limited comparison of the two texts had been made often enough, I was interested in probing a little further into the texts, as well as bringing into the discussion the commentaries on the theme when the play began to be translated into a wide range of languages in the eighteenth and nineteenth centuries. The attempt here is to see how the theme was treated in different historical periods and why there was this difference.

This became a veritable treasure hunt with pointers which have taken me far from the epic and the play, but which I nevertheless think are relevant. Given the nature of the forms in which these variations were presented, the interface of culture and history inevitably crept in. And so like Alice, it grew and grew and given half a chance it would grow still more. But I have decided to pause at this point. The intention of the essay is not to present a definitive study of the narrative and its treatment, but rather to suggest that when a theme changes in accordance with its location at a historical moment, the change can illumine that moment, and the moment in turn may account for the change. It is not an attempt to include all references to the narrative, only those which I think reflect varying nuances of the interplay between culture and history, underlining the changes in the historical context and the effect of the latter on the former. The essay is largely only in the nature of a comment, first on the variant versions and then on the readings of the Kālidāsa play. Hence the interventions of the translated texts and the statements of those who gave the story a direction. This is therefore an 'essay' in the literal sense and has been an enjoyable, at times even a light-hearted, diversion from some of the other history that I have been writing.

The links between culture, history and gender are briefly touched upon in the first section. In the second section the version of the story as given in the *Mahābhārata* is discussed, largely in the context of how the epic tradition treated the narrative. The third section introduces the striking change in the narrative and the meanings of the embellishments, now treated as a work of literature in the tradition of courtly culture through the Kālidāsa play, *Abhijñāna-śākuntalam.* The fourth section refers to the continuation of the tradition of the narrative in various more popular forms, although still within the framework of Sanskrit writing, and contrasts it with some glimpses at a different level of how it was viewed by literary theorists around A.D. 1000. The span from the popular to the courtly culture is itself of some interest. The fifth section changes tack, as it were, and moves to a discussion of adaptations and translations of the Kālidāsa play, initially in Braj-*bhāṣā* and then in Urdu. These are very different in spirit from the translations in English and other European languages, where the reception of the play in nineteenth century Europe and India made it a part both of European literary movements and British perceptions of Indian culture; these are discussed in the sixth and seventh section. Tagore's essay on the play becomes the focus of the eighth section, which also considers the modern Indian context within which the play was viewed. The representations have not always been in a literary form, and visual forms are touched on in passing, where relevant.

The choice of illustrations is not entirely arbitrary. Where possible depictions of the same events have been chosen to highlight the contemporising of the story even in the manner of illustrating it. The reading of the Bhita plaque as the arrival of Duṣyanta at the hermitage is in a different style from the deposition of the same event in the miniature paintings from Nalagarh. Śakuntalā with her companions was clearly a favourite theme in the nineteenth century. The obvious "Orientalist" mood of the sketches illustrating the translation by Monier-Williams is quite strikingly unhistorical. The focus at one level is on different versions of the narrative seen essentially in terms of historical change. But the underlying argument is that there are manifestations of culture and cultural ideologies in the way Śakuntalā is projected as a woman, and to that extent there is a historical interface between culture and gender.

I was first introduced to the story from family photograph albums, in one of which there were photographs of the presentation of the play—duly abridged—in my mother's school where she, as a young girl, played the lead. When I reached the age of going to the movies—and it was much later then than it is now—I was taken to see Shantaram's *Shakuntala*, much talked about as a box-office hit. Later, the Kālidāsa play had to be read for a Sanskrit exam, an activity which destroys sensitivity to poetry. But I returned to it many years later, intrigued by the difference in character in this version and that of the epic, and perceived fresh nuances of meaning with each reading. This essay has proceeded from those readings.

I would like to thank those who read an earlier draft and offered comments: Kesavan Veluthat, Kunal Chakrabarti, Kumkum Roy and K.N. Panikkar. They would have preferred a fuller treatment, but I shall leave that to someone else. Kalpana Sahni kindly provided me with some facets of how the play was received in Russian literary circles. Muzaffar Alam brought the Braj and Urdu versions to my attention, the existence of which was something of a revelation to me. Sujit Mukherjee's comments on the essay by Tagore provided yet another perspective. I would also like to thank the participants at a conference on "Conceptualising Culture—the Indian Experience", organised by K.N. Panikkar and held at Wagamon in Kerala, with whom I discussed the general theme. Their comments were very helpful in clarifying some of my ideas.

A Senior Fellowship at the Nehru Memorial Museum and Library provided me some leisure from other research, for writing this essay.

ROMILA THAPAR

New Delhi
March 1999

Śakuntalā

1. Preliminaries

THIS essay is primarily concerned with the interface between literature and history. Historians comb literature for historical facts, references to events or descriptions of a particular historical time: all of which continues to be a legitimate historical enterprise. My intention here is to change the focus somewhat. I would like to take a literary item—such as a narrative—retold a few times and treat this repetition as a prism through which to view points of historical change. These are provided by the same story being retold in variant ways. At a later stage, translations of one of these variants and the commentaries thereon also become part of this biography of a narrative, and provide a perspective on the historical moments conditioning their reception. Underlying this exercise is the suggestion that an item of literature, as a narrative, relates to history, not for what it says which is anyway fictional, but for what it might indicate as being historically significant.

The narrative I have chosen focuses on a young woman, Śakuntalā. That each variant of the story created at different historical periods projects her differently, not only allows a historical view on the story, but also introduces a gender perspective. This is the perspective from which the interface between literature and history will be viewed in this essay. The form which the variants take, the later extensive translations of one among these into European and Indian languages, and the cultural interpretations which they foster, makes the narrative an item of cultural history. The variants of the narrative take on the character of cultural representations. In effect therefore, tracing the history of this narrative itself becomes an even more complex interface between literature, history, gender and culture. It is not my intention here to explore it in depth, rather to demonstrate that it is a viable activity which will direct us to many unexplored dimensions of both our past and our present.

In the conceptualising of Indian culture today, a question which is implicit concerns the relationship of pre-colonial culture to the colonial and that which has followed. My attempt will be to delineate this relationship in broad terms by using one significant narrative which has been part of a cultural construction at many points in Indian history. Its repeated occurrence, although in variant forms, has in the past been treated as a relatively unchanging continuity. I would like to argue that the narrative, like an actor, plays many parts, some accommodating and others contesting its earlier forms, and that it has an intimate relationship with its historical context. How then does the narrative interface with the historical moment? In this essay, I hope to show how cultural symbols, idioms, icons, are changed in differing historical contexts; and to underline the kind of disjuncture introduced by colonial intervention. The imprint of the latter can, and often does, colour our reading of the pre-colonial past. This is not to suggest that prior to colonial readings the view was linear and unbroken, but rather to argue that the colonial intervention has made for a more emphatic imprint on our contemporary life than earlier historical interventions. This becomes pertinent if one argues, as I do, that the delineation of the past can often be a reconstruction drawing on the needs of the present.

Related to this is the question of the centrality of the notion of being critical or analytical about the interfaces of cultural expression. Are such analyses associated only with modern times, assuming that there was little or no intellectual confrontation earlier, or that the social underpinnings of cultural articulations are as yet not familiar to those investigating the early past? Even more significant is the question of when an issue of cultural articulation breaks away from being viewed as part of the controversy within an authentic, prior tradition, to being seen as one of contemporary importance. It is linked to the assertion, by some, that culture evolves naturally through the interaction of people and is therefore not created or cultivated by particular groups. The Nature versus Culture debate, much discussed in eighteenth and nineteenth century Europe, was crucial not just to Romantic poetry but also to some European perspectives on human society.

The concept of "culture" as a literary form in relation to the early past implies an intersecting of disciplines, of which history is foundational. In the Indian situation it involves not only the original text and its historical context, but often the Orientalist reading of it and the internalising of this reading by Indian commentators of the last two centuries. Understanding this process entails questioning, or at least contextualising, the Orientalist representation and being conscious of the paradigms of European perspectives which have been brought to bear on Indian culture. An understanding of the tradition does not mean merely negating these paradigms but contextualising the elements of what is sought to be defined as "the tradition".

Understanding a cultural item historically also involves some comprehension of what it was identified with and the ideology which it represented. Identities in the past have been various, and any one item can have multiple identities which change at historical moments. Creative articulations in the form of cultural items relate to the dominant ideology in various ways ranging from endorsing to confronting it; the relationship has been directed to questions of caste, class, ethnicity, gender and so on, although those dictating the dominant ideology tend to project it as free of contestation. This combination of identity and ideology means that culture has a historical dimension as seen in the forms selected for the creation of a cultural item, and a social dimension in the assumption that the ideologies of the dominant groups are the ones sought to be imprinted.

I would like to touch on some of these ideas, using the narrative of Śakuntalā. My focus therefore is not on the play per se, but on the treatment of the central figure, the woman who transforms the narrative. It is also to consider the reasons for changes in the narrative and the relation which its various forms have with their historical context, as seen through the changing representation of Śakuntalā. Some viewing of gender relations in variant times and places thus becomes a part of the theme.

My interest in looking at variations of the same theme at different points of time has to do with how the past is viewed by the present—wherever the present is located in time. There is therefore a constant dialogue between the past and the present. Because of this, the same theme often undergoes change, such change acting as an indicator of the dialogue, and of different readings and histories. A popular theme becomes multi-layered because of its varying forms: perhaps some of the many pasts which contributed to its present form can be prised apart. The present selects items from the past which are used to invent or refashion what comes to be called a "tradition".[1] These are generally items which the present finds attractive and which legitimise its various codes of behaviour and belief. The making of a tradition becomes yet another dialogue with the past. It is often a perceived past which contributes to the construction of history, although in effect it may well derive from the perspectives of the present.[2]

I would like to illustrate this by taking up the theme of Śakuntalā, a young woman who features in the earlier Sanskrit texts and whose character and personality change with new renderings of her story or with later comments on them. The representation of Śakuntalā in varied historical contexts, where each of these, it seems to me, dominates the reading of the original character, also becomes an appropriate entry point for looking at facets of the history of that time. That she is a woman introduces the dimension of gender, and it is striking that her representation as a woman alters radically over the centuries. This is evident not just from the way in which she is presented in the different versions of the story, but also in the assessment of her significance in its modern interpretations. This touches not merely on the narrative but also on her identification with what surrounds her. The perception of this identification changes interestingly with the treatment of the woman in the various versions.

The earliest narration occurs in the epic, the *Mahābhārata*, in the form of *kāvya*/poetry. An expanded treatment of the narrative is best known as the play, *Abhijñāna-śākuntalam* by Kālidāsa which, although it borrows the story from the epic, nevertheless differs from it significantly. The dramatic form was a deliberate distancing from the epic since the two genres reflected diverse literary and social interests. The interface between literary forms and their social context can be ways of exploring the social order, especially when the form changes so radically. That Sanskrit was the language of the epic meant that it was not restricted to ritual compositions, and its more commonly used version, which Pāṇini refers to as *Bhāṣā*, was employed in non-liturgical compositions. This was further strengthened when royal inscriptions in Indian languages came to be composed in Sanskrit and not exclusively in Prākrit, as they were in the Mauryan period. The earliest Sanskrit inscriptions are associated with rulers of northern and western India and with dynasties which we now describe as foreign. There is an identity of language in the epic and the drama, but the two genres mould the language in distinctive ways.

Whenever Śakuntalā is mentioned we think immediately of the play by Kālidāsa which has been, and continues to be, valued both by Indian commentators as well as others who have read it in Sanskrit, or in translation. Given the status of Kālidāsa as a poet, the fine quality of the play in terms of language and structure, and the evocations of masterly metaphors, it is not surprising that it has always been held as an exemplar of Sanskrit drama. An understanding of the play is furthered if one is familiar with what existed before, how it was later constantly reshaped in translations—both literary and visual—which followed from it, and the perspectives from which it was viewed. Each new treatment provides an aspect which either illuminates the text or is a reflection of the historical moment when its particular perspective came into being.

The theme was selected by Kālidāsa from an earlier source, the *Mahābhārata*, and treated very differently in the creation of the play, but the earlier source tends to be excluded from discussions about the play, in part perhaps to subordinate historical exegesis. Yet for many centuries, Indian audiences would have known both versions of the story, versions which were dissimilar in important respects. Since they belong to two different historical periods and relate to diverse social backgrounds, there is more than just a variance in literary style. The choice today of the Kālidāsa version as almost the sole narrative is an endorsement of the views of both classical Sanskrit and Orientalist scholarship, which affirmed the superiority of the play and therefore the centrality of its narrative. Jones' declaration that Kālidāsa was "the Shakespeare of India" is still widely quoted. That Sanskrit literary criticism centuries earlier had given it the same status was not foregrounded in this assessment. It had been evaluated in terms of dramaturgy and literary quality, whereas now what is more popularly commented upon is the leading character of the play, Śakuntalā herself. Evaluation in terms of dramaturgy implied that the depiction of the woman was not autonomous but in accordance with the requirements of dramatic theory. Literary critics of our times were less concerned with evaluating the two literary forms, *kāvya* and *nāṭaka*. Orientalism, in using the play as an articulation of Indian culture—and particularly as reflected in the depiction of Śakuntalā—could well have drawn on a comparison of the woman in the two genres, but did not do so.

Orientalism of the eighteenth and nineteenth centuries influenced many cultural choices of the Indian middle class, among them being a perception of what was regarded as the Indian cultural tradition. The question of Indian womanhood was an important dimension of this perception, and Kālidāsa's Śakuntalā was seen to epitomise the Indian woman. What is regarded as "tradition" however, is always selective and needs to be understood in terms of why particular selections were made at particular moments.

The epic as narrative is believed to predate Kālidāsa by a few centuries and, possibly, has an even earlier origin in the oral tradition.[3] Dating the *Mahābhārata* has been a perennial debate. As an oral epic it may well go back to earlier centuries, but at some point it was converted into a text, although left open to interpolations. The bracket of 400 B.C. to A.D. 400 would probably be the most appropriate for the text. Similarly the date for Kālidāsa varies but he is generally placed in about the fourth century A.D. This allows of two possibilities: that the epic version predated the play or, that the two were closer in time, but evolved from dichotomous social contexts and addressed different audiences. Neither possibility disallows a discussion of the differences in both and some analysis of the reasons for these.

The two versions belong to different genres and their literary and social purpose differs; divergences would therefore be expected. The epic version was initially bardic recitation, as part of the oral performance of such narratives for an audience of chiefs and clansmen. Epics were stitched together from bardic fragments where the fragments often observe the morphology of folk narratives.[4] Such fragments had their origin in stories of heroic feats, myths and possibly a community memory of what were believed to have been events which had taken place in earliest times. It was in part a recital of what was claimed to be family history and the deeds of actual or fictive ancestors, for many later clans sought status through linking themselves with the earliest established clans. The oral nature of the epic made it prone to narrative stereotypes, repetition of actions and formulaic verses. It was also prone to interpolations which were inserted as and when required, or for that matter to deletions of some portions if thought necessary. The final text therefore takes on the quality of a palimpsest.

This was different from a court drama, written in finely honed and crafted language, performed before a select audience on a special occasion, and familiar to a literate, formally educated, sophisticated segment of society—the urban *nāgarakas*. It was the legitimation by paradigm not of the clan but of the court and the dynasty, and moulded in the tradition of the romantic comedy where the sport of kings was articulated in hunting and romantic love. Themes were often taken from the epic or earlier compositions which would make them familiar to the audience, and in doing so there would have been some reflective search for links, but not in too apparent a fashion. Yet it is likely that the Śakuntalā of the epic would have been more widely known at the popular level than the heroine of the drama. Taking a story from the epic repertoire and converting it into a play with the highlighting of a mood, an emotion or a situation was common to other cultures as well, and the Greek tradition comes immediately to mind.

Differences in cultural preference are often socially conditioned and socially functional. The Kālidāsa version could have been seen as a refinement of the epic version. Court culture inevitably was associated with the ruling class, particularly in well-stratified societies. Even the later version of the narrative in Braj-*bhāṣā*, intended for the court, had limited audiences among the aristocracy of the eighteenth century. Although they considerably widened the social span by adapting the story to more commonly spoken languages, the adaptations nevertheless remained a part of court culture. Translations of the Kālidāsa play into modern European languages introduced further historical dimensions, such as German Romanticism and British Orientalism, and these in turn influenced the modern Indian perception of the significance of the narrative. But the modern treatment of high culture allows for many foci which are expressed simultaneously, and so the theme of Śakuntalā is depicted in painting, read as a Sanskrit text by students, and made into popular films.

2. The Narrative from the *Mahābhārata*

WHAT appear to be the mythical pre-epic origins of the narrative of Śakuntalā occur in some parts of the Vedic corpus. An early but passing reference to her is made in the *Śatapatha Brāhmaṇa*,[5] where she is linked to the preeminent clan of the Bharatas, whose greatness could not be superceded by any. It is said that the *apsarā* Śakuntalā conceived Bharata at Nāḍapit (which a later text glosses as the location of the *āśrama* of the *ṛṣi* Kaṇva). Bharata, the son of Duḥṣanta, performed a gigantic *aśvamedha* sacrifice, where seventy-eight horses were bound near the Yamunā river and fifty-five near the Gaṅgā, a fantasy on the preeminence of the Bharatas. He conquered the earth and brought more than a thousand horses for Indra's sacrifice. This in itself marks him out as extraordinary, for horses were imported from the north-west and much prized. The exaggerated figure for the number of horses therefore is more an indication of the esteem in which Bharata was held and the presumed efficacy of the sacrifice, than a literal accounting of the numbers involved. The connection between the deity Indra and the lineage of Bharata was close, and is often reiterated. The mother of such a hero was clearly special.

Another passing reference is made to Bharata in the *Aitareya Brāhmaṇa*[6] where Dīrghatamas is said to have anointed Bharata, who then conquered in every direction and performed many *aśvamedhas*. The number of horses involved increases a hundredfold in this version and the number of cows gifted runs into thousands. The name Dīrghatamas—literally, deep darkness—supports the legend that he was born blind, and in later life set adrift in a river which took him to the Aṅga country in the east where he married outside the social pale.[7] His son Kakṣīvant was therefore a *dāsi-putra brāhmaṇa*, by birth a *brāhmaṇa* of lower status, but an established category nevertheless. The association of Bharata with Dīrghatamas is somewhat unexpected, since it hints at the hero being befriended by a priest who may have had access to non-orthodox rituals and shamanistic practices. If such practices were a recognised alternative ritual, then the hero would be drawing on more than one culture.

The story is related at length in the *Mahābhārata* where it occurs as one among the ancestral legends of the Pūru lineage in the *Ādi parvan* or "the book of the beginning" as it has been called, containing origin myths and genealogies. It is told as the *Śakuntalopākhyāna*,[8] *ākhyānas* being narratives of past heroes. The Pūru lineage was part of the Candravaṃśa, (Lunar line) one of the two *kṣatriya* lineages—the other being the Sūryavaṃśa (Solar line)—to which most clans claiming *kṣatriya* status were assigned. Many dynasties in later Indian history also claimed descent from these two royal lineages. The Candravamśa traces itself back to the androgynous Iḍā who was the ancestress to Yayāti and his successors, such as Pūru and their descendent, Bharata. These heroes are eulogised in spite of Pūru being of uncertain social origin according to the Vedic corpus.[9] Clearly origins could be invented for those who had power, wealth to bestow on the creators of genealogies, and the ability to protect their clansmen. Both the Kauravas and the Pāṇḍavas were said to belong to the Pūru lineage, and therefore the opening book of the *Mahābhārata* sets out the legends of their ancestors. The irony however is that neither of the two, the Pāṇḍavas and Kauravas around whom the present text revolves, were related by blood to the Pūru lineage as they were sired by

Kṛṣṇa Dvaipāyana (the son of the sage Parāśara and the fisher-woman Satyāvatī), and their mothers were the daughters of the *rājā* of Kāśī, also unrelated to the Pūrus. Nevertheless the origin myth had to be maintained and the links insisted upon by reiterating these stories. Bharata is a key figure in the genealogical record as he is among those who consolidate the clans. The story of Śakuntalā is significant in the narrative of their ancestors, because she was the mother of Bharata.

Analyses of the structure and content of the *Mahābhārata* have led to the view that the original epic was subjected to many additions and interpolations. Thus two categories of composition have been recognised, variously called epic and psuedo-epic or narrative and didactic.[10] Because of the constant additions, the compilation of the *Mahābhārata* extended over a few centuries, and according to some between 400 B.C. to A.D. 400. Bardic fragments are likely to have been composed in an earlier period as there are references to a few of these heroes and clans in the early texts of the Vedic corpus. It is thought that the Bhṛgu *brāhmaṇas*, specialists in *dharmaśāstra* and *nītiśāstra*, edited the existing versions and interpolated the didactic sections focusing on social obligations and polity, thus converting the epic from bardic literature to a high culture text. Interpolations acted as mechanisms of legitimising not only religious cults and sects such as Bhāgavatism, but also the socio-political changes involved in the transition from a lineage-based society to a monarchy.[11] In its own context heroic literature was the literature of the elite, the chiefs and the ruling clans, but it incorporated the folk narratives of lesser groups more readily. Originating in forms that facilitated recitation with a frequent resort to dialogue, the epic was easy to follow. With the emergence of courtly literature, the language became more complex and cultivated, with the new elites regarding the literature of the older elites as, occasionally, being of lower status. The continuity of the epic in India as a legitimising agency allowed it to remain a part of the high culture, but somewhat at the more popular end of the scale, together with the *Purāṇas*. Many of the earlier books of the *Mahābhārata* are narrative in content with some later interpolations. By contrast, the *Śānti parvan* and the *Anuśāsana parvan* are intended as didactic texts concerned with matters related to *rāja-dharma*, the theory of governing; and *mokṣa-dharma*, of attaining liberation from rebirth, the performance of rituals, sacred duty and such like. The conversion of the epic into religious literature—the literature of Vaiṣṇava Bhāgavatism—a mutation which the *Rāmāyaṇa* also underwent, changed its character but ensured its transmission. Some of the earlier fragments from the narrative section do however retain their epic character.

The historical context to these stories is a lineage-based society, with chiefdoms moving towards incipient kingdoms. Authority is concentrated in the ruling clans and its distribution is linked to birth and closeness to the senior clans. Genealogies and origin myths are therefore of crucial importance, as are the legends of those believed to be ancestors. Power lies with kinsmen and this makes the presence of sons imperative. Kinship connections frequently function as administrative aids. Cattle-keeping and the cultivation of crops sustained society, the former requiring control over large acres of pasture land, some in forested regions. Hunting was also a mechanism for asserting control over grazing grounds. Cattle-raids or raiding for tribute were recognised ways of augmenting wealth and these encouraged the system of prestations—the voluntary (in theory) tribute paid to the chief on special occasions. The major sacrificial rituals relating to chiefship such as the *abhiṣeka* or initiation, the *rājasūya*, *aśvamedha* and *vājapeya*, were intended for establishing claims to power, territory and suzerainty over others, and took the form of a kind of potlatch. The sacrificial occasion was one when wealth was collected by a *rājā* and was then partly destroyed in the course of the ritual, with the rest being given as *dāna*/gift and *dakṣiṇā*/fee, to the *brāhmaṇas*[12] performing the ritual. The role model for the hero is the god Indra, an important deity but soon to be in confrontation with the *ṛṣis* and overshadowed by the popularity of Viṣṇu and Śiva. Indra's ambivalent relationship with the *ṛṣis* which occasionally became antagonistic, is apparent in the epic. The turning away from the sacrificial ritual—the *yajña*—and the seeking of alternative ways of liberating the soul—*mokṣa*—such as *dhyāna*, *yoga* and *tapas*, were in part responsible for the questioning of the sacrificial ritual. The didactic sections were added later and reflect conditions when monarchy had been established, and therefore assume the existence of kingdoms. The term *rājā*, translated consistently as "king" in the past is now being seen as more nuanced. Depending on the context it may be better translated as "chief" in many of the early texts.[13] In the re-editing of the *Mahābhārata*, some chiefdoms were undoubtedly transmuted into the now more familiar kingdoms.

The central location of epic events was the Indo-Gangetic watershed and the Gaṅgā-Yamunā *doāb* as well as the fringes of this area. This was *madhya-deśa*, the middle country. The geography of the Śakuntalā episode is confined to an *āśrama* in the foothills of the Himalayas, what would today be called the terai, and the town of Hastināpur, not too far away. The identification of the latter has been made with the village of the same name in Meerut district, an identification which is not certain. The *āśrama* would have been on the edge of the heavier Gangetic forests and would have represented the movement of the people of the plains into the hills and forests nearby. *Āśramas* were frequently the vanguard of those who followed as settlers. A mound at Hastināpur close to the Gaṅgā has been excavated;[14] its occupation would suit the period of the early composition of the epic but there is no easy correlation between the epic and archaeological data. Only the name of the village provides a possible identity with the epic Hastināpur, together with the destruction of the early settlement by flood, attested to in the epic and corroborated from excavations. Far from its being the resplendent home of the mighty Pauravas, the excavations suggest a rather poor settlement to begin with, and some improvement in the next phase with wattle-and-daub houses and a few iron artefacts. A closer parallel is suggested by the third phase, around the mid-first millennium B.C., subsequent to a time of floods, and this phase points to some degree of urbanisation and more sophisticated life-ways. Clearly a one-to-one equation between excavated sites and literary texts cannot be made.[15] There is also the problem of the imaginative overlay in the latter, where, with many retellings of the story over many centuries, the original wattle-and-daub house may well have ended up as a marble palace.

Women are important to such a society, where being the mother of the first-born male child provided immediate status; for the mother this became almost symbolic of property. The women of the *Mahābhārata* are strong personalities, cherishing their autonomy and willing to argue for their rights. Social norms and customs do not follow a linear pattern and, taken as a whole, tend to be hopelessly confused, partly because of the telescoping of time in an epic, and partly because of a varied range of societies being interlinked. There were also the celestial women, the *apsarās*. They had their own codes of behaviour and were not subject to the rules of human society, although quite a few played an ancestral role in genealogies.

In the *Mahābhārata*, the narrative of Śakuntalā is told by Vaiśampāyaṇa to Janámejaya in the course of reciting the epic on the occasion of a major sacrificial ritual.

*Mahābhārata, Ādi Parvan**

Janámejaya said:

62

I have heard fully from you, O brahmin, how the Gods, Dānavas, and Rākṣasas, and also the Gandharvas and Apsarās, descended to earth with a portion of themselves. Now I wish you to tell me from the beginning in the presence of these brahmins and seers, O brahmin, how the dynasty of the Kurus came into being.

Vaiśaṃpāyana said:

A dynast of the Pauravas was a mighty hero called Duḥṣanta, herdsman of all the earth to her four horizons, O best of the Bhāratas. This triumphant king enjoyed the earth entire with all four quarters, and also countries that are surrounded by the ocean; and the pleasure of this scourge of his enemies extended as far as the barbarians and forest tribes to all lands that are skirted by the pearl-rich ocean and peopled by the four classes.

There was no miscegenation, no one needed to plough or mine the earth, nobody did evil while this king reigned. All the people were bent on Law and Profit, cherishing a joy in their own Law, while he, O tiger among men, lorded the countryside. There was no fear of theft, my friend, no fear whatever of starvation, nor fear of disease, while he lorded the countryside. The classes delighted in their own Laws and lacked all selfishness in their acts of worship. Relying on him as the guardian of the earth, they met with no danger from anywhere. The rain god rained in time and the crops were ample; earth abounded with all gems and flowed with wealth. The youthful king, of miraculous great prowess, hard as a diamond, could have lifted Mount Mandara and carried it in his arms with its woods and forest. He

---

**Ādi parvan*, Chapters 62-69 translated by J.A.B. van Buitenen in, *The Mahābhārata*, Vol. 1, The Book of the Beginning. University of Chicago Press, Chicago: 1973, pp. 156-71.

In an otherwise impressive translation, van Buitenen unfortunately translates *kṣatriya* and *śūdra* as baron and serf, which is historically inaccurate for the context of the *Mahābhārata*.

was equally accomplished with the bow as with the club, in swordsmanship, on elephant and horseback. In his might he matched Viṣṇu, in radiance the sun, in imperturbability the ocean, in endurance the earth. A well-esteemed ruler he was, with town and realm serene, who dwelled among a people noted for law-minded intentions.

Vaiśaṃpāyana said:

63

Upon a time this strong-armed king rode out, with ample strength of men and mounts, to a dense forest, escorted by hundreds of horses and elephants. He progressed surrounded by hundreds of warriors, carrying swords and lances, brandishing clubs and maces, wielding javelins and spears. And as the king went on, the lion roars of his warriors, the blasts of conches and drums, the thunder of the chariot rims reinforced by the trumpeting of the grand elephants, the whinnying of the horses, and the growls and arm-slapping of the men rose to a tumultuous noise. From the balconies of their terraced palaces the womenfolk gazed upon the hero, who made his own fame, in all his regal magnificence. And watching their king, equal of Indra, slayer of foes, warder-off of enemy elephants, they thought of him as the Thunderbolt-Wielder himself. "He is a tiger among men, of wondrous prowess in battle, before the strength of whose arms no enemy keeps his life!" Such were the words that the women spoke; and with love they sang his praises and strew rain bursts of flowers on his head. Everywhere he went the brahmins lauded him; and thus, with the greatest joy, he went out to the forest hunting. Town and country folk followed him a long way, until the king finally dismissed them and they returned.

The overlord of earth filled earth and the heavens with the thunder of his chariot that flew like the Fair-Winged Bird. And as he rode, the alert king chanced to see a wood like Indra's paradise, wooded with *bilva* and *arka* bushes and *khadira* trees, abounding with trees and plants such as *kapitthas* and *dhavas*, rolling with hills and plateaus, overspread with boulders, which was empty of water and people for a stretch of many leagues.

And in this wood, which teemed with herds of deer and beasts of prey that stalk the forest, Duḥṣanta, tiger among men, with retainers, escort, and mounts wrought havoc, killing game of many kinds. Many families of tigers he laid low as they came within range of his arrows; he shot them with his shafts. Those that were in the distance the bull among men shot down with his arrows; others that came up close he cut down with his sword; and antelopes he brought down with his spear, the powerful spearman, who also knew all the points of the circular club swing and whose courage was boundless. He stalked about killing wild game and fowl with javelin, sword, mace, bludgeon, halberd. And when the wondrously valiant king and his warlike warriors raided the great forest, the big game fled it. The herds of deer, their flocks dispersed, their leaders killed, cried out for help everywhere. The river they sought out was dry; and thin with despair for water, their hearts exhausted with exertion, they dropped down, unconscious. Overcome by hunger and thirst, they fell prostrate on the ground, exhausted. There were some that were eaten raw by starving tiger men; other woodsmen built a fire, lit it, cut their meat in proper pieces, and ate it. There were mighty elephants that were wounded by swords and ran mad; turning up their trunks, they panicked and stampeded frantically. Dropping dung and urine and streaming with blood, the wild tuskers trampled many men. The forest, darkened by a monsoon of might and a downpour of arrows, its big game weeded by the king, now seemed overrun by buffalo.

Vaiśaṃpāyana said:

64

Having killed thousands of deer, the king with his plentiful mounts entered into another wood in search of deer. Supremely strong, though hungry and thirsty, he penetrated by himself into the depths of the forest till he came to a vast wilderness that was dotted with holy hermitages, a joy to the heart and a feast for the eye. He crossed beyond it and made for still another wood where a cool breeze was blowing, a wood sprinkled with blossoming trees and most prosperous grasslands. It was a wide woodland that echoed with the sweet warblings of birds. All around stood trees that threw pleasant shade and burst with their shoots; their creepers were aswarm with bees, and a sovereign beauty reigned over it. No tree lacked bloom or fruit, no tree was thorny, nor was there one undarkened by bees in that wood. Atwitter with birds, adorned with blossoms, and wooded with trees that bloomed in all seasons, with surpassing-good grasslands, it was a most enchanting wood, and the great bowman entered it. Richly blossoming trees shaken by the wind again and again let loose a colorful downpour of flowers. Brushing the skies, alive with the sweet music of birds, the trees stood resplendent in their many-colored robes of blossoms. And among their shoots, which bent under the burden of bloom, birds and bees sang their gentle songs.

As he gazed upon the many stretches adorned by an outpouring of flowers and surrounded by creepers that were twined into pavilions, adding to his heart's delight, the puissant king became filled with joy. With its blossoming trees whose branches interlaced, the wood seemed to shine with as many maypoles. A pleasantly cool and fragrant breeze that carried the pollen of flowers ran around the woods and accosted the trees as though to make love to them. Such was the woodland upon which the king gazed, grown in the embrace of a river, enchanting, lofty like flagmasts.

Looking at the forest with its wildly excited birds, he saw an idyllic and heart-fetching hermitage, covered with all kinds of trees and alight with blazing fires. Ascetics and anchorites peopled it and groups of hermits. Fire halls aplenty were scattered all over, and carpets of flowers. It seemed to shine forth with its large bays of water on the bank of the river Mālinī, holy and gladdening stream, which, O King, bestrewn with flocks of all kinds of fowl, added loveliness to this wilderness of austerities. And on seeing beasts of prey and deer peaceably together, the king was filled with the purest joy.

Thereupon the illustrious warrior drew nigh to the hermitage that most enchanting everywhere, was the image of the world of the Gods. He saw the river that embraced the hermitage with her holy water spreading out like the mother of all creatures, her banks swarming with *cakravāka* birds, her current carrying blossoms and foam—the habitation of Kiṃnaras that was frequented by monkeys and bears. The sound of holy Vedic lessons wafted over the river; sandbanks strung pearls upon her; rutting elephants, tigers, and mighty snakes visited her.

When he saw the hermitage and the river that enclosed it, the king set his mind upon entering. And he entered the deep woodland, with its necklace of the Mālinī of the shining isles and lovely banks; it appeared like the dwelling place of Nara and Nārāyana, adorned by the Ganges, loud with the shriek of madly dancing peacocks. Having drawn near to the hermitage that resembled Citraratha's park, the lord of men, intending to see the great seer and ascetic Kaṇva Kāśyapa, surpassingly virtuous and of indescribable brilliance, halted his escort of chariots with footmen at the gate of the wood and said to his army, "I shall go to see Kāśyapa, that dispassionate hermit of rich austerities. Remain here until my return." And upon entering that wood, like another paradise of Indra, the lord of men shed his hunger and thirst and became overjoyed. Discarding his regalia and accompanied only by councillor and priest, he walked to the grand hermitage to see the seer who had piled up austerities everlasting.

He saw the hermitage that mirrored the world of Brahmā, echoing with the humming of bees and aswarm with all kinds of fowl. He, tiger among men, heard hymns of the *Ṛgveda* that were being recited, both wordwise and stepwise, as the rituals were spun out by the foremost of Bahvṛca brahmins. The hermitage was radiant with strict priests of boundless spirit who strode their strides, experts on sacrifices and the branches of the *Veda*. Great scholars of the *Atharvaveda*, esteemed by the assembled sacrificers, recited the *Saṃhitā* in both wordwise and stepwise modes. Other brahmins, who spoke with refinement of speech, made the hermitage ring so that it gloriously resembled the worlds of Brahmā. It resounded with priests who knew sacrifice and sacrament, who were conversant with the stepwise recitation and phonetics, and accomplished in the knowledge of the rules of interpretation and the significance of the principles thereof—past masters of the *Veda*, proficient in the combination and connection of all kinds of sentences, schooled in a variety of rites, intent upon Salvation and Law, who had acquired knowledge of the final truth through argumentation, objection, and conclusion and were the foremost of practitioners. Everywhere the slayer of enemy champions saw grand and perfected brahmins, controlled and strict in their vows, engaged in the muttering of spells and the offering of oblations. The lord of the earth saw colorful, flower-decked seats that had been carefully set out, and he was amazed. And seeing brahmins doing *pūjā* to the sanctuaries of the Gods, this most strict king thought himself attending the worlds of Brahmā. Watching the great and sacred hermitage, protected by Kāśyapa's austerities and hallowed by the multitudes of its ascetics, he could not watch enough.

And thus the slayer of foes, with councillor and priest, set foot in Kāśyapa's sanctum, which was everywhere crowded with seers rich in austerities, solitary, most enchanting, holy.

Vaiśaṃpāyana said:

65

Thereupon the strong-armed king dismissed his councillors and went on alone. He did not find the seer of strict vows in the hermitage. Failing to find the seer and finding the hermitage empty, he spoke in a loud voice, thundering over the woodland: "Who is here?" Hearing his cry, a young maiden appeared, like Śrī incarnate, and came out of that hermitage, wearing the garb of a female hermit. No sooner had the black-eyed girl seen King Duḥṣanta than she bade him welcome and paid him homage. She honored him with a seat, with water to wash his feet, and a guest gift, and asked, O King, the overlord of men about his health and well-being.

After honoring him properly and inquiring about his health, she said with a faint smile, "What can I do?" The king, seeing that she had a flawless body and having been honored properly, replied to the sweet-spoken girl, "I have come to pay my worship to the venerable seer Kaṇva. Where has the reverend gone, my dear? Tell me, my pretty."

Śakuntalā said:

My reverend father has gone out of the hermitage to gather fruit. Wait a while, you will see him return.

Vaiśampāyana said:

The king, having failed to find the seer, looked at the girl who had addressed him and saw that she had beautiful hips, a lustrous appearance, and a charming smile. She was radiant with beauty, with the sheen of austerities and the calm of self-restraint. The king now said to the maiden, as perfect of shape as of age, "Who are you? Whose are you? Why, fair-waisted girl, have you come to this wilderness? Endowed with such perfection of beauty? From where are you, my pretty? For one look at you, lovely, has carried my heart away! I want to know about you, tell me, my pretty."

At these words of the king in the hermitage she laughed and said in a very sweet voice, "I am regarded as the daughter of the venerable Kaṇva, Duḥṣanta, the great-spirited and famous ascetic and equable scholar of the Law."

Duḥṣanta said:

The reverend lord, whom the world worships, has never spilled his seed! The God Law himself might stray from his course, but not this saint of strict vows. How could you have been born his daughter, fair maiden? I have great doubts on this, pray dispel them!

Śakuntalā said:

Then listen, my king, how this story has come to me, and how this once came to be, and how in fact I became the hermit's daughter. One day a seer came here who raised questions about my birth, and hear how the reverend spoke to him, sire.

"Viśvāmitra, as you know," he said, "performed of yore such huge austerities that he bitterly mortified Indra himself, lord of the hosts of Gods. Fearful lest the ascetic, whose puissance had been set ablaze by his austerities, would topple him from his throne, the Sacker of Cities therefore spoke to Menakā. 'Menakā, you are distinguished in the divine talents of the Apsarās. Take my welfare to heart, beautiful woman, and do as I ask you, listen. That great ascetic Viśvāmitra, who possesses the splendor of the sun, has been performing awesome austerities that make my mind tremble. Menakā of the pretty waist, Viśvāmitra is your burden. This unassailable man of honed spirit is engaged in dreadful austerities; and lest he topple me from my throne, go to him and seduce him. Obstruct his asceticism, do me the ultimate favor! Seduce him with your beauty, youth, sweetness, fondling, smiles, and flatteries, my buxom girl, and turn him away from his austerities'!"

Menakā said:

The reverend lord is a man of great heat and always of great austerity and irascible. And you yourself, sir, know that he is like that. Should I not fear him of whose heat, austerity, and fury you yourself stand in fear? Him, who divorced the venerable Vasiṣṭha from his beloved sons? Who was born a baron and by brute force became a brahmin? Who created an unfordable river of plentiful waters just to wash himself, a most sacred river that people know as the Kauśikī, where of yore at a time of disaster the law-abiding royal seer Matanga, having become a hunter, supported the great-spirited seer's wife, and later, when the famine was past, the mighty sage returned to the hermitage and gave the river the name of Pārā—the same river where he, pleased with Matanga, himself officiated at his sacrifice and you yourself, from fear, came rushing to drink the Soma? Viśvāmitra, who angrily created a new galaxy of counter-constellations from Śravaṇā onward, with a wealth of asterisms over and beyond the old galaxy? One who wrought such deeds I fear greatly. Inform me, my ubiquitous lord, how shall I escape being burned by his rage? With his heat he could burn down the worlds, quake the earth with his feet, knead the mighty Mount Meru into a ball and spin it around! A man of such austerity, blazing like a fire, master of his senses—how could a young woman like me ever touch him? His mouth is a blazing offering, fire, sun and moon are the pupils of his eyes, Time itself is his tongue—how could one like me touch him, O best of Gods? Him of whose might even Yama and Soma and the great Seers and all the Sādhyas and Vālakhilyas stand in awe, one like me should not fear, why? Yet, having been so ordered by you, how can I fail to approach the seer, O lord of the Gods? But contrive to protect me, king of celestials, so that under your protection I can do your bidding. But the wind had better blow open my skirt when I am playing before him, and Manmatha must be my helpmate in this enterprise, O god, by your grace. And let a fragrant breeze blow from the woods at the hour that I shall be seducing that seer!

"So be it," he said, and when it had thus been disposed, she repaired to the hermitage of Kauśika.

Śakuntalā [repeating the words of Kaṇva] said:

66

"Indra, at Menakā's words, gave orders to the ever-moving wind, and Menakā at once departed with the wind. Then Menakā, callipygous nymph, set timid eyes on Viśvāmitra, who, all his evil burned off by his austerities, was yet engaged in more in his hermitage. She greeted him and began to play in front of him. Off with the wind went her moonlight skirt, the fair-skinned nymph dropped to the ground embracing it, bashfully smiling at the wind. And so that strictest of seers saw Menakā nude, nervously clutching at her skirt, indescribably young and beautiful. And remarking the virtue of her beauty the bull among brahmins fell victim to love and lusted to lie with her. He asked her, and she was blamelessly willing.

"The pair of them whiled away a very long time in the woods, making love when the spirit seized them, and it seemed only a day. And on Menakā the hermit begot Śakuntalā, on a lovely tableland in the Himālayas, by the river Mālinī. Once the baby was born, Menakā abandoned her on the bank of the Mālinī; and, her duty done, she returned rapidly to Indra's assembly.

"Birds, seeing the baby lying in the desolate wilderness that was teeming with lions and tigers, surrounded her protectively on all sides. Lest beasts of prey, greedy for meat, hurt the little girl in the forest, the birds stood guard around Menakā's child. Then I chanced to come to the river to rinse my mouth and saw her lying in the deserted and lonely woods surrounded by birds.

I took her home and adopted her as my daughter. In the decisions of Law they quote three kinds of fathers respectively: the one who begets the child's body, the one who saves its life, and the one who gives it food. And, since she had been protected by birds in the desolate wilderness, I gave her the name Śakuntalā. Thus, you should know, did Śakuntalā become my daughter, good friend, and innocently Śakuntalā thinks of me as her father."

In this manner did Kaṇva describe my birth to the great seer who had questioned him, and thus overlord of men, should you know me for Kaṇva's daughter. For I think of Kaṇva as my father, never having known my own. So, sire, I have told you exactly as I have heard it.

Duḥṣanta said:

67

And very clear is it that you are the daughter of a king, the way you told it, beautiful girl. Be my wife, buxom woman! Tell me, what can I do for you? Today I shall bring you golden necklaces, clothes, earrings wrought of gold, and sparkling gems from many countries, my pretty, and breast plates and hides. Today all my kingdom will be yours; be my wife, my pretty! Come to me, timid and lovely, according to the rite of the *Gāndharvas,* for my girl of the lovely thighs, the *Gāndharva* mode is cited as the best of marriage rites!

Śakuntalā said:

My father has gone out of the hermitage to gather fruits, O King. Wait a while. He himself will give me away to you.

Duḥṣanta said:

I want you to love me, flawless girl of the beautiful hips! Here I stand for you, for my heart has gone out to you. Oneself is one's own best friend, oneself is one's only recourse. You yourself can lawfully make the gift of yourself. There are eight forms of marriage known in total as being lawful—*brāhma, daiva, ārṣa, prājāpatya, āsura, gāndharva, rākṣasa,* and lastly *paiśāca.* Manu Svāyaṃbhuva has declared their lawfulness in this order of descent. The first four are recommended for a brahmin, you must know; the first six, innocent girl, are lawful for the baronage, in descending order. The *rākṣasa* mode is set forth for kings, the *āsura* marriage for commoners and serfs. Three of the five are lawful, the other two are held to be unlawful. The *paiśāca* and *āsura* forms are never to be perpetrated. Marriage can be done according to this rite, for such is known to be the course of the Law. *Gāndharva* and *rākṣasa* marriages are lawful for the baronage, have no fear of that—either one or the two mixed may be held, without a doubt. You are in love with me as I am in love with you, fair girl—pray become my wife by the rite of the *Gāndharvas*!

Śakuntalā said:

If this is the course of the Law, and if I am my own mistress, then, chief of the Pauravas, this is my condition in giving myself in marriage, my lord. Give your own true promise to the secret covenant I make between us: the son that may be born from me shall be Young King to succeed you, great king, declare this to me as the truth! If it is to be thus, Duḥṣanta, you may lie with me.

Vaiśaṃpāyana said:

Without hesitation the king replied, "So shall it be! And I shall conduct you to my city, sweet-smiling woman, as you deserve. This I declare to you as my truth, my lovely." Having thus spoken, the royal seer took his flawlessly moving bride solemnly by the hand and lay with her. And he comforted her and departed, and said many times, "I shall send an escort for you, with footmen, horses, chariots, and elephants; and with that I shall take you to my castle, sweet-smiling Śakuntalā!"

With such promises, Janamejaya, the king departed, and as he went he worried in his heart about Kāśyapa. "What may the venerable hermit not perpetrate when he hears of it, with all his ascetic power . . ."; and with this worry he entered his own capital.

Kaṇva himself returned to his hermitage a little while after the king's departure, and Śakuntalā was too embarrassed to dare approach her father. But Kanva, great ascetic, was gifted with divine knowledge and knew all. Seeing with his divine eyes, the master was pleased and said, "What you, of royal descent, ignoring me, have done, this your intercourse with a man, is not a transgression of the Law. For the *gāndharva* style of marriage is said to be the best for a baron, 'done in secret, without formulas, between a loving man and a loving woman.' Duḥṣanta, the man you went to lovingly, is a good man, Śakuntalā, great-spirited and law-minded. There shall be born a man of great spirit in the world—a son, yours, of great strength, a king who shall sway this entire earth to the corners of the oceans. When he marches out, the sovereign Wheel of that great spirited Turner of the Wheel shall forever roll unimpeded."

She washed the feet of the weary hermit, put down his burden, laid out the fruit he had gathered. And she said to him, "I have chosen this good man, King Duḥṣanta, for my husband. Please bestow your grace upon him and his ministers."

Kaṇva said:

I have grace for him, fair Śakuntalā, for *your* sake. Ask a boon from me, for *his* sake, whatever you wish.

Vaiśaṃpāyana said:

Thus did Śakuntalā, wishing to prosper Duḥṣanta, choose as her boon that the Pauravas would be firm in the Law and never stumble from their kingdom.

Vaiśaṃpāyana said:

68

When Duḥṣanta had returned to his seat after making his promises to Śakuntalā, the woman with the lovely thighs gave birth to a son of boundless might, after bearing him for a full three years, O Janamejaya, a son radiant like a blazing fire, enriched with all the virtues of beauty and generosity, true scion of Duḥṣanta. Kaṇva, best minister to the sacred, administered solemnly upon him the sacraments of birth, and others, as he grew in wisdom. He was a large child, with shining and pointed teeth, solid like a lion, wearing on his palm the sign of the wheel, and illustrious, large-headed, and strong. The boy, who appeared like the child of a God, grew up rapidly there. When he was six years old, the child in Kaṇva's hermitage would fetter lions and tigers, boars, buffaloes, and elephants to the trees around the hermitage and run about playing and riding and taming them. Hence the hermits who dwelled in Kaṇva's hermitage gave him a nickname: "He shall be Sarvadamana, for he tames everything!" So the boy became known as Sarvadamana, and he was endowed with prowess, might, and strength.

Watching the boy and his superhuman exploits, the seer told Śakuntalā, "It is time for him to become Young King." Since he knew how strong he had grown, Kaṇva said to his students, "Today you must quickly take Śakuntalā here with her son from our hermitage to her husband—she is blessed with all the marks that bespeak a good wife. For it is not good for women to live too long with their kinsmen; it imperils their reputation, good conduct, and virtue. Therefore take her without delay!"

"So be it," they said; and the mighty anchorites all started out and followed Śakuntalā and her son to the *City of the Elephant.* Taking her lotus-eyed son, who was like the child of an Immortal, the radiant woman left the woodland that Duḥṣanta had known. She went with her son to the king, her son shining with the brilliance of the morning sun, and was recognized and admitted. Śakuntalā paid proper homage to her king and said, "This is your son, sire. Consecrate him as Young King! For he is the godlike son you have begotten on me, king. Now act with him as you promised, greatest of men. Remember the promise you made long ago when we lay together, man of fortune, in Kaṇva's hermitage!"

When the king heard these words of hers, he remembered very well, yet he said, "I do not remember. Whose woman are you, evil ascetic? I do not recall ever having had recourse to you, whether for Law, Profit, or Love. Go or stay, as you please, or do what you want!"

At these words the beautiful and spirited woman was overcome with shame and, stunned with grief, stood motionless like a tree trunk. Her eyes turned copper red with indignant fury, her pursed lip began to tremble, and from the corner of her eyes she looked at the king with glances that seemed to burn him. Yet, although driven by her fury, she checked her expression and controlled the heat that had been accumulated by her austerities. For a moment she stood in thought, filled with grief and indignation, and looking straight at her husband, she said angrily, "You know very well, great king! Why do you say without concern that you do not know, lying like a commoner? Your heart knows the truth of it! Good sir, alas you yourself are the witness to your truth and your lie—do not despise yourself! He who knows himself to be one way and pretends it is another way is a thief who robs his own soul—what evil is beyond him? You think you are alone with your self, but don't you know the ancient seer who dwells in your heart? Him who knows your evil deeds? It is before him that you speak your lie!

"A man who has done wrong thinks, 'Nobody knows me.' But the Gods know him, and his own inner soul. Sun and Moon, Wind and Fire, Heaven, Earth, and Water, and his heart and Yama, and Day and Night, and both the Twilights, and the Law all know the doings of each man. Yama Vaivasvata takes away the evil one has done when the soul in his heart, witness to his doings, remains content with him. But when the soul is discontented with the wicked man in whom it dwells, then Yama takes away the evildoer. A man who despises his soul and dissembles will find the Gods of no avail and his soul of no benefit.

"Do not despise me, who have been a faithful wife, because I have come on my own. You fail to honor me with the guest gift that is due me, your wife, who have come to you of my own accord! Why do you slight me in your assembly as though I were a commoner? I am surely not baying in a desert—why don't you hear me? Duḥṣanta, if you do not do my word as I am begging you, your head will burst into a hundred pieces! A husband enters his wife and is reborn from her—thus the old poets know this as a wife's wifehood. The offspring that is born to a man who follows the scriptures saves with his lineage the forebears that died before. Svayaṃbhū himself has said that a son is a *putra* because he saves his father from the hell named Put. She is a wife who is handy in the house, she is a wife who bears children, she is a wife whose life is her husband, she is a wife who is true to her lord. The wife is half the man, a wife is better than his best friend, a wife is the root of Law, Profit, and Love, a wife is a friend in a man's extremity. They who have wives have rites, they who have wives have households, they who have wives are happy, they who have wives have luck. Sweet-spoken wives are friends in solitude, fathers in the rites of the Law, mothers in suffering. Even in the wilderness she means respite for the man who is journeying. A man with a wife is a trustworthy man. Therefore a wife is the best course. Only a faithful wife follows even a man who has died and is transmigrating, sharing a common lot in adversities, for he is forever her husband. A wife who has died before stands still and waits for her husband; and a good wife follows after her husband if he has died before. This, sire, is the reason why marriage is sought by man, where a husband finds a wife for now and eternity.

"A son, the wise say, is the man himself born from himself; therefore a man will look upon the mother of his son as his own mother. The son born from his wife is as a man's face in a mirror; and looking at him brings as much joy to a father as finding heaven brings to a saint. Men, burned by the sorrows of their hearts and sickly with disease, rejoice in their wives, as overheated people do in water. No matter how aggravated, a man should say no unkind things to his loving women, for in them he sees contingent his love, his joy, and his merit. Women are forever one's sacred field of birth—are even the seers able to have children without one? A son stumbles and covered with dirt embraces his father—is there joy beyond that?

"And you, why do you reject frowningly a son who of his own accord has come to you and fondly looks at you? Ants carry their own eggs and never break them—you, so wise in the Law, won't keep your son? Neither clothes nor loving women nor water are so good to touch as the infant son you embrace. Of two-footed men the brahmin is best; of four-footed beasts the cow is worthiest; of respected men the guru is the first; and of all things to touch a son is the choicest. Embrace and touch your handsome son! There is no feeling on earth lovelier than to feel a son. For three full years I have borne this son, lord of kings, for him to kill your grief. When I was giving birth to him a voice came from the sky, saying, O Paurava, 'He shall be the offerer of a hundred Horse Sacrifices.'

"Do not men who had gone to another village take their sons lovingly on their laps and kiss their heads and feel happy? From the *Vedas* themselves, as you too know, the twiceborn recite these verses at the birth ceremony of their sons, 'From each limb hast thou come forth, thou art born from my heart, thou art myself with the name of son, live thou a hundred autumns! For my nourishment lies with thee, and my eternal lineage—therefore live thou, my son, in all happiness for a hundred autumns!' He has been born from your limbs, one man from another: look on my son as your other self, as your reflection seen in a clear pond. Just as the *āhavanīya* fire is carried forward from the *gārhapatya* hearth, so is he born from you, and you, being one, have been made two.

"In time past while you were going on a chase and were led off by a deer, you approached me, a young girl, in my father's hermitage. Urvaśī, Pūrvacitti, Sahajanyā, Menakā, Viśvācī, and Ghṛtācī are the six greatest Apsarās. And from among them it was the beautiful Apsarā Menakā, daughter of Brahmā, who came from heaven to earth and bore me by Viśvāmitra. The Apsarā Menakā gave birth to me on a peak of the Himālayas and abandoned me pitilessly and went, as if I were another's child. What evil deeds have I done before in another life that in my childhood I was abandoned by my kin, and now by you? Surely when you forsake me I shall go to my hermitage—but pray do not forsake your own son!"

Duḥṣanta said:

I do not know that this is my son you have born, Śakuntalā. Women are liars—who will trust your word? Menakā, your mother, was a merciless slut who cast you off like a faded garland on a peak of the Himālayas! Viśvāmitra, your merciless father, who, born a baron, reached for brahminhood, was a lecher! Menakā is the first of the Apsarās, Viśvāmitra the first of the seers—how can you call yourself their daughter, speaking like a whore? Are you not ashamed to say such incredible things, especially in my presence? Off with you, evil ascetic! An ever-awesome seer, an Apsarā like Menakā—are related to you, a wretch that wears a hermit's garb! Your son is too big, and he is strong even while still a child; how can he have shot up like a *Śāla* tree in such a short time? Your own birth is very humble, and you look like a slut to me. So Menakā happened to give birth to you from sheer lust? Everything you say is obscure to me, ascetic. I do not know you. Go where you want!

Śakuntalā said:

69

King, you see the faults of others that are small, like mustard seeds, and you look but do not see your own, the size of pumpkins! Menakā is one of the Thirty Gods, the Thirty come after Menakā! My birth is higher than yours, Duḥṣanta! You walk on earth, great king, but I fly the skies. See how we differ, like Mount Meru and a mustard seed! I can roam to the palaces of great Indra, of Kubera, of Yama, of Varuṇa; behold my power, king!

The lesson I shall teach you is the truth, impeccable prince, to instruct you, not to spite you, so listen and forbear. As long as an ugly man does not see his face in a mirror he will think that he is handsomer than others. But when he sees his ugly face in a mirror, he knows how inferior he is. A very handsome man never despises anyone, but the constant babbler becomes a foul-mouthed slanderer. A fool who hears the gossipers speak good and evil always eats up the evil as a swine eats up dung. An intelligent man who hears the gossipers speak good and evil always finds the good as the swans find milk in water. As sorry as a good man who reproaches others, so happy is an evil man reproaching others. Just as good people find joy in speaking well of the aged, so the fool finds joy in berating an honest man. Happily live they who know no evil; happily the fools who look for it. When the good are belittled by others they call such people enemies. There is nothing more ludicrous found in the world than that the wicked call the honest wicked. Even a heretic fears a liar like a virulent poisonous snake; how much more the orthodox! He who does not accept the son he himself begot as his equal will see the Gods destroy his fortune and will never find the worlds. For the ancestors call a son the foundation of family and lineage, the highest of all merits of Law—therefore one should never abandon a son. Manu cites six kinds of sons—

the one begotten on one's wife; and these five: obtained as gift, bought, reared, adopted, and begotten on other women. Sons give men merit of Law and a good name, they foster the happiness of their fathers' hearts and, once born, save the ancestors from hell like ferries of the Law.

Tiger among kings, do not forsake your son, as you protect yourself, your word, and your Law, O lord of the earth. Do not stoop to deceit, lion among kings. The gift of one pond is better than a hundred wells, one sacrifice is more than a hundred ponds, one son more than a hundred sacrifices, one truth more than a hundred sons. A thousand Horse Sacrifices and truth were held in a balance, and truth outweighed all thousand. Speaking the truth, O king, may or may not be equaled by learning all *Vedas* and bathing at all sacred fords. There is no Law higher than truth, nothing excels truth; and no evil is bitterer on earth than a lie. Truth, O king, is the supreme Brahman, truth is the sovereign covenant. Do not forsake your covenant, king, the truth shall be your alliance.

If you hold with the lie, if you have no faith of your own in me, then I shall go. There is no consorting with one like you. Even without you, Duḥṣanta, my son shall reign over the four-cornered earth crowned by the king of mountains!

Vaiśaṃpāyana said:

Having said all this to the king, Śakuntalā departed. Then, a disembodied voice spoke from the sky to Duḥṣanta, as he sat surrounded by his priests, chaplain, teachers, and councillors. "The mother is the father's water sack—he is the father who begets the son. Support your son, Duḥṣanta; do not reject Śakuntalā. The son who has seed saves from Yama's realm, O God among men. You have planted this child. Śakuntalā has spoken the truth. A wife bears a son by splitting her body in two; therefore, Duḥṣanta, keep Śakuntalā's son, O King. This is ruin: what man alive will forsake a live son born from himself?

"Paurava, keep this great-spirited scion of Duḥṣanta and Śakuntalā; for he is yours to keep, and so is our behest. And as you keep him, he will be known by the name of Bharata."

King Paurava heard the utterance of the celestials and, much delighted, spoke to his chaplain and councillors, "Listen, good sirs, to what the Envoy of the Gods has spoken! I myself knew very well he was my son. But if I had taken him as my son on her word alone, suspicion would have been rife among the people and he would never have been cleared of it."

The king, having thus cleared himself of all suspicions, through the words of the Envoy of the Gods, now happily and joyfully accepted his son, O Bharata. He kissed him on the head and embraced him lovingly; and he was welcomed to the court by the brahmins and praised by the bards. The king upon touching his son became filled with the greatest joy; and, knowing his duty, he honored his wife according to it. His majesty made up to her and said, "The alliance I made with you was not known to my people; that is the reason why I argued, so that I might clear you, my queen. People would think that I had a bond with you because you are a woman, and that I had chosen this son for the kingdom. That is why I argued. And if you have spoken very harsh words to me in your anger, dear wide-eyed wife, it was out of love, and I forgive you, beautiful woman."

Thus spoke King Duḥṣanta to his beloved queen, and he honored her, O Bhārata, with clothes, food, and drink. Thereupon King Duḥṣanta invested his son by Śakuntalā with the name Bharata and anointed him Young King. And the glorious Wheel of the great-spirited Bharata rolled thundering through the worlds, grand, radiant, divine, unvanquished. He defeated the kings of the earth and made them his vassals; he lived the Law of the strict and attained to sublime fame. He was a king, a Turner of the Wheel, a majestic worldwide monarch. He sacrificed many sacrifices, he was an Indra, lord of the winds. Like Dakṣa, he had Kaṇva officiate at a richly rewarded sacrifice, and, an illustrious king, Bharata offered a Horse Sacrifice that was styled Vast-in-Cows, at which he gave a thousand lotus counts of kine to Kaṇva.

From Bharata springs the Bhārata fame, from him the Bhārata race and those other ancient men who are famed as Bhāratas. In the continuing lineage of Bharata there arose great and puissant kings, the likes of Gods, the likes of Brahmā, whose names are famous beyond measure everywhere. I shall celebrate those among them who were their chiefs, O Bhārata, the fortunate and godlike ones, given to truth and honesty.

The epic version highlights certain facets of the story, some similar and some different from the later versions. It sets out the origin myth of the founder of the Bharata clan, an origin endorsed by a divine proclamation. It also requires the approval of the clansmen since, evidently, the status of the *rājā* was not absolute. The *rājā* is described as the *goptā*—the herdsman of the earth, and even though the earth is said to be extensive and as far as the settlements of the *mleccha* (social outcastes) and the forest peoples, it is not a title which would have been used in a sophisticated court. The pastoral connotation is evident and *goptā* is indicative of a relatively small, well-knit society, even if Duḥṣanta is described as the *goptā* of the earth. The extent of territory is diminished by the uncertainty of its borders since the settlements of the *mleccha* and the forest peoples were not too far from Hastināpur. In effect this was a small area where attacks against the forest people could be initiated with the intrusion of a hunt into an erstwhile closed area. To describe the settlements of forest peoples as on the distant boundary would suggest that they may have been seen as alien.

A series of contrasting settings frames the scenes: the ferocity of the hunt, the gentle calm of the hermitage, each presenting a different face of nature, of the forest, the *araṇya*. The hunt is at one level an onslaught on nature, but is also suggestive of a surrogate battle or raid in which territorial claims are being established. The *rājā* goes on a hunt accompanied by a large entourage of heavily armed soldiers. The graphic account of the hunt reads like a war against nature. One is reminded of another vivid description of the destruction of the forest, the Khāṇḍava-vana consumed by fire[16] to provide a sufficient clearing in the forest for the establishing of Indraprastha.

The hermitage is set so deep in the forest that it is almost another world—a magical world of translucent green, lush growth on both banks of the river Mālinī. It is liminal space, the bridge between the two contrasting ecological cultures of the *grāma*/settlement and the *araṇya*/forest. As a hermitage it parallels the forest retreats described in the *Brāhmaṇas*, but also provides a genesis to the *agrahāra* which came to be established later, where land was donated to *brāhmaṇas* who had it cultivated, and combined the functions of substantial landowners with those of the hermitage. But the epic hermitage has much of the natural world. The trees provide a cool shade, the earth is soft and covered with clusters of flowering trees and creepers, the birds and the bees are undisturbed and even the predatory animals are gentle. The Vedic recitations link it to the world of the hero and Duḥṣanta imagines he has entered the world of Brahmā. Vedic recitations in accordance with the well-known mnemonic devices of the *pada-pāṭha* and the *krama-pāṭha* suggest an *āśrama* with a large number of celibate students. Yet in every other way it is more suggestive of the habitat of forest dwellers—the *āṭavikas* and *vanavāsis*—with whom we are told Duḥṣanta has been in conflict. Can the story, at one level, be viewed as symbolic of an opposition between the society of the hero and the people of the forest ? The hunt as an onslaught on nature would also then take on the character of an attempted domination over forest dwellers, which was of course an aspect of the process of clearing land and establishing settlements on the part of chiefdoms on the way to acquiring greater power. The bi-polarity of the forest and the court is a theme which consistently runs through the many versions of the story.

Duḥṣanta arrives at the hermitage almost by accident, following a deer. The hero chasing a deer during a hunt and arriving at an unexpected place is well known to folk literature, and in the Indian context the deer enticing the *kṣatriya* is familiar from other sources as well, not least the

Rāmāyaṇa. The enticement is into an *āśrama*, and the otherness of the world of the hermitage is emphasised by Duḥṣanta entering it unaccompanied by his entourage. The power of asceticism is being respected for the *ṛṣi* can destroy the universe or create fear even in Yama, the god of Death. Śakuntalā receives him alone and is forthright and welcoming. She replies at length to his questions and without any shyness or embarrassment, even when describing how she came to be born.

The birth and childhood of Śakuntalā would not be extraordinary given the other narratives on this theme in the epic. Perhaps the closest parallel is that of Kuntī to whom the *ṛṣi* Durvāsas gives the secret formula of calling up any deity to father a son on her. She tests it whilst yet unmarried and bears a son to Sūrya, the sun-god. But because she is unmarried she cannot keep the child, so he is placed in a basket and set adrift on a river to be picked up by persons of the low *sūta* caste. He grows into one of the anti-heroes of the epic, Karṇa.[17] The birth is not associated with a marriage, the child is forsaken and when Kuntī discovers Karṇa to be her lost first-born and reveals it to him, he is torn between the joy of discovering his actual mother and the knowledge that, as his mother, she is about to make an impossible demand of him: the preservation of his enemies, the Pāṇḍavas, three of whom are his step-brothers. Women in the epic are, at times, devoted mothers or mothers who have their individualistic ways of expressing what the relationship between parent and child should be—this need not involve conforming to the routine.

Duḥṣanta, much taken by "the flawless girl with the beautiful hips", offers marriage and also what seems to be a kind of bride-price—jewels, gems, clothes and even his kingdom. Śakuntalā makes the marriage conditional. The decision to marry Duḥṣanta is hers alone and is later endorsed by her foster-father. The exceptionally long gestation of Bharata underlines his special status. He grows up in the hermitage and is taken to the capital when he is of an appropriate age, in accordance with the wishes of Kaṇva. Hastināpur is almost incidental, its description being minimal. There is no mention of any elaborate court and it seems to be the residence of a chief rather than a king. The dialogue between Duḥṣanta and Śakuntalā at the court is down to earth, to say the least, and although he refers abusively to her parents, she replies to him with dignity and does not allow herself to be brow-beaten.[18] She is a forthright, free, assertive, high-spirited young woman who demands that her conditions, as stipulated at her marriage, be fulfilled. Less concerned with herself she is ready to return to the forest (although she lectures the king on the necessity of a wife), but insists that the son be recognised. The issue is less that of the marriage, more the question of proving the paternity of the child, the crux of this story. The birth of a male child provides status to the mother and allows her to make claims on the father's clan. This is made clear in the statement of the celestial voice which says that the mother is the bag for containing the seed, but it is to the father that the child belongs, and a son can save the father from going to the abode of Yama. This statement becomes something of a formulaic verse in some of the later texts paraphrasing the narrative. A woman's power lies directly in her actions, and symbolically in the existence of her son. But the statement of the celestial voice also implicitly raises the question of Duḥṣanta's morality: of the need for Duḥṣanta to accept responsibility for the child. The divine proclamation establishes the status of Bharata and makes him acceptable to the clansmen, a requirement which preconditions his initiation into the clan.

In the dialogue with Duḥṣanta, Śakuntalā seems to be the more assertive, as her appeal is to the truth of her claim; she does not stoop to abusing him. Her reference to the various functions of a wife aimed at propitiating the husband, makes one wonder whether this passage was not a later interpolation, at a time when the forthrightness of Śakuntalā may have become somewhat unpalatable, and was modified. The delineation of Śakuntalā marks a counterpoint to the notion of the *pativratā*, the ideal wife, which is referred to elsewhere in the text in the later didactic sections. Interpolating passages was regularly resorted to in the epics and would have been one way of mediating a different social ethic. The personality of Duḥṣanta, by comparison, is more weakly defined and his pretence of not recognising her can hardly be regarded as appropriate to the ethic of the hero. Yet this again is not the only occasion for such an incident, for it looms equally large in the narrative of the *Rāmāyaṇa* in the attitude of Rāma towards Sītā when they return to Ayodhyā. Perhaps it has less to do with the ethic of the hero and more to do with the testing of the heroine.

One may well ask, who in fact is Śakuntalā ? She is depicted as being almost a woman of the *āṭavika/vanavāsi* society, whose social origin was disguised by making her the daughter of an *apsarā*. Such a reading would change the social contours of the relationship and explain why the *rājā* should have ignored her existence after he left the hermitage of Kaṇva although he remembered his sojourn with her. It might also underline her independence and, to that extent, a distancing from the *rājā*. Her attitude is not that of a submissive subject. She is a woman from a different society who sees herself as equal in status to the man, characteristic of the society of forest dwellers whose egalitarianism would be more evident than that of Hastināpur. She can confidently go back to her dwelling in the forest and leave Duḥṣanta to come to terms with the boy. The *gāndharva* marriage frequently takes place between a *rājā* and a woman of the forest. Was this literally so, until the *apsarā* became the synonym for such a woman? The hint of bride-price in the proposal of marriage would again point to her belonging to a society conditioned by a different set of norms from those of Hastināpur.

Apsarās feature prominently in the legends woven around heroes. They frequently enter the scene at the start of a lineage or when there is a break in it.[19] They could represent a claim to status or else a marriage with a woman from an obscure or socially marginalised family who is then raised in rank by being projected as an *apsarā*. They are depicted as water-nymphs in the *Ṛgveda* and the goddess of speech, Vāk, is said to be born of the waters.[20] The *Atharvaveda* speaks of the *apsarās* living in trees such as the *nyagrodha*/banyan and *aśvattha*/peepal, trees which were important to Vedic ritual.[21] One is of course reminded of those Indus seals which depict a woman within a tree. This perhaps links them not only to the continuing worship of trees as part of fertility rituals, but also to later representations of the rite which sometimes required a virgin to touch a tree with her foot to encourage it to bloom; and the *Śālabhañjikās*, sculptural representations of women associated with trees, where women are seen as a symbol of fertility and sexuality. In other sections of the epic reference is made to a number of *tīrthas* named after *apsarās*, places of pilgrimage often near water sources.[22] *Apsarās* are generally not bound in marriage and when they have succeeded in seduction, they return to their usual pursuits although some may remain longer with their human lovers. But their virginity is not questioned, and as seductresses they are symbols of rejuvenation and of the power of femininity. This does not make them into "celestial prostitutes" as some would describe them, for there is a difference between a prostitute and a seductress. Their seductions are generally only of a single *ṛṣi* and the context is that of using one kind of power to break another. The sexuality of the *apsarās* is comprehended less by us today, since it comes from a world with very different mores from those of the Judeo-Christian tradition, which we frequently subscribe to now. Śakuntalā's faithfulness to Duḥṣanta is not characteristic behaviour for an *apsarā*. They are however, often the victims of a curse which, in the examples from the *Mahābhārata*, converts them into unattractive creatures.[23] The curse is intended to lower their pride and humiliate them, and to create a binary opposition between *kāma* and *tapas*, first asserted in the *Ṛgveda*.[24] *Tapas* begets *kāma* but *kāma* can become the test of *tapas*. The *apsarā* was a beautiful woman made for dalliance, the fantasy woman of the world of the heroes. In later times the *apsarās* fade when the goddesses become prominent. The *apsarās* are not, therefore, the same as women of the earth, they have their own order and their own codes of behaviour and authority. In a sense they are a counterweight to the insistence on the *pativratā* as the ideal woman—the life-long, devoted, self-effacing wife to her husband—and to that extent alleviate the dreariness of the didactic sections of the epic with their heavy male-dominated pronouncements.

There is a continuing association of *apsarās* with heroes, as for instance in the hero-stones of later times, which show the hero being taken up to heaven by *apsarās* after he has died in battle.[25] There is also an association with heavenly musicians, the Gandharvas. In the epic version, the identity of Śakuntalā as an *apsarā* is reiterated by the small details which make her different from an ordinary woman.

Yet she is in the mould of the other epic heroines—Draupadī, Kuntī, Gāndhārī—strong women who as mothers and wives dominate the story and whose individuality cannot be overlooked. Epic heroines are sometimes associated with the knowledge of a treasure which the hero seeks, or else they protect the treasure. In the narrative of Śakuntalā the treasure may be symbolised by the son she brings to the hero, a son who was to be unique in the lineage of the Pūrus. The eulogies on Bharata in the later tradition, exalting him as the ancestor of a famous clan (even though his children died and he was succeeded by an adopted son); marking him out as a major figure in the lineage not only requires introduction through an unusual birth—namely, a three-year gestation with a mother who could be either an *apsarā* or a forest dwelling woman—it also ensures that the story of Śakuntalā remains in the consciousness of those who live in the land of Bharata.

The epic story appears to have been represented in other forms as well in the period around the Christian era. These were largely visual, and although its identity is uncertain it may be suggested that the story had some currency.

The representation of narrative in art was popularised through the depiction of the *Jātaka* stories and events from the life of the Buddha on Buddhist monuments constructed just prior to and after the Christian era. In such places the narrative tends to give priority to space over time and frequently focuses either on the central episode of the story (that which makes it recognisable) or else arranges the events within a single frame.[26] In both cases it assumes that the story is well-known. Buddhist sites often depict the story within a medallion, a form which has parallels with decoration on mirrors. The story has been identified in a low relief at the Ranigumpha cave in Orissa, dating to about the second century B.C. A king is shown as arriving with soldiers and hunting deer, whilst a beautiful woman rests on a low hanging branch of a tree with a deer at her feet. The king is then shown as putting away his bow and conversing with her. Although the identification has been contested it seems plausible.[27]

A more evocative graphic narrative is the one on a disc made of shell, inlaid with mother-of-pearl, strips of gold and coloured glass, which was found in the excavations at Ai-Khanum—a town on the Oxus—and has been dated prior to 145 B.C. It appears to have been deposited in the treasury, therefore could have been brought from India as a luxury item, being either the back of a mirror or the lid of a box. Various scenes are depicted: a royal procession through a landscape with deer and peacocks; three persons riding in a chariot-and-four, over one of whom is held an umbrella and the group escorted by three riders; a group under an arched roof look on at the scene; a seated couple are conversing; a building with three pinnacles is depicted, and a quadrangular pond. Stylistically it is suggestive of Sanchi and Vidisha and is thought to be the work of a specialist in shell carving.[28]

A clay disc from Bhita has a scene of a hunt and a hermitage.[29] It is a circular terracotta plaque, stylistically suggesting the period of the Christian era and perhaps contemporary with Sanchi, especially if the original matrix was ivory, as is thought. It depicts a forest landscape with deer and peacocks and the huts of hermits. A woman fills water in a vessel and there is also a chariot-and-four in which there are two persons; another two seem to be in conversation behind a barrier.

That two of the beautifully crafted objects with scenes apparently depicting this story were expensive items, suggests that it was appreciated among the wealthy and may even have had currency in court circles. The mirror focuses attention on the gaze, the subject looking at herself or himself. It has been argued that the depiction of the gaze was a form of courtly romance, and the repeated evoking of "the gaze" in the play of Kālidāsa would support this.

It would seem that the epic version of the story was being depicted, given the absence of those episodes which distinguish the play from the epic story. If the scenes shown were those of the Śakuntalā story—and they could also have been from any other story linking a hunt to a hermitage and to a couple—it would by now have been widely known and recognised from the themes, since none of these objects carry labels of identification. But this popularity was to be considerably enhanced by the conversion of the story into a play by Kālidāsa.

Terracotta plaque from excavations at Bhita, which has been interpreted as depicting the scene of the arrival of Duṣyanta at the hermitage of Kaṇva

Menakā and Śakuntalā (Ravi Varma)

3. The *Abhijñāna-śākuntalam* of Kālidāsa

WHEN we turn to the play by Kālidāsa, the *Abhijñāna-śākuntalam*, not only have the context and the story changed but, more pertinently, the character of Śakuntalā is a contrast to the woman in the epic. There is almost a contestation with the epic version which, in the presentations of modern times, has been marginalised. In Kālidāsa's version we are in the realm of delicacy and romance, of anguish and imminent tragedy, of pathos and finally, of happiness. The emotional range is infinite when compared to the epic narrative, but in the intermeshing of the emotions, the image of Śakuntalā undergoes a transformation. Kālidāsa takes the theme from the epic but fills it out with sub-plots involving a curse and a signet ring. In adapting a known theme he was following the theoretical rules relating to heroic comedies, in which earlier stories from the epics were frequently reworked. It could be said that the sub-plots are almost as important as the main story, for they may be the cause of both the separation of the lovers and ultimately of their coming together again. Such sub-plots are also used by Kālidāsa in the other plays, where some of the action revolves around a curse and a reunion. The sub-plots draw in those elements which are of the supernatural and the magical, and introduce the unpredictable and irrational, acting as counterpoints to the otherwise rather straight romantic narrative.

Kālidāsa remoulded a well-known story to the extent that it became unusual and changed the essential mood of the narrative, but he was not the only one making such innovations. His predecessor, Bhāsa had also written plays, some deriving their themes from the *Mahābhārata,* and such plays helped to position old narratives in a different genre. Familiarity with the foundational story meant that innovations would be easily recognised. Court circles and urbanites would still be familiar with the narratives from the oral tradition, although some of them were now prescribed in a new format. In writing this play Kālidāsa selected a theme from the epic, but the sub-themes may well have come from folk literature. A flavour of this is found in some of the *Jātakas* which were popular tales, each with a moral conforming to Buddhist ethics. The *ākhyāna* or narrative from the epic was converted into a *nāṭaka*, the two being very different literary genres. In the process there is a selection of an item from the past, a conscious looking back at it and the creating of a new form, compatible with contemporary perspectives.

Elaborating on the origin myth of the Bharatas constituted a deliberate turning to the past, possibly with the unstated thought of drawing some parallels with the present. Given the history of northern India in the early centuries A.D. there would have been contesting identities, particularly among those competing for power. If viewed as an entity, the works of Kālidāsa do suggest the structuring of a royal identity, different perhaps from that of most pre-Gupta courts; the lavish performance of the rituals pertaining to *kṣatriya* status is one example of the difference.

The play follows the outline of the epic story but introduces some changes which weave in elements of stereotypes from other sources, the whole being structured into a sophisticated dramatic form. This was a characteristic feature of the *nāṭaka*, typically, heroic drama of a romantic nature; the theme was based on a well-known story, often from the *itihāsa-purāṇa* tradition, but added to it was an element of originality and innovation.[30] The quality of the language, and the finely intermeshed dialogue and plot lift it from the conventional to the unique. At a broader level the high culture of the play is reflected in the nuanced relationships between the characters. The play was intended for performance, not for recitation, and was performed at the court or at a court festival for a small, discerning and sophisticated audience.

There is no certainty about Kālidāsa's dates but he is likely to have lived in about the fourth century A.D. Some would prefer an earlier date. His version of the story could therefore have been written some centuries subsequent to that of the epic. A number of arguments have been made to suggest that he was associated with the Gupta court and, although none are conclusive, he could well have been a contemporary. The basic argument is itself circuitous, in that Kālidāsa is associated with the Gupta period in order to prove the theory of its being the. "Golden Age". It is viewed by some as the reassertion of an Indian dynasty after the long rule of the foreign Indo-Greeks, Śakas and Kuṣāṇas, but there is little consciousness of this in most contemporary texts. The use of Sanskrit in inscriptions was a continuation of an earlier practice started by the Kṣatrapas, and the propagation of the cults of Viṣṇu or Śiva were familiar from patronage given to them by earlier royal families and their associates. An imprint of Śaiva worship implicit in the *Abhijñāna-śākuntalam* has been recognised.[31] There is curiously little of Buddhism or Jainism in it, which is surprising considering that both Ujjain and Mathura were associated with them and Malwa and central India were familiar to Kālidāsa, as is evident from his *Meghadūtam*.

Among the more interesting legends about Kālidāsa is the one related by the Tibetan, the Lama Tāranātha in the seventeenth century, in which Kālidāsa, a handsome cowherd, is transformed from a fool to a poet largely through the grace of the goddess Kālī and the support of the princess Vāsantī.[32] Interestingly, it is the intervention of a woman in this legend which reveals his accomplishment as a poet. There is a certain inversion of reality in this version as Kālidāsa, although said to be a cowherd, writes a highly classical form of Sanskrit. His use of language established a norm, imitated by subsequent playwrights and poets. It is curious that authors such as Vālmīki and Kālidāsa should be the subject of legends which show them as being initially fools or knaves.

The romantic play as a genre of literature spotlighted the sport of kings—hunting (both literally and symbolically) and romantic love, set in a courtly background. The hunt can also be seen as a metaphor of courtly love: pursuit, contesting emotions and ultimately, submission. The play is seen as focussing on the tension between *kāma* and *dharma*, desire and duty, manifest in the relation between the two dominant *rasas* of *Śṛṅgāra-rasa* and *vīra-rasa*, the erotic and the heroic, a theory developed by later commentators on the play.[33] The former has to be controlled and the latter exercised. This is also part of the scheme of *puruṣārtha*, where the balance between *dharma*, *artha* and *kāma*, are said to bring about *mokṣa*/liberation from rebirth. But perhaps the focus is not on a canvas as broad as that of *puruṣārtha*; it can be argued that there are other tensions too. Hunting, or the alternative of going into battle, provided the opportunity for heroic acts. To this context may be added the necessity of *viraha* at some point so that separation creates the tragic element which is finally resolved by the lovers coming together. Love-in-union and love-in-separation are important components in romantic plays, and more so in those of Kālidāsa. Themes picked up from legends of the past entail some looking back and some reformulating. There was no insistence on staying within the confines of the original story and no hesitation in making it more contemporary. The tautness of the play and the interlocking of locations were intended for audiences appreciative of these elements. The action is set in an earlier period but

Kālidāsa introduces features from his own times, particularly when he indirectly endorses requirements stated in the *dharmaśāstras* as, for example, in references to the behaviour of a wife in her husband's home or the duties of the king.

There is in the play a rhetoric of political power based on the monarchical state. The fourth century A.D. was a period of well-established monarchies with their appurtenances of administration, revenue and coercive agencies. The court at Hastināpur is now the focus of those in authority and kingly authority was expressed in various ways, for example in the taking of impressive titles such as *mahārāja-adhirāja*. This would have a quite different effect from the epic, where Duḥṣanta is referred to as the *goptā* and the *rājā*. The duties performed by the king exceed that of simply protecting his subjects, as he is now responsible for their welfare, and for maintaining equilibrium in society. The latter is accomplished through a hierarchy of administration in which the court is central, and is provisioned through taxes. The centrality of succession based on birth remained necessary to dynastic rule, and the legitimacy of succession continued to be a major concern.

The up-grading, as it were, of monarchy is also suggested in the closeness of kings to deities, a feature common to many literary works of this time. Duṣyanta (as he is named in the play) is called upon for assistance by Indra when the latter is threatened by *asuras*. The association between *rājās* and gods was earlier said to derive from the king being constituted of divine particles—a step towards his being seen as the human parallel to deity. Still later, claims would be made on occasion, to kings being an incarnation of deity, frequently Viṣṇu. This did not mean creating an icon of the king to be worshipped as deity, rather such "incarnations" were often attempts at manipulating the power of the king.

But closeness to deity is not the only claim made. The

alternative authority of the *ṛṣi* is also drawn upon in the term *rājaṛṣi,* by which his control over his domain is seen to be similar to the discipline of the *ṛṣi,* as indeed the authority of the *ṛṣi* would enhance kingship.[34] Apart from this, the visibility of Brahmanical high culture is evident and was a dominant part of the classicism with which Kālidāsa is associated. The *āśrama* is an incipient *agrahāra*—a settlement of *brāhmaṇas* on land donated by the king. In earlier times the former was a clearing in the forest where *ṛṣis* settled, whereas the latter had the legal status of being a grant from a governmental authority. In the post-Gupta period settlements such as the *agrahāras* became powerful nuclei and networks of upper caste culture and learning. There was a consciousness of elite behaviour being conditioned (at least in theory) by the norms of the *dharmaśāstras*, and the play reflects the values of elite society, largely conditioned by upper caste mores.

There is a greater distancing between the king and those living in the *āśrama* of Kaṇva, in part expressed by their deference to the king. Some have attributed the shyness of Śakuntalā to her being overawed by the king. Kings were beginning to make donations of land to learned *brāhmaṇas*; sometimes the donation was of waste land so that the *brāhmaṇa* settlement also functioned to open it up to cultivation and to Sanskritic culture. The *āśrama* with its self-contained activities suggests a parallel with an *agrahāra.*[35] *Āśramas* were exempt from taxes, the argument being that their pious activities accumulated merit, part of which accrued to the king who could also be called upon to protect them. When the *vidūṣaka* says that the rice growing in the *āśrama* of Kaṇva should be taxed, he is rebuked by the king who explains that the revenue from the *āśrama* lies in the merit gained from the activities of those who live there. The cultivation of privately held and state controlled land was a major source of revenue, and a hierarchy of taxes became familiar. This was very different from the skirmishes and cattle-raids of the epics which were a means of garnering resources. A further source of revenue was commerce, an activity which had reached out to virtually every part of the subcontinent by now. There was overland trade with west and central Asia and maritime trade with the Red Sea and south-east Asia. Control over territory was important but the nature of control had changed. Territory was the *rāṣṭra* and the collection of revenue was central. Hunting was now but a pale shadow of the hunts of earlier times, for land was controlled through military conquest and administration.

The play opens with a brief hunting scene, far gentler and less destructive than that of the epic. Duṣyanta eventually narrows the hunt to a deer, significantly the much valued blackbuck, and the chase takes him to the *āśrama*. The parallels between Śakuntalā and the deer are frequent: they symbolise the serenity of the *āśrama*, are innocent and given to tenderness, and are also physically close, for the deer the king is hunting is a fawn nurtured by Śakuntalā. This seems to hint at the predator being the king and Śakuntalā being the prey, as is mentioned in passing by the *vidūṣaka*. It also hints, again in passing, at Śakuntalā being the mother of the king's son. Curiously, although the last Act is set in an *āśrama,* there are no deer in it and this has been read as suggestive of a different Śakuntalā.[36] The meekness and gentleness implicit in the analogy of the deer have vanished, and she is now presented as a woman who has experienced the vicissitudes of life. Hunting as the recreation of kings was regarded as enviable expertise, but hunters who hunted for food—the Vyādhas, Niṣādas and such like—were placed low in the social hierarchy and treated as sinful.[37] The *kṣatriya* can indulge in the same activity blamelessly because it is in a different social context. The hunt was a physical cleansing of the hunter, dispensing with bile, phlegm, fat and sweat; it was a means of acquiring proficiency in the use of weapons and an understanding of the fears of animals.[38] The hunt could become a court event when the entourage was large, and at times even included the royal women. The opening hunt in the play is not confined to the individual huntsman, as the king rides through the forest in his chariot accompanied by his *vidūṣaka* and others. But on entering the *āśrama* he leaves them behind, removes his royal regalia and weapons and hands them to the charioteer. This has been interpreted as the king casting off the royal image as he is entering another world,[39] presumably one which is the antonym of the royal court. But at the same time this was almost a fantasy world, the threshold of romantic imaginings and magic, enhanced by the *nayikā*/heroine being not an ordinary woman but one born of an *apsarā*. This argument could be taken further: that the *āśrama* although protected by the king, is in some ways outside his realm, since those who live in it do not pay taxes to the state nor do they observe the requisite social obligations.

The play is an elaboration of the skeletal story in the epic. Doubtless courtly drama required a teasing out of the story to provide dramatic effects and to induce a romantic mood. The *āśrama* which the king enters is the epitome of gentleness, harmony and peace. Parrots rest on trees, pecking scattered grains of rice, stones have a veneer because of the oily nuts which have fallen on them, water drips from the clothing of bark hung out to dry, the deer feed without fear, streams meander noiselessly through the forest and the smoke rises from the sacrificial fires of the *ṛṣis*. The *āśrama* is also a counterpoint to the hunt since the ritual of sacrifice uses only domesticated animals and cultivated cereals as offerings. In no case are wild animals used for this purpose,[40] although the forest provides pastures for the village animals.[41]

The *āśrama* is said to be protected by the king, which is also suggestive of its being parallel to the *agrahāra*; this is indicated by the king at first pretending to be an officer in royal employ, concerned with the well-being of *āśramas*. It is not as isolated as the forest in the epic although it is also located in the Himalayan foothills, a few hours travel from Hastināpur. The acolytes greet the king with deference and the wish that he may have a worthy son—a premonition of the essential story. Śakuntalā therefore is left to receive guests. The conversation is almost entirely between him and the two young women who are Śakuntalā's companions, Priyaṁvadā and Anasūyā; compared to Śakuntalā they are far more worldly. The two friends mediate between Śakuntalā and Duṣyanta and in this, too, the play differs from the epic where the story is told virtually as a dialogue between the protagonists, with almost no participation by other persons either of the *āśrama* or the court. Priyaṁvadā generally takes the initiative; for instance, explaining Śakuntalā's birth and identity to the king, also stating that she is eligible for marriage, and later suggesting that Śakuntalā write a letter to the king; or indeed, asking the king to banish the anguish of her friend and pleading with Durvāsas to mitigate the effect of the curse. Priyaṁvadā is closer in spirit to the independent and competent Śakuntalā of the epic version, and is therefore a foil to the helplessness of Śakuntalā in the play. It is likely that if Priyaṁvadā had accompanied Śakuntalā to the court she may well have forced the king to recognise her friend! Duṣyanta has to enquire into the *varṇa* status of Śakuntalā as he is the protector of the *varṇāśramadharma,* and it would be inappropriate if he himself broke the social code. Therefore he is relieved that she is Viśvāmitra's daughter, thus ranking as a *kṣatriya.*

Śakuntalā herself is extremely shy and retiring, the romanticised persona of a woman of upper caste culture. Initially she does not even address the king directly, speaking to him through her friends. She is almost pushed into conversation with him, and he makes it obvious that he is deeply attracted to her. She reciprocates his sentiment, and is so motivated by romantic love that after only an initial hesitation, she accepts his offer of a *gāndharva* marriage. The erotic undertones are evidenced in various ways: the motif of the bee hovering around Śakuntalā's face which makes Duṣyanta envious of the bee; or Śakuntalā asking her friends to loosen her bark clothing; or the creeper entwining itself around the mango tree.[42] These undertones build up to the more open expression of the erotic in Act III. In signalling the erotic, glances initially replace the desire to touch. Śakuntalā looks back longingly as she moves away, encouraging Duṣyanta to believe that she shares his feelings. Her parentage combines the contradiction of an *apsarā* who conquers through the erotic, and the *ṛṣi* who conquers through eliminating the erotic, even if in this case he has succumbed to it. The contrast between eroticism in Act III and its absence in the final Act VII when the hero and heroine are re-united, provides a tension even to the erotic. The *nāndī* or invocation to the play has also been read as attempting to establish what some literary critics have emphasised, namely, the preponderance of the *śṛṅgāra-rasa*, the mood of love.

Kaṇva is informed of all that has happened by a celestial voice which adds that Śakuntalā's child will act for the good of the earth, and Kaṇva approves of her marriage with Duṣyanta. It is almost as if the prophecy regarding the reign of Bharata is the justification for accepting an otherwise independent decision on the part of Śakuntalā. In this version she makes no conditions. The initiative is repeatedly taken by the king. Duṣyanta says that he will send for her on his return to the capital. It is Anasūyā who asks the practical question: a king has many loves, therefore will there be sorrow in the life of Śakuntalā once he leaves the *āśrama*? The king answers emphatically in the negative. Their courting takes place in a garden-like part of the forest where the trees and flowers are those generally also found in palace gardens, such as the *bakula*, lotus, mango, *saptaparṇa* and so on. Gardens are necessary to courtly poetry and are the rendezvous of lovers. The blossoming of flowers hints at the blossoming of love. The imagery of creepers twining around sturdy trees, such as the oft–

mentioned jasmine creeper which embraces the mango tree, reflects the same sentiment.

The introduction of the two motifs of the curse and the signet ring (*nāma muḍra*) change the purpose of the story, and was probably encouraged by the incorporation of *viraha* into the *śṛṅgāra*, the separation of the lovers for a brief period, essential to the attainment of a love fulfilled. Both motifs are stereotypical items of folk literature and have a contrapuntal relationship: the curse acts as an impediment to the action, the ring as a token of recognition resolves the problem. Signet rings had become fashionable with the coming of the Yavanas—the Indo-Greeks—and those associated with Mediterranean trade.[43] It was thought to be especially potent since it encapsulated the power of the person in addition to being the object prompting recognition. The theme is familiar from other texts—Sītā recognising the signet ring of Rāma in the *Rāmāyana*, and its even more central role in the play by Viśākhadatta, the *Mudrarākṣasa*. The ring is initially offered as a pledge to Śakuntalā's companions in the First Act, but is not thought to be necessary. It is also a means of revealing the identity of the king. His giving the ring to Śakuntalā at the time of leaving was the more serious pledge, and her losing it could be suggestive of a certain casualness on her part.

The finding of the ring in the belly of a fish has its own meaning. Symbolic connections with fish occur in the legends of the *kṣatriyas* such as that of Vasu Uparicara and the birth of Satyāvatī. The ring disguises the crux of the dilemma, the question of the paternity of the child. Had she been wedded through one of the higher forms of marriage, the ring would have been superfluous, for witnesses would have vouched for the marriage and the bride would have accompanied her husband to his home. Equally important, the ring frees the king from any blame for rejecting the woman he had married. It binds the events of the story and its centrality is clear from the title of the play: "the recognition/recollection of Śakuntalā".

The ring causes a double disappearance: for Śakuntalā the king disappears symbolically; for him, she disappears literally.

The ring also highlights the centrality of memory in the play, where remembering becomes a device for recalling emotion, both the emotion of union and of separation.[44] It hints at two kinds of power: that of the *ṛṣi* and that of the king. In the conflict between the two the power of the *ṛṣi* would seem to be greater as it controls the events. To the extent that the past is essential to the reality of the present, the loss of the past or even a part of it, changes the texture of the present. There is a disjuncture between the experience of the past, the exterior world and the continuity from the past. The intervention of memory, or rather the loss of it in this case, creates the possibility of viewing both protagonists through dichotomous situations, one of an emotion fulfilled in the *āśrama* and the other of rejection at the court. The time change in the last act crystallises the encrustations of the intervening years. Barbara Stoler Miller writes evocatively that memory has the power to shatter the logic of mundane life: it makes the invisible visible, abolishes distances, and reverses chronologies.

The question has been asked as to whether Kālidāsa uses memory to introduce us into the universe of imagination evoked by beauty, as has been asserted by a later commentator, Abhinavagupta.[45] It can also be linked to love, where *smara* has a double meaning of both memory and love.[46] Does memory recall past love or does love recall the memory of it? In the play memory and love are interlinked. Is memory also the forgetting of the present, for it comes to be superimposed as the vision of the past onto our perceptions of the present? Duṣyanta's amnesia is also a comment on memory. That it is unreliable is apparent from the effectiveness of the curse, which raises the question of who forgets and why. Did the *vidūṣaka* remember the romance of the king with the girl from the *āśrama*, but prefer not to remind his companion of it? Memories are personal but also involve a sharing of the vision of the past. How then is memory reconstructed—in the abstract or visually? Duṣyanta's attempt to capture the memory of his love in a painting is also an attempt at re-experiencing a past event, however fragmented and momentary this re-experiencing may be.

The use of a token-ring in a story is well-known and occurs in many folk tales as well as other narratives.[47] In a Greek story, Pelecritus threw his ring into the sea and it was returned to him after six days by a fisherman who had found it in the belly of a fish. Was Kālidāsa familiar with this story, as has been suggested?[48] The Indian version of stories associated with these sub-plots are known, as for instance, in the stereotypical narrative which tells of a man, away from home, who falls in love with a woman and leaves his ring with her as a token of his identity.[49] This is told in a Buddhist *Jātaka* story, refashioned to suit a Buddhist ethic, where the ring is a token not only of identity but also the legitimacy of the wife and the son born to her—in fact, of importance for the same reason as in the Kālidāsa play. It is possible the idea of introducing the signet ring was borrowed by Kālidāsa from the *Kaṭṭhahāri-Jātaka*,[50] or that it may have come from the common source of an oral tradition.

*Kaṭṭhahāri Jātaka**

Once on a time in Benares, Brahmadatta the king, having gone in great state to his pleasaunce, was roaming about looking for fruits and flowers when he came on a woman who was merrily singing away as she picked up sticks in the grove. Falling in love at first sight, the king became intimate with her, and the Bodhisatta was conceived then and there. Feeling as heavy within as though weighed down with the bolt of Indra, the

*E.B. Cowell (ed. and trans.), *The Jātaka*, published by the Pali Text Society, Luzac and Co., London, 1969, Vol. I, pp. 28-29.

woman knew that she would become a mother, and told the king so. He gave her the signet-ring from his finger and dismissed her with these words:—"If it be a girl, spend this ring on her nurture; but if it be a boy, bring ring and child to me."

When the woman's time was come, she bore the Bodhisatta. And when he could run about and was playing in the playground, a cry would arise, "No-father has hit me!" Hearing this, the Bodhisatta ran away to his mother and asked who his father was.

"You are the son of the King of Benares, my boy." "What proof of this is there, mother?" "My son, the king on leaving gave me this signet-ring and said, 'if it be a girl, spend this ring on her nurture; but if it be a boy, bring ring and child to me.'" "Why then don't you take me to my father, mother?"

Seeing that the boy's mind was made up, she took him to the gate of the palace, and bade their coming be announced to the king. Being summoned in, she entered and bowing before his majesty said, "This is your son, sire."

The king knew well enough that this was the truth, but shame before all his court made him reply, "He is no son of mine." "But here is your signet-ring, sire; you will recognise that." "Nor is this my signet-ring." Then said the woman, "Sire, I have now no witness to prove my words, except to appeal to truth. Wherefore, if you be the father of my child, I pray that he may stay in mid-air; but if not, may he fall to earth and be killed." So saying, she seized the Bodhisatta by the foot and threw him up into air.

Seated cross-legged in mid-air, the Bodhisatta, in sweet tones repeated this stanza to his father, declaring the truth:—

Your son am I, great monarch; rear me, Sire!
The king rears others, but much more his child.

Hearing the Bodhisatta thus teach the truth to him from mid-air, the king stretched out his hands and cried, "Come to me my boy! None, none but me shall rear and nurture you!" A thousand hands were stretched out to receive the Bodhisatta; but it was into the arms of the king and of no other that he descended, seating himself in the king's lap. The king made him viceroy, and made his mother queen-consort. At the death of the king his father, he came to the throne by the title of King Kaṭṭhavāhana—the faggot-bearer—and after ruling his realm righteously, passed away to fare according to his desserts.

The skeletal story in this version is the same, but without the curse, a powerful addition introduced by Kālidāsa. The curse is the stereotypical impediment of the folk-tale; its object is a woman and therefore she becomes responsible for the turn of events. It could be argued that since marriage and procreation are generally not associated with an *āśrama*, the marriage of Śakuntalā affected its purity. The curse was an attempt to erase this impurity. It becomes the antidote of the *gāndharva* marriage since, in effect, it annuls the marriage; it is the negation of the emotion which has nurtured the sentiment of love. Both the curse and the signet ring are allegorical. The ring, especially a signet ring, binds, and signifies a person placing himself in the hands of the other; this continues the flow of action. The curse stops the flow of action or diverts it to other realms and distinguishes between the one who is under a curse, and others. The link is not accidental for the ring is required to make the curse effective as well as to resolve the problem of separation. The curse and the ring, seemingly the sub-plot of the narrative, alter it substantially. The sub-plot indirectly introduces the power of those who supercede the human—the *ṛṣi* and the deity—and their opposition as symbolised in the relationship between Indra and the *ṛṣis*; the curse takes on the form of fate and brings about a situation of immanent tragedy, providing the conflict necessary to the exploration of moral values. It introduces an intervention beyond human manipulation—and even the gods cannot or do not wish to intercede. Nor is it a completely fatalistic fate, since it has an evident cause—Śakuntalā's neglect of Durvāsas. Such an intervention adds to the narrative, but also lifts the play out of the original narrative frame and provides another dimension which, although it is not pursued in the play, could be the source for philosophical speculation.

The epic does not directly introduce Durvāsas into the Śakuntalā story, he occurs in association with Kuntī.[51] In reassuring Pāṇḍu that she can bear sons, Kuntī explains that when she was young and in her father's house, she was required to honour visiting guests and this led her to welcome Durvāsas, a *brāhmaṇa* with an awesome reputation. He was so pleased by her attention that as a boon, he taught her a magical spell by which she could call on any god who would then be in her power, and from whom she could procreate a son. Thus she became the mother of many sons, of Karṇa and of the three eldest Pāṇḍavas. Is there a hint here of hospitality including more than the customary *arghya*, the washing of feet and the offering of food?[52] It seems unusual that a *brāhmaṇa* should encourage a virgin to invite gods to procreate sons on her, merely in return for the *arghya*. Kālidāsa reverses the Kuntī episode and makes Śakuntalā neglect the required hospitality to Durvāsas. Was Śakuntalā's neglect incidental, or deliberate because it may have involved a different kind of hospitality for which she was not willing? Was this the cause of Durvāsas' wrath, or had this notion of hospitality been discarded by the time of Kālidāsa? In some societies the provision of a nubile woman, preferably of status, would have been required hospitality. The guest could be a deity in disguise or a harbinger of good or ill fortune, and should therefore be propitiated. Above all, hospitality was an aspect of gift exchange and therefore reciprocal, demanding the recognised requirements.

Were the curse and the ring also introduced because they gloss over the real tension between Śakuntalā and Duṣyanta, namely, the paternity of her child? Śakuntalā now does not have to defend the right of her son, since the flow of events is beyond human control. Duṣyanta cannot be blamed for his behaviour as he is under a spell. On the king refusing to acknowledge Śakuntalā as his wife,

Śārṅgarava and Śāradvata—the disciples of Kaṇva accompanying Śakuntalā to the court—angrily accuse the king of being a liar, a thief and a king who wilfully opposes that which is his righteous duty. To all these accusations the king can innocently reply that he is not guilty, since he has no recollection of Śakuntalā. By extension therefore, he is not going to allow a woman, however beautiful, to be imposed on him as his wife. Is Kālidāsa avoiding the moral issue of condemning Duṣyanta's action in rejecting Śakuntalā, and would such an avoidance not have been regarded as contemptible in those times? The epic version does at least raise the issue through the celestial voice; the play, on the other hand, introduces extraneous elements which detract from commenting on the injustice of Duṣyanta's treatment of Śakuntalā.

The opening scene at the court is a song of the bee flitting from flower to flower, which the *vidūṣaka* pointedly compares to Duṣyanta. This is a premonition of what is to come. The *kañcukī*/chamberlain, pronounces upon the king's duties of upholding the *dharma*, which is almost an invocation to a subsequent scene when this becomes a matter of concern. We now see the other aspect of the king functioning within the formalities of the court, only too conscious of having to protect his subjects and to judge, punish or reconcile those involved in disputes. This is a glimpse of the dilemma which Śakuntalā's claim will pose for the king—should he risk abandoning a wife or taint himself by accepting the wife of another man? A kind of parallel is introduced in the matter of the king having to decide whether to confiscate the property of a merchant who had died intestate, and in a distant place. This was a bitter law, objected to in later times. Duṣyanta is willing to give up his right in favour of the merchant's pregnant wife and further, considers abolishing the law. It is a comment on the idea that the king taking another man's property was acceptable, but taking his wife was taboo.

As she enters the court Śakuntalā's right eye twitches,

said to be a bad omen. It is a counterpart to the throbbing in Duṣyanta's right arm when he enters the *āśramas* of Kaṇva and Mārīca. Śakuntalā meets with rejection from Duṣyanta. As far as the court is concerned, the king's rejection has less to do with the legality of the *gāndharva* marriage[53] than with the paternity of the child. Duṣyanta's statement that the female *kokila* bird leaves its eggs to be hatched in the nest of others unrelated to it, implies that Śakuntalā is doing the same. Duṣyanta's rejection angers Śakuntalā and she refers to him as *anārya*/ignoble, a man falsely preaching *dharma,* like a deceptive well overgrown with weeds. But her anger is brief as she is embarrassed at having lost the ring, which slipped off her hand while she was worshipping at the sacred pool of the shrine of Indra's consort, Sacī. The loss of the ring creates the dilemma of her remaining unrecognised and unable to prove the paternity of her child. It is the ring here that binds the events together. In this version Śakuntalā is not the spirited woman who argues her right. Weeping and helpless at this turn of fate, she calls upon Mother Earth to receive her back, whereupon Menakā appears and whisks her away in a flash of lightning. Again this echoes the episode in the *Rāmāyaṇa* when Sītā, in distress, calls upon her mother, Earth, to take her back and the earth opens up to receive her. Interestingly both women are not human- born. But such disappearances do hold out hope of some alternative to injustice although, significantly, the alternative takes the negative form of going away from the scene of injustice. Śakuntalā is taken to the *āśrama* of Mārīca, which is of a higher status than that of Kaṇva, where she gives birth to Bharata and is symbolically, her maternal home.

It has been suggested that in some recensions in manuscript, the king's insulting remarks on Śakuntalā—such as placing her child in another's nest—draw out an angry response from Śakuntalā; she questions the right of men to be the sole judges of both the truth and that which is conducive to the welfare of the world, denying this right to women.[54] In some other editions (particularly in the printed editions of the nineteenth century) this response is replaced by her weeping but accepting the rejection. Was there a choice between representing her as accepting the rejection or objecting to it, and did the later redacters choose the first version? Even if this were so, however, there is much else in the play which suggests her submitting to what she regarded as her fate.

When the ring is brought to the king he recalls his love for Śakuntalā, and regrets not only her departure but also the loss of a son. The need for a son becomes obsessive because he fears that the Pūru lineage may terminate with him. His remorse at what he has done leads him to paint a picture of her and her companions in the *āśrama,* thus seeking an illusory presence, a presence which reinforces her absence. The *viraha* is dramatic in the fullness of his regret. For the audience, Śakuntalā's separation from him is modulated by the presence of the *apsarā,* Sānumatī, who remains invisible but comments on the scene in the palace garden, where the king expresses regret, remorse and grief at not having recognised Śakuntalā. In a somewhat throwaway statement, Sānumatī refers to the imminent reunion of Duṣyanta and Śakuntalā, because the gods are once more eager to partake of the oblations offered at ancestral sacrificial rituals. For this to take place, however, the presence of Duṣyanta's son is necessary. For Kālidāsa, this decision lies with the gods, not with Duṣyanta and Śakuntalā. It also pertains to the relationship between deities and *ṛṣis*: do the gods have the power to annul the curse of the *ṛṣi,* or has the power of the *ṛṣi* already been exercised through the recovery of the ring? The nuances of this relationship become more evident when the final reunion of the lovers takes place at the intervention of Indra.

The last act sees Duṣyanta travelling in Indra's air-borne chariot and alighting at the *āśrama* of Mārīca.[55] The initial action interestingly is not his recognition of

Śakuntalā, but of the son. The tension between *kāma* and *dharma* is resolved in the birth of the son.[56] The son as successor is a requirement of the *dharma* of the king and in this case, is the fruition of his *kāma*. The king is irresistibly drawn to his son in whom he recognises the marks of a *cakravartin*/monarch of the universe. Playing with a lion cub signals association with royalty, for there were no lions in the high Himalayas and are unlikely to have been conjured up in an *āśrama* associated with deities. The son had to be declared the *yuvarāja* to ensure continuity. From the moment she recognises the king, Śakuntalā does not hesitate to welcome him, continually referring to him as her noble husband, and addressing him as *āryaputra*. Mārīca explains the problem created by the curse of Durvāsas at which Duṣyanta is declared to be blameless, and Śakuntalā is relieved that she was not rejected by her husband. Supernatural intervention was the cause of the separation. The final scene of Duṣyanta entering the *āśrama* is reminiscent of the opening scene.[57] The duplication is indirectly underlined by Duṣyanta's arrival through the agency of a hunt in the opening scene—where the hunting of predators and deer simulates a campaign—and by his return from an actual campaign against the *asuras* in the last scene. In the first Act Śakuntalā is living in unison with the members of the *āśrama*, whereas in the closing Act she is the separated wife, therefore distinct from the others in the *āśrama*.

Generic to the epic form is the duality of the home, and exile. In the Homeric epic, exile took the form of Ulysses traversing the seas; in the Indian epics, exile is the period spent in the forest. The settlement and the forest then become foundational dualities referred to in a variety of texts as *grāma* and *araṇya*, or *kṣetra* and *vana*, or even *pura* and *janapada*. This duality might have influenced Kālidāsa in building the structure of the play on such an opposition. Even the characterisation of the two protagonists focuses on Śakuntalā as the woman of the *āśrama*—the forest—and Duṣyanta as the man of the court. Can this be seen as the duality of nature and culture?

The themes of romantic drama in Sanskrit focussing on *śṛṅgāra*/love sometimes reinforce this duality when it is woven around the complementary themes of *saṃbhoga śṛṅgāra* or love in union, and *vipralamba śṛṅgāra* or love in separation.[58] Kālidāsa emphasises the two moods through a range of bi-polarities: of location, of character, of events. In this play the two aspects are clearly demarcated in two locations, which interestingly are dichotomous locations, the *āśrama* and the royal court. The major part of the play is divided between the *āśrama* of Kaṇva and the court of Duṣyanta, both of which are involved in the creating of dramatic tension. More distantly, and almost like a double exposure in a photograph, are the superior court of Indra, which is spoken of but not actually shown, and the *āśrama* of Mārīca, where the tension is resolved. The latter two are inaccesible to mortals without divine assistance. Both sets of locations are differentiated, and within each set, both reinforce the duality of *āśrama* and court.

The structure of the play therefore underlines a dichotomy familiar from many texts. The *araṇya*/forest represents that which is natural, even disordered and wild, untamed initially—as symbolised in the hunt, a part of which is eventually controlled in the form of the *āśrama* despite its closeness to nature. The *grāma* is that which has been disciplined, and is orderly and settled from its inception, as symbolised in the court. The creation of this dichotomy probably came into being from a situation not only of encroachment into the forest, but the clearing of land which was then cultivated. The wandering of the hunter-gatherer and the pastoralist is curbed by the need to cultivate a more limited area of land. Where hunter-gatherers lived off what was available to them in natural form, be it plant or animal, pastoralists modified this through the domestication and breeding of animals, and agriculturalists changed the landscape by their dependence on cultivated grain. The elementary forms of social organisation associated with those who live on what the forest provides, are transmuted to more complex forms among those who live by cultivating land.

Kālidāsa plays on these dichotomies but, interestingly, reverses their functions. The *āśrama* provides the context for the *śṛṅgāra-rasa* and becomes the location of love-in union, although ideally this should be precluded from an *āśrama*. The royal court which witnesses comments on the king's *dharma* and on *vīra-rasa,* and is generally the background to romantic love, is in this case the location for love-in-separation. Neither of these categories is absolute but the story plays on them both, directly and by inversion. There would seem to be a dialogic relationship between the two as represented in the relationship between Duṣyanta and Indra, and Kaṇva and Mārīca, as there is between the two courts and the two *āśramas*. This bipolarity is evident in the figure of the *ṛṣi* and the *rājā*. The *ṛṣi* opts out of social obligations and establishes an alternative system, distanced from society, in the *āśrama* set in a forest. He draws his power individually, through asceticism, and can accumulate so much of it that even the gods feel threatened. The *rājā* upholds social obligations and, through the protecting of the *varṇāśramadharma,* ensures that the equilibrium of society is maintained. He draws his power from interaction with others, through the laws of governance and through various coercive agencies. This power is never sufficient for the *rājā* to compete with the gods.

The hunt is not an onslaught on nature, as in the epic, for by now kingdoms had far greater control over the forest than before. The forest was wasteland but was nevertheless part of the king's domain; it is a less agressive domination, although the continuing duality evokes confrontation, if not conflict, on occasion. The communion with nature is through the *nāyikā,* the heroine, but the relationship is a little ambivalent.

Kaṇva's *āśrama* is less austere than that of Mārīca and the extent to which it symbolises a forest, suggests more subdued forms. Such *āśramas* were different from the unknown, demonic forest, since they were the vanguards of the settlement. The clearing in the forest was a preliminary to establishing a hermitage. This activity was intensified in the first millennium A.D. with grants of land—either waste or cultivated—by kings to *brāhmaṇas*. The dichotomy of the forest and the settlement continued into post-Gupta times. Kaṇva's *āśrama* mediates between the forest and the court. It is liminal space idealised as being in unison with nature; it is the space where the *grāma* and the *araṇya* can sometimes merge. Its vulnerability is demonstrated both by the king hunting the deer and his wooing a young woman of the *āśrama*. It does not evolve naturally, as would the settlements of forest-dwellers—it is a deliberate imposition on the forest. In romanticising the *āśṛama*, one may well ask if Kālidāsa is not reflecting a nostalgia for the forest which seems to have already overtaken urban culture. Asceticism, because it breaks away from social obligations, requires a location distant from society. Institutions such as *āśramas* are collectives of renouncers who are not necessarily ascetics, and therefore represent an alternative way of life to that dependent on normal social obligations.[59] Kaṇva's asceticism is not of the extreme kind. His *āśrama* has similarities with the *vānaprastha* stage, in that it has *parivrājakas* and *vaikhānasas* rather than *samnyāsins*. It therefore displays a familiarity with court etiquette. Kaṇva is aware of the social norms of caste and marriage. When bidding Śakuntalā farewell, he reiterates what he would regard as the ideal life-cycle for her: childhood in the hermitage identified with nature; dutiful wifehood in a royal household; and a return to the hermitage when social obligations have been fulfilled and her son is ruling. Kālidāsa seems to be adding to the *āśrāma* of Kaṇva some of the characteristics of what was to emerge later as the *agrahāra*. The king's protection through his officers was a right claimed by such institutions. Permitting the eroticism of the lovers is not therefore an absolute infringement on ascetic rigour—this is required in Mārīca's *āśrama*, which becomes an austere extension of Kaṇva's.

Mārīca's hermitage is located in a distant mountainous region, inaccesible to humans, and is visited by Duṣyanta, it would seem at the instigation of Indra.[60] It is as high in status as an *āśrama*, as is Indra's court among royal courts. Mārīca, descended from Brahmā, lives here with his wife, Aditi. The *ṛṣis* here perform various physical austerities; such as the one who is half-buried in an ant-hill, seated so still that he has the slough of a snake for a sacred thread, is covered with creepers and has birds nesting in his hair. They seem to live on air and are undisturbed by visiting *apsarās*. This is the conventional description of extreme asceticism. Yet there is also an element of fantasy in it for it is set in a forest of *kalpa-vṛkṣas* or wish-fulfilling trees, the ascetics meditate on jewel-encrusted marble and the water has a golden hue from lotus pollen. This ensures an even higher status for this *āśrama*. There are no deer in this hermitage and the vegetation is sparse. The king does not visit here on a hunting expedition but out of respect for Mārīca. The Mārīca *āśrama* is carefully crafted, with little of the interface between nature and culture since there is essentially so little of nature in it.

Aśramas were partially places of exile, more so in the case of Mārīca's hermitage than in Kaṇva's. Yet the power of the *ṛṣi* is conceded in both places and this power can control human destiny; this is apparent in the curse of Durvāsas. The king is respectful towards the ascetics both in the *āśrama* and when they come to his court, accompanying Śakuntalā. He is said to be the protector of the ascetics, which was probably necessary if they were encroaching into the forest territory of the *āṭavikas*, or forest-dwellers. The protection is often projected in terms of keeping away the demons and evil spirits, the *rākṣasas*, *pretas*, *daityas*, partly fantasy and partly synonymous with those who were obstructing this encroachment. Curiously, the link between the two *āśramas* is Śakuntalā, a woman, who was a child of the first *āśrama* and a personification of innocence. She has now been through the travail of an unrecognised marriage and motherhood to arrive at eventual recognition in the second *āśrama*.

Representing the *grāma* or settlement are the two royal courts of Indra and Duṣyanta. The power of Indra seems to vacillate. He is generally fearful of *ṛṣis*, and it was at his behest that Menakā seduced Viśvāmitra. This provides an indirect association between Indra and Śakuntalā, a link which recurs in other instances such as Śakuntalā losing her ring at the shrine of Sacī. He requires Duṣyanta's aid in battle against the demons, partly because of the king's prowess but also perhaps to reaffirm his tie with the king. The description of Duṣyanta's court attempts to elevate the mundane into something more poetic. The court is resplendent as is the palace garden, but both are distanced from the forest and from nature. The foil to the king's status is the *vidūṣaka*, his companion, an unlikely *brāhmaṇa* who plays a necessary role. There is also the intervention of the hierarchy of ministers. The jealousies of the queens become a matter for comment and indicate intrigue, which was absent in the *āśrama*. The formality of activities at the court, and to some extent even certain objects, encourage a sense of artificiality. Thus the king momentarily addresses his painting of Śakuntalā as if she were actually there in the flesh. The reality and the mirage are interwoven. The picture is hidden at the approach of the queen although it is well known that the king is pining for Śakuntalā.

The town is effectively a place where the officers are violent and corrupt, and this again is in contrast to the hermitage. The guards are rough with the fisherman, accuse him of stealing the ring and make fun of his low caste, a vignette on normal social confrontations. (Not surprisingly, such vignettes are not included in the picture often presented of "the Golden Age" portrayed in the works of Kālidāsa.) The guards threaten to kill him but when the messenger arrives with a gift of money from the king for the fisherman, they are eager to share it. The fisherman knows that as a man belonging to the powerless lower strata, it would be to his advantage to do so. The magistrate and the fisherman, the former obviously of a high caste and the latter very low, both leave together for the wine shop to celebrate the latter's good fortune. Urban pleasures, it would seem, do not stand in the way of caste regulations—higher castes are able to consume the wealth of the lower in a mood of togetherness. Or else, caste regulations were more lax than has been assumed. The contrast between *araṇya* and *grāma* is thus reiterated, not merely in the movement from Kaṇva's *āśrama* to the court and the town, but also in the emphatic difference between these and the two later locations which are crucial to the resolution of the play, even if briefly.

The contrast between forest and court is generic to the epic but is emphasised in this particular play more directly than in others by Kālidāsa, partly as a concession to the story being taken from the epic; it could also be because he was romanticising the *āśrama* and the polarity was sharper in his own perception of their difference. The forest was a place of exile for those who were court-based, but also endorsed the sentiment of exile for those *ṛṣis* who were in the process of acquiring supernatual powers. The court is the focus of a different kind of power and there is often a tension between the two. In the play, Duṣyanta in court demonstrates royal power. It could be argued that this was sublimated by him in his relationship with Śakuntalā in Kaṇva's *āśrama*. That he had finally to come to Mārīca's *āśrama* to recover his wife and son, is not merely a resolution of the tension but also a concession to the superior power of the ascetic. That the gods created a situation which would bring them together becomes a sub-plot.

The tension is also apparent in more direct forms. On one occasion it is said that there is agitation in the *āśrama,* and the king realises that it is caused by his entourage looking for him, upsetting the discipline of the *āśrama.* The word used for the entourage is significantly, *paura,* of the *pura*/settlement or town. When the ascetics Śārṅgarava and Śāradvata, both disciples of Kaṇva accompanying Śakuntalā, arrive at Hastināpur, they are clearly contemptuous of life at the court. The palace to them is a house on fire and the town, mired in filth. These remarks underline the hostility of the *āśrama* to the city and the palace and all that they symbolise—the sickness of urban living. Such sentiments also reflect the earlier suspicion of urban living voiced in some of the *dharmsūtras*, and contrast sharply with Buddhist and Jaina renouncers who, although they live on the outskirts of urban centres, are dependent upon them for alms. Moreover, they see them as part of the community with whose welfare they are concerned.

The characterisation of Duṣyanta and Śakuntalā is also an aspect of this tension, for his is the culture of the townsman, and she is a child of the *āśrama.* Early on, he comments that the women of the forest have a beauty rarely seen in royal palaces. It has been argued that patriarchal ideologies project "nature" as feminised and "culture" as masculine, where nature is passive and culture, authoritative.[61] If this be so then the identification of Śakuntalā with nature would be, as we shall see, an extreme form of feminising, counter-balanced by the culture of the king and the court as masculine.

But the dichotomy between nature and culture, touched upon in the literature of many societies, is particularly visible in European literature and philosophy of the nineteenth century. Notions of nature and culture relate to specific conditions, and the association of gender with culture varies in different situations. Each is a relativised concept with a significance which derives from a specificity.

There are only shifting boundaries between their semantic fields.[62] What is more commonly found is the differentiation between the wild and the planted, where the former is forest and woodland and the latter requires kinship and the recognition of clan and territory—a parallel perhaps to the spatial and social division of *grāma* and *araṇya*. This does not however signify that women symbolise nature and the wild, and men, the planted.

Śakuntalā appears to be a counterpoint to the other women in the play, most evidently to her companions, Priyaṁvadā and Anasūyā, as well as the women of the court. The forthright, free-speaking Śakuntalā of the epic, making her bargain with Duḥṣanta undergoes a radical change in the play; here she is an innocent child of the *āśrama*, grappling with the emotions of love, bewildered by the instincts of sexual desire with which she was hitherto unacquainted: the natural woman of the forest who knows no deceit. She is persuaded to the *gāndharva* marriage and makes no conditions as did the epic Śakuntalā. She encapsulates the romantic image of forest-dwellers in the mind's eye of the urbanite, an image used in poetry, even when the forest peoples became problematic to encroaching agriculture and to hunting expeditions. She lives in the depth of the forest, difficult of access; she is born of an *apsarā* and is initially nurtured by birds of prey, again symbolic of an innate gentleness recognised even by these birds! She grows up among the fawns and they drink fearlessly from her hand. She is clothed in bark and adorned with flowers. There is an abundant use of similes in which she is compared to plants: her lips are the colour of the lotus bud, her arms are like the two stalks of the lotus, she calls herself the sapling of the sandalwood, the jasmine is her sister, and so on. The trees bend towards her as she passes by, and she is blessed by the guardian deities of the forest. When she writes a letter to the king expressing her love for him, she does so on a lotus leaf. However, as a woman of the forest she may not have been literate, nor was it necessary that such women be. Perhaps Kālidāsa assumes that all upper caste women, irrespective of where they live, have enough literacy to be able to write a love letter. The image of the *apsarā* reinforces Śakuntalā's closeness to nature. When she leaves the forest to go to Duṣyanta's court, nature shares in the sorrow of her farewell: the grass drops from the mouth of the doe, the peacock stops dancing, the *cakravāka* does not answer his mate, and the creepers shed their leaves which fall like teardrops. Yet at the same time, Kaṇva through his power as a *ṛṣi* is able to materialise jewels for Śakuntalā from the forest, although these are required only when she is leaving for the court: a transformation of nature into culture? Both the jewels and the advice which Kaṇva gives her are concessions to the culture of the court.

This enhanced portrayal of her almost as a part of nature is in direct contrast to the epic Śakuntalā, who was as real as the Śakuntalā of the play is illusory. The latter is shy, retiring and modest. The portrayal is projected as so irresistible that it excludes even the minimum concerns of the epic Śakuntalā. In the final Act when Duṣyanta recognises her, Śakuntalā's reactions are very revealing. She consoles herself by stating that Duṣyanta did not really spurn her, he merely lost his recollection of her for a while. She goes on to explain to herself that she was reaping the consequences of some wrong-doing in her last birth—a curious remark from one born of an *apsarā* and unlikely to have been subjected to rebirth. Her explanations are attempts to exonerate her husband. The question of whether his actions even require forgiveness on her part, does not enter her mind. Significantly it is only in this final scene that Duṣyanta is submissive and expresses his regret for his past actions.

The image of Śakuntalā as the child of the *āśrama* is hemmed in by the way in which a woman is viewed in a wider context, which view is apparent from other comments in the play. It is a view that reinforces submission and inferiority. It is said that a woman can be virtually a goddess but remains emotionally vulnerable, therefore weak. Kaṇva expresses relief when he decides to send Śakuntala to her husband for, he says, a daughter is a possession which eventually belongs to someone else. Kaṇva's blessing reiterates the Pūru connection, hoping that her husband will treat her the way Yayāti treated Śarmiṣṭhā. In the same way that she bore him Pūru, Śakuntalā may bear Duṣyanta a *samrāṭ*: the husband and the son fulfill her life. He wishes her to observe the social norms, be a subservient wife to her husband, live in friendship with her co-wives and be considerate to the servants. The female ascetics in Kaṇva's *āśrama,* when bidding her farewell, bless her and wish that she becomes the Chief Queen, that she be the mother of heroes and that she be respected by her husband.

In his rejection of her Duṣyanta is uncomplimentary about women whom he describes as designing, shrewd and with an untaught cunning, such as that of the cuckoo laying her egg in another's nest. This contrasts with the epic version, where Duḥṣanta is abusive towards Śakuntalā and *her* parentage, but not about women in general. In the play there is scant mention of her illegitimacy or the charge of immorality against her parents. The subservience of a wife to her husband is stated not only by Kaṇva when she is leaving the hermitage, but also by Kaṇva's disciples who accompany her to the court. They advise her to remain there, even in servitude, because better that a wife be as a servant in the home of her husband, than live away from him. Duṣyanta is free to either abandon her or accept her, for the husband's authority over a wife is unlimited.

In the transition from the epic story to the play there is a decline in the empowerment of women. The epic emphasises empowerment through Śakuntalā having borne the son of Duḥṣanta; in the play the romantic mood is primary—the woman of these times does not make conditions. (The importance of the son becomes a focus only in the latter part of the play.) Romantic love hides the loss of empowerment and gradually becomes a fantasy, for if Śakuntalā claims to be the wife of Duṣyanta then she must behave like a *pativratā*, the ideal wife, devoted to her husband. In an upper caste, polygamous situation, romantic love is always available to a husband, but obviously not to a wife. The king's rejection of Śakuntalā does not become a moral issue: it is glossed over through the introduction of the motifs of the curse and the ring. Whereas in the epic the question of the king's morality is implicitly raised in the statement of the celestial voice endorsing Śakuntalā's claim to the truth, in the play it is not an issue. The play is a celebration of romantic love where the woman, before she is acknowledged as a wife, exercises the freedom to choose and to act. But romantic love has to be transmuted into the ideal of a *pativratā*. The conversion from one mood to the other requires the reiterating of rules which bind the woman. Romantic love becomes almost a reversal of wifely devotion.

A comparison of the depiction of Śakuntalā in the epic and the play indicates the influence of patriarchy in conceptualising the role of a woman of the upper castes, but perhaps we should tease out the nature of this change. Patriarchal norms need not always be introduced as a binary alternative. Indian society has always had a multiplicity of segmented forms which make generalisations about the totality complicated. Each segment would have experienced change and would have related to change differently. There is not only polygamy; sometimes each new marriage may be legalised through any one of the eight forms of marriage. Thus a king could be married through the most respectable form of *kanyā-dāna,* the gifting of a daughter by her father, or through paying a bride-price, or through a *gāndharva* marriage. Each form pertained to caste and custom. In such societies, the identification of a linear change in patriarchy would lose some of the nuances in the variations.

Upper caste, patriarchal attitudes towards women are reflected not only in the statements quoted above, but also in the hint of ambiguity about the *gāndharva* marriage which might have been seen as something of an anachronism in the time of Kālidāsa. Deriving from the assumption that women are objects of pleasure, the *gāndharva* marriage is not generally associated with ritual; its declaration was doubtless intended more to legitimise the birth of a son than the status of the woman. Kaṇva regards it as a lawful marriage; although he might have preferred a *kanyā-dāna,* the gifting of the daughter, he also realised that the daughter of an *apsarā* may not have fitted that role. In a late section of the play, the king refers to Śakuntalā as his *dharmapatnī*, his lawfully wedded wife, the *kṣetra*/field in which he has planted his *bīja*/seed. This is a change from the epic reference to the woman as the sac or bag. The simile of the field and the seed becomes more common. Indra's charioteer, Mātali, also speaks of Śakuntalā as the king's *dharmapatnī*. The ambiguity of the *gāndharva* marriage stems from Śārṅgarava's description of it as a secret marriage with a hint of seduction, and the rebuke that the elders were not informed. Sārṅgarava is sharp with the king and says that Kaṇva has pardoned him for his behaviour with the girl, but that he was now behaving like a thief in rejecting her. Such rebuke does make the king anxious about his own honour. But Śārṅgarava is also hard on Śakuntalā, perhaps because he resented a woman transgressing patriarchy and choosing her own husband. He finds her independence irksome. Nevertheless the legality or morality of the marriage is not a major concern.

Meant generally for *kṣatriyas*, presumably as a solution to the roving eye of royalty especially when away on hunts, it is described by Manu as a sexual union arising out of desire.[63] The association with the Gandharvas makes such a marriage appropriate for an *apsarā*. The symbolism of the hunt then takes on another dimension. The woman has in any case to be of the right status since the marriage was regarded as legally binding. Hence Duṣyanta's apprehension that Śakuntalā might be the daughter of a *brāhmaṇa*, and his envy of the bee kissing Śakuntalā because it does not have to first determine her *varṇa* status! His relief at discovering that her father was a *kṣatriya* is great. Her parentage is made known to the king, not by her as in the epic version, but by her rather more talkative companions. As a well-bred young woman she herself cannot be so free with a potential suitor. He is also reassured by her companions that she is eligible for marriage. Śakuntalā's identity hinges on her relationship with the various male members of her family: with her father Viśvāmitra for her *kṣatriya* status; with her foster-father Kaṇva; with her husband Duṣyanta; and finally as the mother of Duṣyanta's son. One is reminded here of the verses in Manu which state that a woman is dependent, in turn, on her father, her husband, and her son as she goes through her life-cycle.[64] That she is taken away by her mother and not forced to become a servant in her husband's house, is a concession to her having recourse to an alternative denied to most other women. Being an *apsarā* allows of this release.

The association of Śakuntalā with the two *āśramas* does not suggest asceticism on her part. In Kaṇva's *āśrama* she experiences not only her childhood and youth but also romantic love and marriage, and in Mārīca's *āśrama*, motherhood. That she is referred to as a *tapasvinī* has sometimes been taken to mean that she was an ascetic doing penance, but this term is often used for heroines in distress. A careful analysis of the use of this word indicates that it refers not only to asceticism, but that it has an alternate meaning—pitiable or miserable or ill-fated, its synonyms in Sanskrit lexicography being *anukampya* and *karuṇa*.[65] What can be assumed is that the term is applied to the heroine when she has to control her frustration—and therefore also her passion—at not being with her beloved. Both are inimical to *tapas*. The conditionality which prevents her from fulfilling her wishes and obtaining the union which she seeks lead her to being called a *tapasvinī*. Interestingly, the word is used in its two different senses by Sānumatī, first with reference to Śakuntalā suffering from the separation (as indeed was the king) and later to mean a female ascetic. The meaning of "ill-fated" is further clarified by its being used to describe Mālavikā in *Mālavikāgnimitram*, where she is a princess in hiding, working for the queen but in love with the king, Agnimitra. This would not be a reference to her doing penance. It is therefore the pitiable condition of Śakuntalā, bereft of her husband, which explains her being called a *tapasvinī*.

The play has other women characters who fill out the picture of the feminine. Śakuntalā's companions, Priyaṁvadā and Anasūyā, are not nature's children, but women well aware of the world outside the *āśrama*. It is they who negotiate the crises in Śakuntalā's life and this heightens the projection of her innocence. It has been said that Śakuntalā's individuality is de-emphasised in order to bring her closer to nature,[66] but it is this closeness which is in effect projected as her individuality. The elderly Gautamī seems to be the mother figure in the *āśrama*. She expresses concern for Śakuntalā when she has been rejected by Duṣyanta and by the disciples of Kaṇva. They show their anger, both at the king but also at the humiliation of Kaṇva's daughter through what they regard as her assertion of independence and her irresponsible behaviour, and so insist on her remaining behind in the palace.

The two queens of Duṣyanta, Vasumatī and Hamsāvatī, are cardboard figures, in effect discarded by the king. Once loved by him, they have taken to intrigue—often said to be the occupation of superceded royal women. Emphasis is placed on the romantic elements of court life, even though we know from other sources that queens were influential as advisors, donors and even administrators. The maids at the court are decorative and ineffectual and therefore appropriately named—Parabhṛtikā, the little cuckoo and Madhukarikā, the little honey-bee. The king also has a Yavanī, a girl attendant who brings him his bow when Indra's charioteer attacks his *vidūṣaka*. Two other women, one behind the scenes, Menakā, and Aditi, are of even higher status than the rest. Menakā is the arch seductress who forsakes her child but whose maternal feelings are aroused when Śakuntalā is in distress. That she takes away her anguished daughter almost exonerates her for abandoning the baby girl. Aditi has the status of a parental deity. The reuinted family being blessed by her at the end signifies divine approval of the marriage. This juxtaposition of the goddess and the *apsarā* may not be accidental, for the centrality of *apsarās* in the legends declines with the waning of heroic society and the emergence of goddesses as figures of power.

These are women of varying status. Irrespective of this they are grouped together by their use of Prākrit which, although considered inferior as a language, was considered appropriate for the dialogue of women. Even the *apsarās* speak Prākrit, as does the child Bharata. Had it been merely that Prākrit was widely spoken even at court, then the men would also have spoken it, leaving the poetry to be composed in Sanskrit. Language is a marker of status and of identity, whereby high status male characters speak Sanskrit and those of low status such as guards, fishermen and minor officials, speak Prākrit. The *Nāṭyaśāstra* prescribes the varieties of Prākrit to be spoken by the various characters, although authors did deviate. The heroine and her friends spoke Śaurasenī, other women of the court spoke Māgadhi, the *vidūṣaka* spoke a related Prācya, the officers, merchants and servants spoke Ardha-Māgadhi and the citizens, Dakṣinātya. In some manuscripts, a *chāyā* is provided, which is a Sanskrit gloss on the Prākrit passages. This hierarchy of dialects suggests almost a caricature of classification but points to the crucial importance of language as a social marker. A status distinction is maintained even in Kanva's *aśrama* where it may not have actually prevailed, but is a reflection of court mores. Prākrit was important to the narrative of events, so that an audience could follow the story clearly, and the use of Prākrits suggests that audiences may have included more than just the members of the court.[67] Nevertheless convention would have required a familiarity with Prākrit even by the most educated of Sanskrit speakers, and the Prākrit used in plays may be viewed as a language for drama.[68] But language alone is not the defining characteristic of popular culture; the contents of what is said are also significant.

The language spoken by a character indicated the status of the person to a discerning audience, except that there is one set of interesting reversals, which suggests that language was also a strategy. The *sūta* or charioteers speak Sanskrit, perhaps to indicate closeness to the king and the ambiguity in the *varṇa* of the *sūta*. Most *dharmaśāstra* texts describe the *sūta* as belonging to a low *pratiloma* caste but some earlier texts had assigned the *sūta* a relatively higher status.[69] Yet the *vidūṣaka* who was virtually on equal terms with the king, spoke Prākrit. The use of more than one language and dialect complicates the focus on the meaning of words. Given that in the presentation of plays there was a minimum of decor and lighting, the impact and use of language would have to have been enhanced.

Counterposed to the king is the *vidūṣaka*, his companion. Both the *Nāṭyaśāstra* and Abhinavagupta maintain that the *nāyaka* and the *vidūṣaka* are the two leading male characters, but the concept of the *vidūṣaka* appears to have been different from the characterisation as it evolved in drama. They meet on an equal footing and call each other by the informal term, *vayasya*/friend, but they are the inverse of each other. The role and personality of the *vidūṣaka* is the creation of the authors of plays as he does not appear as a court figure in royal biographies, nor is there any such role even for a low-grade *brāhmaṇa* in the texts on kingship and governance. It is thought that the *vidūṣaka* may have originated from the farces of the folk tradition, from where the character was appropriated by courtly drama.[70] His non-conforming to the brahmanical function is a deliberate intervention by the authors of plays; it allows him to be a commentator on events and situations without having to prove his bonafides for doing so, or having to support given norms. The origins of the *vidūṣaka* can possibly also be traced back to the scapegoat in Vedic ritual in which case he can even take on the impurity of the king.[71] The *vidūṣaka* is a *brāhmaṇa* but he speaks Prākrit and this makes him out to be a lesser *brāhmaṇa*; not a ritual specialist but performing the role of confidante to the king, one who through his witticisms provides a humorous counterpoint to the love-lorn king. The latter wishes to talk about his love, as do all lovers, and the *vidūṣaka* alone can keep his secret even if he caricatures his romantic inclinations. This introduces a comical element which reduces the emphasis on the king's romantic feelings; it also punctures the hero's intangible constructions of emotion and fantasy.[72] There is almost an element of indifference to the anguish of the king; to this extent the *vidūṣaka* does not participate in the two major *rasas* of the play, but introduces another *rasa*, that of laughter at a lower level. He is loyal to the king to the point where there is no need either of sycophancy or flattery. He is therefore a foil to the king and consciously distances himself from any idealism.[73] As such he has to be a *brāhmaṇa,* for his being of the lower *varṇas* would be *lèse majesté*. Not only is he a foil to the king, he is also a scapegoat for the king's foibles. The *vidūṣaka* is apparently mocking him and thereby potentially subverting the hero. He is also mocking the *brāhmaṇa* through being the kind of person he is; and this might even have been a counterpoint to the *purohita* at the court. Yet he insists on being recognised as a *brāhmaṇa*. The ritualisation of behaving contrary to social norms was not unknown. The *vrātyas* mentioned in Vedic texts were among such groups as were, later, a number of sects, frequently Śaiva, such as the Kapālikas, the Pāśupatas and the Aghoris. The intention was to reverse the norms so as to claim the independence of being outside them. This is partially reflected in the construction of the *vidūṣaka*. He is not a trickster but he does invert the hierarchy. Non-brahmanas and those lower down in society may well have seen some *brāhmaṇas* in this image—shrewd, greedy, and enjoying the good things of life.

The *vidūṣaka*'s aversion to the forest and the hermitage where, according to him, one lives like a savage, and his longing to return to the pleasures of the court is even more ironic coming from a *brāhmaṇa*. He complains that the hunt has shaken up his joints. He refers to oily-haired ascetics and suggests that they be taxed fifteen per cent on the wild rice in the *āśrama*, at which suggestion he is rebuked by the king. He objects to drinking tepid water from the streams, to eating scorching hot meat at odd hours, to the noise of the elephants and horses at night, and of the bird-catchers. He declares that his purpose in life is to be comfortable and live on a diet of soft and sweet food. Physically he is said to be ugly both in body and face, heightening the contrast with the handsome, romantic hero. His hostility to life in the forest is again an opposition which stems from the court, the settlement. The *vidūṣaka* is permitted to be much more critical of life in the *āśrama* or the forest than any other person from the court. This is a freedom which, in later times and in the literature of the regional languages, could take the form of the *vidūṣaka* expressing radical opinions.[74] This was permitted because he was speaking in the local language and was given the status of a *brāhmaṇa*. The *vidūṣaka* in *Abhijñāna-śākuntalam* is articulating both the tension between hermitage and court, as well as the reality which has to pierce the romantic fantasy. To this extent his presence is suggestive of a link between the more earthy epic story and the romance of Kālidāsa. This link surfaces in a variety of texts, written subsequent to Kālidāsa but not always telling the story as he does. The range of these texts, some including the narrative and others focusing on a discussion of the play as dramatic form and the language as poetry, provides a glimpse of the new roles which the story was to play, where some of these forms pertained to popular culture and others to high culture.

*Śakuntalā and the Ring of Recollection**

by Kālidāsa

TRANSLATED BY BARBARA STOLER MILLER

CHARACTERS

Players in the prologue:
DIRECTOR: Director of the players and manager of the theater (*sūtradhāra*).
ACTRESS: The lead actress (*naṭī*).

Principal roles:
KING: Duṣyanta, the hero (*nāyaka*); ruler of Hastināpura; a royal sage of the lunar dynasty of Puru.
ŚAKUNTALĀ: The heroine (*nāyikā*); daughter of the royal sage Viśvāmitra and the celestial nymph Menakā; adoptive daughter of the ascetic Kaṇva.
BUFFOON: Māḍhavya, the king's comical brahman companion (*vidūṣaka*).

Members of Kaṇva's hermitage:
ANASŪYĀ and PRIYAṀVADĀ: Two young female ascetics; friends of Śakuntalā
KAṆVA: Foster father of Śakuntalā and master of the hermitage a sage belonging to the lineage of the divine creator Marīci, and thus related to Mārīca.
GAUTAMĪ: The senior female ascetic.
ŚĀRṄGARAVA and ŚĀRADVATA: Kaṇva's disciples.

---

*Translated as: *Śakuntalā and the Ring of Recollection*, by Barbara Stoler Miller, in, Barbara Stoler Miller (ed.), *Theater of Memory* (New York: Columbia University Press, 1984) pp. 85-176.

Various inhabitants of the hermitage: a monk with his two pupils, two boy ascetics (named Gautama and Nārada), a young disciple of Kanva, a trio of female ascetics.

Members of the king's forest retinue:
CHARIOTEER: Driver of the king's chariot (*sūta*).
GUARD: Raivataka, guardian of the entrance to the king's quarters (*dauvārika*).
GENERAL: Commander of the king's army (*senāpati*).
KARABHAKA: Royal messenger.

Various attendants, including Greco-Bactrian bow-bearers (*yavanyaḥ*).

Members of the king's palace retinue:
CHAMBERLAIN: Vātāyana, chief officer of the king's household (*kañcukī*).
PRIEST: Somarāta, the king's religious preceptor and household priest (*purohita*).
DOORKEEPER: Vetravatī, the female attendant who ushers in visitors and presents messages (*pratīhārī*).
PARABHṚTIKĀ and MADHUKARIKĀ: Two maids assigned to the king's garden.
CATURIKĀ: A maidservant.

City dwellers:
MAGISTRATE: The king's low-caste brother-in-law (*śyāla*); chief of the city's policemen.
POLICEMEN: Sūcaka and Jānuka.
FISHERMAN: An outcaste.

Celestials:
MĀRĪCA: A divine sage; master of the celestial hermitage in which Śakuntalā gives birth to her son; father of Indra, king of the gods, whose armies Duṣyanta leads.
ADITI: Wife of Mārīca.
MĀTALI: Indra's charioteer.
SĀNUMATĪ: A nymph; friend of Śakuntalā's mother, Menakā.
Various members of Mārīca's hermitage: two female ascetics, Mārīca's disciple Gālava.

BOY: Sarvadamana, son of Śakuntalā and Duṣyanta; later known as Bharata.

Offstage voices:
VOICE OFFSTAGE: From the backstage area or dressing room (*nepathye*); behind the curtain, out of view of the audience. The voice belongs to various players before they enter the stage, such as the monk, Śakuntalā's friends, the buffoon, Mātali; also to figures who never enter the stage, such as the angry sage Durvāsas, the two bards who chant royal panegyrics (*vaitālikau*).
VOICE IN THE AIR: A voice chanting in the air (*ākāśe*) from somewhere offstage: the bodiless voice of Speech quoted in Sanskrit by Priyaṁvadā (4.4); the voice of a cuckoo who represents the trees of the forest blessing Śakuntalā in Sanskrit (4.11); the voice of Haṁsapadikā singing a Prakrit love song (5.1).

Aside from Duṣyanta, Śakuntalā, and the buffoon, most of the characters represent types that reappear in different contexts within the play itself, an aspect of the circular structure of the play in which complementary relations are repeated. In terms of their appearance, the following roles might be played by the same actor or actress:
Kanva—Mārīca
Gautamī—Aditi
Anasūyā and Priyaṁvadā
Sānumatī and Caturikā
Two Ascetic Women in the hermitage of Mārīca
Charioteer—Mātali
Monk—Śārṅgarava
General—Chamberlain
Karabhaka—Priest

The setting of the play shifts from the forest hermitage (Acts 1–4) to the palace (Acts 5–6) to the celestial hermitage (Act 7). The season is early summer when the play begins and spring during the sixth act; the passage of time is otherwise indicated by the birth and boyhood of Śakuntalā's son.

ACT ONE

The water that was first created,
the sacrifice-bearing fire, the priest,
the time-setting sun and moon,
audible space that fills the universe,
what men call nature, the source of all seeds,
the air that living creatures breathe—
through his eight embodied forms,
may Lord Śiva come to bless you! (1)

PROLOGUE

DIRECTOR (*looking backstage*): If you are in costume now, madam, please come on stage!
ACTRESS: I'm here, sir.
DIRECTOR: Our audience is learned. We shall play Kālidāsa's new drama called *Śakuntalā and the Ring of Recollection.* Let the players take their parts to heart!
ACTRESS: With you directing, sir, nothing will be lost.
DIRECTOR: Madam, the truth is:

I find no performance perfect
until the critics are pleased;
the better trained we are
the more we doubt ourselves. (2)

ACTRESS: So true . . . now tell me what to do first!
DIRECTOR: What captures an audience better than a song? Sing about the new summer season and its pleasures:

To plunge in fresh waters
swept by scented forest winds
and dream in soft shadows
of the day's ripened charms. (3)

ACTRESS (*singing*):

Sensuous women
in summer love
weave
flower earrings
from fragile petals
of mimoṡa
while wild bees
kiss them gently. (4)

DIRECTOR: Well sung, madam! Your melody enchants the audience. The silent theater is like a painting. What drama should we play to please it?

ACTRESS: But didn't you just direct us to perform a new play called *Śakuntalā and the Ring of Recollection?*

DIRECTOR: Madam, I'm conscious again! For a moment I forgot.

The mood of your song's melody
carried me off by force,
just as the swift dark antelope
enchanted King Duṣyanta. (5)

(*They both exit; the prologue ends. Then the king enters with his charioteer, in a chariot, a bow and arrow in his hand, hunting an antelope.*)

CHARIOTEER (*watching the king and the antelope*):

I see this black buck move
as you draw your bow
and I see the wild bowman Śiva,
hunting the dark antelope. (6)

KING: Driver, this antelope has drawn us far into the forest. There he is again.

The graceful turn of his neck
as he glances back at our speeding car,
the haunches folded into his chest
in fear of my speeding arrow,
the open mouth dropping
half-chewed grass on our path—

watch how he leaps, bounding on air,
barely touching the earth. (7)

(*He shows surprise.*)
Why is it so hard to keep him in sight?

CHARIOTEER: Sir, the ground was rough. I tightened the reins to slow the chariot and the buck raced ahead. Now that the path is smooth, he won't be hard to catch.

KING: Slacken the reins!

CHARIOTEER: As you command, sir.
(*He mimes the speeding chariot.*)
Look!

Their legs extend as I slacken the reins
plumes and manes set in the wind, ears angle back;
our horses outrun their own clouds of dust,
straining to match the antelope's speed. (8)

KING: These horses would outrace the steeds of the sun.

What is small suddenly looms large,
split forms seem to reunite,
bent shapes straighten before my eyes—
from the chariot's speed
nothing ever stays distant or near. (9)

CHARIOTEER: The antelope is an easy target now.
(*He mimes the fixing of an arrow.*)

VOICE OFFSTAGE: Stop! Stop, king! This antelope belongs to our hermitage! Don't kill him!

CHARIOTEER (*listening and watching*): Sir, two ascetics are protecting the black buck from your arrow's deadly aim.

KING (*showing confusion*): Rein in the horses!

CHARIOTEER: It is done!
(*He mimes the chariot's halt. Then a monk enters with two pupils, his hand raised.*)

MONK: King, this antelope belongs to our hermitage.

Withdraw your well-aimed arrow! Your weapon
should rescue victims, not destroy the innocent! (10)

KING: I withdraw it.
(*He does as he says.*)

MONK: An act worthy of the Puru dynasty's shining light!

> Your birth honors
> the dynasty of the moon!
> May you beget a son
> to turn the wheel of your empire! (11)

THE TWO PUPILS (*raising their arms*): May you beget a son to turn the wheel of your empire!

KING (*bowing*): I welcome your blessing.

MONK: King, we were going to gather firewood. From here you can see the hermitage of our master Kaṇva on the bank of the Mālinī river. If your work permits, enter and accept our hospitality.

> When you see the peaceful rites of devoted ascetics,
> you will know how well your scarred arm protects us. (12)

KING: Is the master of the community there now?

MONK: He went to Somatīrtha, the holy shrine of the moon, and put his daughter Śakuntalā in charge of receiving guests. Some evil threatens her, it seems.

KING: Then I shall see her. She will know my devotion and commend me to the great sage.

MONK: We shall leave you now.

(*He exits with his pupils.*)

KING: Driver, urge the horses on! The sight of this holy hermitage will purify us.

CHARIOTEER: As you command, sir.

(*He mimes the chariot's speed.*)

KING (*looking around*): Without being told one can see that this is a grove where ascetics live.

CHARIOTEER: How?

KING: Don't you see—

> Wild rice grains under trees
> where parrots nest in hollow trunks,
> stones stained by the dark oil
> of crushed iṅgudī nuts,
> trusting deer who hear human voices
> yet don't break their gait,
> and paths from ponds streaked
> by water from wet bark cloth. (13)

CHARIOTEER: It is perfect.

KING (*having gone a little inside*): We should not disturb the grove! Stop the chariot and let me get down!

CHARIOTEER: I'm holding the reins. You can dismount now, sir.

KING (*dismounting*): One should not enter an ascetics' grove in hunting gear. Take these!

(*He gives up his ornaments and his bow.*)

Driver, rub down the horses while I pay my respects to the residents of the hermitage!

CHARIOTEER: Yes, sir!

(*He exits.*)

KING: This gateway marks the sacred ground. I will enter.

(*He enters, indicating he feels an omen.*)

> The hermitage is a tranquil place,
> yet my arm is quivering . . .
> do I feel a false omen of love
> or does fate have doors everywhere? (14)

VOICE OFFSTAGE: This way, friends!

KING (*straining to listen*): I think I hear voices to the right of the grove. I'll find out.

(*Walking around and looking.*)

Young female ascetics with watering pots cradled on their hips are coming to water the saplings.

(*He mimes it in precise detail.*)

This view of them is sweet.

> These forest women have beauty
> rarely seen inside royal palaces—
> the wild forest vines far surpass
> creepers in my pleasure garden. (15)

I'll hide in the shadows and wait.

(*Śakuntalā and her two friends enter, acting as described.*)

ŚAKUNTALĀ: This way, friends!

ANASŪYĀ: I think Father Kaṇva cares more about the trees in the hermitage than he cares about you. You're as delicate as a jasmine, yet he orders you to water the trees.

ŚAKUNTALĀ: Anasūyā, it's more than Father Kaṇva's order. I feel a sister's love for them.
(*She mimes the watering of trees.*)
KING (*to himself*): Is this Kaṇva's daughter? The sage does show poor judgment in imposing the rules of the hermitage on her.

The sage who hopes to subdue
her sensuous body by penances
is trying to cut firewood
with a blade of blue-lotus leaf. (16)

Let it be! I can watch her closely from here in the trees.
(*He does so.*)
ŚAKUNTALĀ: Anasūyā, I can't breathe! Our friend Priyaṁvadā tied my bark dress too tightly! Loosen it a bit!
ANASŪYĀ: As you say.
(*She loosens it.*)
PRIYAṀVADĀ: (*laughing*): Blame your youth for swelling your breasts. Why blame me?
KING: This bark dress fits her body badly, but it ornaments her beauty . . .

A tangle of duckweed adorns a lotus,
a dark spot heightens the moon's glow,
the bark dress increases her charm—
beauty finds its ornaments anywhere. (17)

ŚAKUNTALĀ (*looking in front of her*): The new branches on this mimosa tree are like fingers moving in the wind, calling to me. I must go to it!
(*Saying this, she walks around.*)
PRIYAṀVADĀ: Wait, Śakuntalā! Stay there a minute! When you stand by this mimosa tree, it seems to be guarding a creeper.
ŚAKUNTALĀ: That's why your name means 'Sweet-talk.'
KING: 'Sweet-talk' yes, but Priyaṁvadā speaks the truth about Śakuntalā:

Her lips are fresh red buds,
her arms are tendrils,
impatient youth is poised
to blossom in her limbs. (18)

ANASŪYĀ: Śakuntalā, this is the jasmine creeper who chose the mango tree in marriage, the one you named 'Forestlight.' Have you forgotten her?

ŚAKUNTALĀ: I would be forgetting myself!
(*She approaches the creeper and examines it.*)
The creeper and the tree are twined together in perfect harmony. Forestlight has just flowered and the new mango shoots are made for her pleasure.

PRIYAMVADĀ (*smiling*): Anasūyā, don't you know why Śakuntalā looks so lovingly at Forestlight?

ANASŪYĀ: I can't guess.

PRIYAMVADĀ: The marriage of Forestlight to her tree makes her long to have a husband too.

ŚAKUNTALĀ: You're just speaking your own secret wish.
(*Saying this, she pours water from the jar.*)

KING: Could her social class be different from her father's? There's no doubt!

> She was born to be a warrior's bride,
> for my noble heart desires her—
> when good men face doubt,
> inner feelings are truth's only measure. (19)

Still, I must learn everything about her.

ŚAKUNTALĀ (*flustered*): The splashing water has alarmed a bee. He is flying from the jasmine to my face.
(*She dances to show the bee's attack.*)

KING (looking longingly):

> Bee, you touch the quivering
> corners of her frightened eyes,
> you hover softly near
> to whisper secrets in her ear;
> a hand brushes you away,
> but you drink her lips's treasure—
> while the truth we seek defeats us,
> you are truly blessed. (20)

ŚAKUNTALĀ: This dreadful bee won't stop. I must escape.
(*She steps to one side, glancing about.*)

Oh! He's pursuing me . . . save me! Please save me! This mad bee is chasing me!

BOTH FRIENDS (*laughing*): How can we save you? Call King Duṣyanta. The grove is under his protection.

KING: Here's my chance. Have no fear . . .

(*With this half-spoken, he stops and speaks to himself.*)

Then she will know that I am the king . . . Still, I shall speak.

ŚAKUNTALĀ (*stopping after a few steps*): Why is he still following me?

KING (*approaching quickly*):

> While a Puru king rules the earth
> to punish evildoers,
> who dares to molest
> these innocent young ascetics? (21)

(*Seeing the king, all act flustered.*)

ANASŪYĀ: Sir, there's no real danger. Our friend was frightened when a bee attacked her.

(*She points to Śakuntalā.*)

KING (*approaching Śakuntalā*): Does your ascetic practice go well?

(*Śakuntalā stands speechless.*)

ANASŪYĀ: It does, now that we have a special guest. Śakuntalā, go to our hut and bring the ripe fruits. We'll use this water to bathe his feet.

KING: Your kind speech is hospitality enough.

PRIYAMVADĀ: Please sit in the cold shadows of this shade tree and rest, sir.

KING: You must also be tired from your work.

ANASŪYĀ: Śakuntalā, we should respect our guest. Let's sit down.

(*All sit.*)

ŚAKUNTALĀ (*to herself*): When I see him, why do I feel an emotion that the forest seems to forbid?

KING (*looking at each of the girls*): Youth and beauty complement your friendship.

PRIYAṀVADĀ (*in a stage whisper*): Anasūyā, who is he? He's so polite, fine looking, and pleasing to hear. He has the marks of royalty.

ANASŪYĀ: I'm curious too, friend. I'll just ask him.
(*Aloud.*)
Sir, your kind speech inspires trust. What family of royal sages do you adorn? What country mourns your absence? Why does a man of refinement subject himself to the discomfort of visiting an ascetics' grove?
ŚAKUNTALĀ: (*to herself*): Heart, don't faint! Anasūyā speaks your thoughts.
KING (*to himself*): Should I reveal myself now or conceal who I am? I'll say it this way:
(*Aloud.*)
Lady, I have been appointed by the Puru King as the officer in charge of religious matters. I have come to this sacred forest to assure that your holy rites proceed unhindered.
ANASŪYĀ: Our religious life has a guardian now.
(*Śakuntalā mimes the embarrassment of erotic emotion.*)
BOTH FRIENDS (*observing the behavior of Śakuntalā and the king; in a stage whisper*): Śakuntalā, if only your father were here now!
ŚAKUNTALĀ (*angrily*): What if he were?
BOTH FRIENDS: He would honor this distinguished guest with what he values most in life.
ŚAKUNTALĀ: Quiet! Such words hint at your hearts' conspiracy. I won't listen.
KING: Ladies, I want to ask about your friend.
BOTH FRIENDS: Your request honors us, sir.
KING: Sage Kaṇva has always been celibate, but you call your friend his daughter. How can this be?
ANASŪYĀ: Please listen, sir. There was a powerful royal sage of the Kauśika clan . . .
KING: I am listening.
ANASŪYĀ: He begot our friend, but Kaṇva is her father because he cared for her when she was abandoned.
KING: 'Abandoned'? The word makes me curious. I want to hear her story from the beginning.
ANASŪYĀ: Please listen, sir. Once when this great sage was practicing terrible austerities on the bank of the Gautamī river, he became so powerful that the jealous gods sent a nymph

named Menakā to break his self-control.

KING: The gods dread men who meditate.

ANASŪYĀ: When springtime came to the forest with all its charm, the sage saw her intoxicating beauty . . .

KING: I understand what happened then. She is the nymph's daughter.

ANASŪYĀ: Yes.

KING: It had to be!

> No mortal woman could give birth to such beauty—
> lightning does not flash out of the earth. (22)

(*Śakuntalā stands with her face bowed. The king continues speaking to himself.*)

My desire is not hopeless. Yet, when I hear her friends teasing her about a bridegroom, a new fear divides my heart.

PRIYAṀVADĀ (*smiling, looking at Śakuntalā, then turning to the king*): Sir, you seem to want to say more.

(*Śakuntalā makes a threatening gesture with her finger.*)

KING: You judge correctly. In my eagerness to learn more about your pious lives, I have another question.

PRIYAṀVADĀ: Don't hesitate! Ascetics can be questioned frankly.

KING: I want to know this about your friend:

> Will she keep the vow of hermit life
> only until she marries . . .
> or will she always exchange
> loving looks with deer in the forest? (23)

PRIYAṀVADĀ: Sir, even in her religious life, she is subject to her father, but he does intend to give her to a suitable husband.

KING (*to himself*): His wish is not hard to fulfill.

> Heart, indulge your desire—
> now that doubt is dispelled,
> the fire you feared to touch
> is a jewel in your hands. (24)

ŚAKUNTALĀ (*showing anger*): Anasūyā, I'm leaving!

ANASŪYĀ: Why?

ŚAKUNTALĀ: I'm going to tell Mother Gautamī that Priyaṁvadā is talking nonsense.

ANASŪYĀ: Friend, it's wrong to neglect a distinguished guest and leave as you like.

(*Śakuntalā starts to go without answering.*)

KING (*wanting to seize her, but holding back, he speaks to himself*):

A lover dare not act on his impulsive thoughts!

> I wanted to follow the sage's daughter,
> but decorum abruptly pulled me back;
> I set out and returned again
> without moving my feet from this spot. (25)

PRIYAMVADĀ (*stopping Śakuntalā*): It's wrong of you to go!

ŚAKUNTALĀ (*bending her brow into a frown*): Give me a reason why!

PRIYAMVADĀ: You promised to water two trees for me. Come here and pay your debt before you go!

(*She stops her by force.*)

KING: But she seems exhausted from watering the trees:

> Her shoulders droop, her palms
> are red from the watering pot—
> even now, breathless sighs
> make her breasts shake;
> beads of sweat on her face
> wilt the flower at her ear;
> her hand holds back
> disheveled locks of hair. (26)

Here, I'll pay her debt!

(*He offers his ring. Both friends recite the syllables of the name on the seal and stare at each other.*)

Don't mistake me for what I am not! This is a gift from the king to identify me as his royal official.

PRIYAMVADĀ: Then the ring should never leave your finger. Your word has already paid her debt.

(*She laughs a little.*)

Śakuntalā, you are freed by this kind man . . . or perhaps by the king. Go now!

ŚAKUNTALĀ (*to herself*): If I am able to . . .

(*Aloud.*)

Who are you to keep me or release me?

KING (*watching Śakuntalā*): Can she feel toward me what I feel toward her? Or is my desire fulfilled?

> She won't respond directly to my words,
> but she listens when I speak;
> she won't turn to look at me,
> but her eyes can't rest anywhere else. (27)

VOICE OFFSTAGE: Ascetics, be prepared to protect the creatures of our forest grove! King Duṣyanta is hunting nearby!

> Dust raised by his horses' hooves
> falls like a cloud of locusts swarming
> at sunset over branches of trees
> where wet bark garments hang. (28)

> In terror of the chariots, an elephant
> charged into the hermitage
> and scattered the herd of black antelope,
> like a demon foe of our penances—
> his tusks garlanded with branches
> from a tree crushed by his weight,
> his feet tangled in vines
> that tether him like chains. (29)

(*Hearing this, all the girls are agitated.*)

KING (*to himself*): Oh! My palace men are searching for me and wrecking the grove. I'll have to go back.

BOTH FRIENDS: Sir, we're all upset by this news. Please let us go to our hut.

KING (*showing confusion*): Go, please. We will try to protect the hermitage.

(*They all stand to go.*)

BOTH FRIENDS: Sir, we're ashamed that our bad hospitality is our only excuse to invite you back.

KING: Not at all. I am honored to have seen you.

(*Śakuntalā exits with her two friends, looking back at the king, lingering artfully.*)

I have little desire to return to the city. I'll join my men and have them camp near the grove. I can't control my feelings for

Śakuntalā.

My body turns to go,
my heart pulls me back,
like a silk banner
buffeted by the wind. (30)

(*All exit.*)

END OF ACT ONE

ACT TWO

(*The buffoon enters, despondent.*)

BUFFOON (*sighing*): My bad luck! I'm tired of playing sidekick to a king who's hooked on hunting. "There's a deer!" "There's a boar!" "There's a tiger!" Even in the summer midday heat we chase from jungle to jungle on paths where trees give barely any shade. We drink stinking water from mountain streams foul with rusty leaves. At odd hours we eat nasty meals of spit-roasted meat. Even at night I can't sleep. My joints ache from galloping on that horse. Then at the crack of dawn, I'm woken rudely by a noise piercing the forest. Those sons of bitches hunt their birds then. The torture doesn't end—now I have sores on top of my bruises. Yesterday, we lagged behind. The king chased a buck into the hermitage. As luck would have it, an ascetic's daughter called Śakuntalā caught his eye. Now he isn't even thinking of going back to the city. This very dawn I found him wide-eyed, mooning about her. What a fate! I must see him after his bath.
(*He walks around, looking.*)
Here comes my friend now, wearing garlands of wild flowers. Greek women carry his bow in their hands. Good! I'll stand here pretending my arms and legs are broken. Maybe then I'll get some rest.
(*He stands leaning on his staff. The king enters with his retinue, as described.*)
KING: (*to himself*):

> My beloved will not be easy to win,
> but signs of emotion revealed her heart—
> even when love seems hopeless,
> mutual longing keeps passion alive. (1)

(*He smiles.*)

A suitor who measures his beloved's state of mind by his own desire is a fool.

> She threw tender glances
> though her eyes were cast down,
> her heavy hips swayed
> in slow seductive movements,
> she answered in anger
> when her friend said, "Don't go!"
> and I felt it was all for my sake . . .
> but a lover sees in his own way. (2)

BUFFOON (*still in the same position*): Dear friend, since my hands can't move to greet you, I have to salute you with my voice.
KING: How did you cripple your limbs?
BUFFOON: Why do you ask why I cry after throwing dust in my eyes yourself?
KING: I don't understand.
BUFFOON: Dear friend, when a straight reed is twisted into a crooked reed, is it by its own power, or is it the river current?
KING: The river current is the cause.
BUFFOON: And so it is with me.
KING: How so?
BUFFOON: You neglect the business of being a king and live like a woodsman in this awful camp. Chasing after wild beasts every day jolts my joints and muscles till I can't control my own limbs anymore. I beg you to let me rest for just one day!
KING: (*to himself*): He says what I also feel. When I remember Kaṇva's daughter, the thought of hunting disgusts me.

> I can't draw my bowstring
> to shoot arrows at deer
> who live with my love
> and teach her tender glances. (3)

BUFFOON: Sir, you have something on your mind. I'm crying in a wilderness.
KING (*smiling*): Yes, it is wrong to ignore my friend's plea.
BUFFOON: Live long!
(*He starts to go.*)

KING: Dear friend, stay! Hear what I have to say!

BUFFOON: At your command, sir!

KING: When you have rested, I need your help in some work that you will enjoy.

BUFFOON: Is it eating sweets? I'm game!

KING: I shall tell you. Who stands guard?

GUARD (*entering*): At your command, sir!

KING: Raivataka! Summon the general!

(*The guard exits and reenters with the general.*)

GUARD: The king is looking this way, waiting to give you his orders. Approach him, sir!

GENERAL (*looking at the king*): Hunting is said to be a vice, but our king prospers:

> Drawing the bows only hardens his chest,
> he suffers the sun's scorching rays unburned,
> hard muscles mask his body's lean state—
> like a wild elephant, his energy sustains him. (4)

(*He approaches the king.*)

Victory, my lord! We've already tracked some wild beasts. Why the delay?

KING: Māḍhavya's censure of hunting has dampened my spirit.

GENERAL (*in a stage whisper, to the buffoon*): Friend, you stick to your opposition! I'll try to restore our king's good sense. (*Aloud.*)

This fool is talking nonsense. Here is the king as proof:

> A hunter's belly is taut and lean,
> his slender body craves exertion;
> he penetrates the spirit of creatures
> overcome by fear and rage;
> his bowmanship is proved
> by arrows striking a moving target—
> hunting is falsely called a vice.
> What sport can rival it? (5)

BUFFOON (*angrily*): The king has come to his senses. If you keep chasing from forest to forest, you'll fall into the jaws of an old bear hungry for a human nose . . .

KING: My noble general, we are near a hermitage; your words cannot please me now.

> Let horned buffaloes plunge into muddy pools!
> Let herds of deer huddle in the shade to eat grass!
> Let fearless wild boars crush fragrant swamp grass!
> Let my bowstring lie slack and my bow at rest! (6)

GENERAL: Whatever gives the king pleasure.

KING: Withdraw the men who are in the forest now and forbid my soldiers to disturb the grove!

> Ascetics devoted to peace
> possess a fiery hidden power,
> like smooth crystal sunstones
> that reflect the sun's scorching rays. (7)

GENERAL: Whatever you command, sir!

BUFFOON: Your arguments for keeping up the hunt fall on deaf ears!

(*The general exits.*)

KING (*looking at his retinue*): You women, take away my hunting gear! Raivataka, don't neglect your duty!

RETINUE: As the king commands!

(*They exit.*)

BUFFOON: Sir, now that the flies are cleared out, sit on a stone bench under this shady canopy. Then I'll find a comfortable seat too.

KING: Go ahead!

BUFFOON: You first, sir!

(*Both walk about, then sit down.*)

KING: Māḍhavya, you haven't really used your eyes because you haven't seen true beauty.

BUFFOON: But you're right in front of me, sir!

KING: Everyone is partial to what he knows well, but I'm speaking about Śakuntalā, the jewel of the hermitage.

BUFFOON (*to himself*): I won't give him a chance!

(*Aloud.*)

Dear friend, it seems that you're pursuing an ascetic's daughter.

KING: Friend, the heart of a Puru king wouldn't crave a forbidden fruit . . .

The sage's child is a nymph's daughter,
rescued by him after she was abandoned,
like a fragile jasmine blossom
broken and caught on a sunflower pod. (8)

BUFFOON (*laughing*): You're like the man who loses his taste for dates and prefers sour tamarind! How can you abandon the gorgeous gems of your palace?

KING: You speak this way because you haven't seen her.

BUFFOON: She must be delectable if you're so enticed!

KING: Friend, what is the use of all this talk?

The divine creator imagined perfection
and shaped her ideal form in his mind—
when I recall the beauty his power wrought,
she shines like a gemstone among my jewels. (9)

BUFFOON: So she's the reason you reject the other beauties!

KING: She stays in my mind:

A flower no one has smelled,
a bud no fingers have plucked,
an uncut jewel, honey untasted,
unbroken fruit of holy deeds—
I don't know who is destined
to enjoy her flawless beauty. (10)

BUFFOON: Then you should rescue her quickly! Don't let her fall into the arms of some ascetic who greases his head with iṅgudī oil!

KING: She is someone else's ward and her guardian is away.

BUFFOON: What kind of passion did her eyes betray!

KING: Ascetics are timid by nature:

Her eyes were cast down in my presence,
but she found an excuse to smile—
modesty barely contained the love
she could neither reveal nor conceal. (11)

BUFFOON: Did you expect her to climb into your lap when she'd barely seen you?

KING: When we parted her feelings for me showed despite her modesty.

"A blade of kuśa grass
pricked my foot,"
the girl said for no reason
after walking a few steps away;
then she pretended to free
her bark dress from branches
where it was not caught
and shyly glanced at me. (12)

BUFFOON: Stock up on food for a long trip! I can see you've turned that ascetics' grove into a pleasure garden.

KING: Friend, some of the ascetics recognize me. What excuse can we find to return to the hermitage?

BUFFOON: What excuse? Aren't you the king? Collect a sixth of their wild rice as tax!

KING: Fool! These ascetics pay tribute that pleases me more than mounds of jewels.

Tribute that kings collect
from members of society decays,
but the share of austerity
that ascetics give lasts forever (13)

VOICE OFFSTAGE: Good, we have succeeded!

KING (*listening*): These are the steady, calm voices of ascetics.

GUARD (*entering*): Victory, sir! Two boy ascetics are waiting near the gate.

KING: Let them enter without delay!

GUARD: I'll show them in.

(*He exits; reenters with the boys.*)

Here you are!

FIRST BOY: His majestic body inspires trust. It is natural when a king is virtually a sage.

His palace is a hermitage
with its infinite pleasures,
the discipline of protecting men
imposes austerities every day—
pairs of celestial bards praise
his perfect self-control,

adding the royal word "king"
to "sage," his sacred title. (14)

SECOND BOY: Gautama, is this Duṣyanta, the friend of Indra?

FIRST BOY: Of course!

SECOND BOY:

It is no surprise that this arm of iron
rules the whole earth bounded by dark seas—
when demons harass the gods, victory's hope
rests on his bow and Indra's thunderbolt. (15)

BOTH BOYS (*coming near*): Victory to you, king!

KING (*rising from his seat*): I salute you both!

BOTH BOYS: To your success, sir!

(*They offer fruits.*)

KING (*accepting their offering*): I am ready to listen.

BOTH BOYS: The ascetics know that you are camped nearby and send a petition to you.

KING: What do they request?

BOTH BOYS: Demons are taking advantage of Sage Kaṇva's absence to harass us. You must come with your charioteer to protect the hermitage for a few days!

KING: I am honored to oblige.

BUFFOON (*in a stage whisper*): Your wish is fulfilled!

KING (*smiling*): Raivataka, call my charioteer! Tell him to bring the chariot and my bow!

GUARD: As the king commands!

(*He exits*)

BOTH BOYS (*showing delight*):

Following your ancestral duties
suits your noble form—
the Puru kings are ordained
to dispel their subject's fear. (16)

KING (*bowing*): You two return! I shall follow.

BOTH BOYS: Be victorious!

(*They exit.*)

KING: Māḍhavya, are you curious to see Śakuntalā?

BUFFOON: At first there was a flood, but now with this news of demons, not a drop is left.

KING: Don't be afraid! Won't you be with me?

BUFFOON: Then I'll be safe from any demon . . .

GUARD (*entering*): The chariot is ready to take you to victory . . but Karabhaka has just come from the city with a message from the queen.

KING: Did my mother send him?

GUARD: She did.

KING: Have him enter then.

GUARD: Yes.

(*He exits; re-enters with Karabhaka.*)

Here is the king. Approach!

KARABHAKA: Victory, sir! Victory! The queen has ordered a ceremony four days from now to mark the end of her fast. Your Majesty will surely give us the honor of his presence.

KING: The ascetics' business keeps me here and my mother's command calls me there. I must find a way to avoid neglecting either!

BUFFOON: Hang yourself between them the way Triśaṅku hung between heaven and earth.

KING: I'm really confused . . .

> My mind is split in two
> by these conflicting duties,
> like a river current split
> by boulders in its course. (17)

(*Thinking.*)

Friend, my mother has treated you like a son. You must go back and report that I've set my heart on fulfilling my duty to the ascetics. You fulfill my filial duty to the queen.

BUFFOON: You don't really think I'm afraid of demons?

KING (*smiling*): My brave brahman, how could you be?

BUFFOON: Then I can travel like the king's younger brother.

KING: We really should not disturb the grove! Take my whole entourage with you!

BUFFOON: Now I've turned into the crown prince!

KING (*to himself*): This fellow is absent-minded. At any time he may tell the palace women about my passion. I'll tell him this: (*Taking the buffoon by the hand, he speaks aloud.*)
Dear friend, I'm going to the hermitage out of reverence for the sages. I really feel no desire for the young ascetic Śakuntalā.

> What do I share with a rustic girl
> reared among fawns, unskilled in love?
> Don't mistake what I muttered
> in jest for the real truth, friend! (18)

(*All exit.*)

END OF ACT TWO

ACT THREE

(A disciple of Kaṇva enters, carrying kuśa grass for a sacrificial rite.)

DISCIPLE: King Duṣyanta is certainly powerful. Since he entered the hermitage, our rites have not been hindered.

Why talk of fixing arrows?
The mere twang of his bowstring
clears away menacing demons
as if his bow roared with death. (1)

I'll gather some more grass for the priests to spread on the sacrificial altar.
(*Walking around and looking, he calls aloud.*)
Priyaṁvadā, for whom are you bringing the ointment of fragrant lotus root fibers and leaves?
(*Listening.*)
What are you saying? Śakuntalā is suffering from heat exhaustion? They're for rubbing on her body? Priyaṁvadā, take care of her! She is the breath of Father Kaṇva's life. I'll give Gautamī this water from the sacrifice to use for soothing her. (*He exits; the interlude ends. Then the king enters, suffering from love, deep in thought, sighing.*)
KING:

I know the power ascetics have
and the rules that bind her,
but I cannot abandon my heart
now that she has taken it. (2)

(*Showing the pain of love.*)
Love, why do you and the moon both contrive to deceive lovers by first gaining our trust?

Arrows of flowers and cool moon rays
are both deadly for men like me—

the moon shoots fire through icy rays
and you hurl thunderbolts of flowers. (3)

(*Walking around.*)

Now that the rites are concluded and the priests have dismissed me, where can I rest from the weariness of this work?

(*Sighing.*)

There is no refuge but the sight of my love. I must find her.

(*Looking up at the sun.*)

Śakuntalā usually spends the heat of the day with her friends in a bower of vines on the Mālinī riverbank. I shall go there.

(*Walking around, miming the touch of breeze.*)

This place is enchanted by the wind.

A breeze fragrant with lotus pollen
and moist from the Mālinī waves
can be held in soothing embrace
by my love-scorched arms. (4)

(*Walking around and looking.*)

I see fresh footprints
on white sand in the clearing,
deeply pressed at the heel
by the sway of full hips. (5)

I'll just look through the branches.

(*Walking around, looking, he becomes joyous.*)

My eyes have found bliss! The girl I desire is lying on a stone couch strewn with flowers, attended by her two friends. I'll eavesdrop as they confide in one another.

(*He stands watching. Śakuntalā appears as described, with her two friends.*)

BOTH FRIENDS (*fanning her affectionately*): Śakuntalā, does the breeze from this lotus leaf please you?

ŚAKUNTALĀ: Are you fanning me?

(*The friends trade looks, miming dismay.*)

KING (*deliberating*): Śakuntalā seems to be in great physical pain. Is it the heat or is it what is in my own heart?

(*Miming ardent desire.*)

My doubts are unfounded!

Her breasts are smeared with lotus balm,
her lotus-fiber bracelet hangs limp,
her beautiful body glows in pain—
love burns young women like summer heat,
but its guilt makes them more charming. (6)

PRIYAMVADĀ (*in a stage whisper*): Anasūyā, Śakuntalā has been pining since she first saw the king. Could he be the cause of her sickness?

ANASŪYĀ: She must be suffering from lovesickness. I'll ask her . . .

(*Aloud.*)

Friend, I have something to ask you. Your pain seems so deep . . .

ŚAKUNTALĀ (*raising herself halfway*): What do you want to say?

ANASŪYĀ: Śakuntalā, though we don't know what it is to be in love, your condition reminds us of lovers we have heard about in stories. Can you tell us the cause of your pain? Unless we understand your illness, we can't begin to find a cure.

KING: Anasūyā expresses my own thoughts.

ŚAKUNTALĀ: Even though I want to, suddenly I can't make myself tell you.

PRIYAMVADĀ: Śakuntalā, my friend Anasūyā means well. Don't you see how sick you are? Your limbs are wasting away. Only the shadow of your beauty remains . . .

KING: What Priyaṁvadā says is true:

Her cheeks are deeply sunken,
her breasts' full shape is gone,
her waist is thin, her shoulders bent,
and the color has left her skin—
tormented by love,
she is sad but beautiful to see,
like a jasmine creeper
when hot wind shrivels its leaves. (7)

ŚAKUNTALĀ: Friends, who else can I tell? May I burden you?

BOTH FRIENDS: We insist! Sharing sorrow with loving friends makes it bearable.

KING:

Friends who share her joy and sorrow
discover the love concealed in her heart—
though she looked back longingly at me,
now I am afraid to hear her response. (8)

ŚAKUNTALĀ: Friend, since my eyes first saw the guardian of the hermits' retreat, I've felt such strong desire for him!
KING: I have heard what I want to hear.

My tormentor, the god of love,
has soothed my fever himself,
like the heat of late summer
allayed by early rain clouds. (9)

ŚAKUNTALĀ: If you two think it's right, then help me to win the king's pity. Otherwise, you'll soon pour sesame oil and water on my corpse . . .
KING: Her words destroy my doubt.
PRIYAMVADĀ (*in a stage whisper*): She's so dangerously in love that there's no time to lose. Since her heart is set on the ornament of the Puru dynasty, we should rejoice that she desires him.
ANASŪYĀ: What you say is true.
PRIYAMVADĀ (*aloud*): Friend, by good fortune your desire is in harmony with nature. A great river can only descend to the ocean. A jasmine creeper can only twine around a mango tree.
KING: Why is this surprising when the twin stars of spring serve the crescent moon?
ANASŪYĀ: What means do we have to fulfill our friend's desire secretly and quickly?
PRIYAMVADĀ: 'Secretly' demands some effort. 'Quickly' is easy.
ANASŪYĀ: How so?
PRIYAMVADĀ: The king was charmed by her loving look; he seems thin these days from sleepless nights.
KING: It's true . . .

This golden armlet
slips to my wrist
without touching the scars

my bowstring has made;
its gemstones are faded
by tears of secret pain
that every night wets my arm
where I bury my face. (10)

PRIYAMVADĀ (*thinking*): Compose a love letter and I'll hide it in a flower. I'll deliver it to his hand on the pretext of bringing an offering to the deity.

ANASŪYĀ: This subtle plan pleases me. What does Śakuntalā say?

ŚAKUNTALĀ: I'll try my friend's plan.

PRIYAMVADĀ: Then compose a poem to declare your love!

ŚAKUNTALĀ: I'm thinking, but my heart trembles with fear that he'll reject me.

KING (*delighted*):

The man you fear will reject you
waits longing to love you, timid girl—
a suitor may lose or be lucky,
but the goddess always wins. (11)

BOTH FRIENDS: Why do you belittle your own virtues? Who would cover his body with a piece of cloth to keep off cool autumn moonlight?

ŚAKUNTALĀ (*smiling*): I'm trying to follow your advice.

(*She sits thinking.*)

KING: As I gaze at her, my eyes forget to blink.

She arches an eyebrow,
struggling to compose the verse—
the down rises on her cheek,
showing the passion she feels. (12)

ŚAKUNTALĀ: I've thought of a verse, but I have nothing to write it on.

PRIYAMVADĀ: Engrave the letters with your nail on this lotus leaf! It's as delicate as a parrot's breast.

ŚAKUNTALĀ (*miming what Priyaṁvadā described*): Listen and tell me if this makes sense!

BOTH FRIENDS: We're both paying attention.

ŚAKUNTALĀ (*singing*):

I don't know
your heart,
but day and night
for wanting you,
love violently
tortures
my limbs,
cruel man. (13)

KING (*suddenly revealing himself*):

Love torments you, slender girl,
but he completely consumes me—
daylight spares the lotus pond
while it destroys the moon (14)

BOTH FRIENDS (*looking, rising with delight*): Welcome to the swift success of love's desire!

(*Śakuntalā tries to rise.*)

KING: Don't exert yourself!

Limbs lying among crushed petals
like fragile lotus stalks
are too weakened by pain
to perform ceremonious acts. (15)

ANASŪYĀ: Then let the king sit on this stone bench!

(*The king sits; Śakuntalā rises in embarrassment.*)

PRIYAṀVADĀ: The passion of two young lovers is clear. My affection for our friend makes me speak out again now.

KING: Noble lady, don't hesitate! It is painful to keep silent when one must speak.

PRIYAṀVADĀ: We're told that it is the king's duty to ease the pain of his suffering subjects.

KING: My duty, exactly!

PRIYAṀVADĀ: Since she first saw you, our dear friend has been reduced to this sad condition. You must protect her and save her life.

KING: Noble lady, our affection is shared and I am honored by all you say.

ŚAKUNTALĀ (*looking at Priyaṁvadā*): Why are you keeping the king here? He must be anxious to return to his palace.
KING:

> If you think that my lost heart
> could love anyone but you,
> a fatal blow strikes a man
> already wounded by love's arrows! (16)

ANASŪYĀ: We've heard that kings have many loves. Will our dear friend become a sorrow to her family after you've spent time with her?
KING: Noble lady, enough of this!

> Despite my many wives,
> on two the royal line rests—
> sea-bound earth
> and your friend. (17)

BOTH FRIENDS: You reassure us.
PRIYAṀVADĀ (*casting a glance*): Anasūyā, this fawn is looking for its mother. Let's take it to her!
(*They both begin to leave.*)
ŚAKUNTALĀ: Come back! Don't leave me unprotected!
BOTH FRIENDS: The protector of the earth is at your side.
ŚAKUNTALĀ: Why have they gone?
KING: Don't be alarmed! I am your servant.

> Shall I set moist winds in motion
> with lotus-leaf fans to cool your pain,
> or rest your soft red lotus feet
> on my lap to stroke them, my love? (18)

ŚAKUNTALĀ: I cannot sin against those I respect!
(*Standing as if she wants to leave.*)
KING: Beautiful Śakuntalā, the day is still hot.

> Why should your frail limbs
> leave this couch of flowers
> shielded by lotus leaves
> to wander in the heat? (19)

(*Saying this, he forces her to turn around.*)
ŚAKUNTALĀ: Puru king, control yourself! Though I'm burning with love, how can I give myself to you?

KING: Don't fear your elders! The father of your family knows the law. When he finds out, he will not blame you.

> The daughters of royal sages often marry
> in secret and then their fathers bless them. (20)

ŚAKUNTALĀ: Release me! I must ask my friends' advice!

KING: Yes, I shall release you.

ŚAKUNTALĀ: When?

KING:

> Only let my thirsting mouth
> gently drink from your lips,
> the way a bee sips nectar
> from a fragile virgin blossom. (21)

(*Saying this, he tries to raise her face. Śakuntalā evades him with a dance.*)

VOICE OFFSTAGE: Red goose, bid farewell to your gander! Night has arrived!

ŚAKUNTALĀ (*flustered*): Puru king, Mother Gautamī is surely coming to ask about my health. Hide behind this tree!

KING: Yes.

(*He conceals himself and waits. Then Gautamī enters with a vessel in her hand, accompanied by Śakuntalā's two friends.*)

BOTH FRIENDS: This way, Mother Gautamī!

GAUTAMĪ (*approaching Śakuntalā*): Child, does the fever in your limbs burn less?

ŚAKUNTALĀ: Madam, I do feel better.

GAUTAMĪ: Kuśa grass and water will soothe your body.

(*She sprinkles Śakuntalā's head.*)

Child, the day is ended. Come, let's go back to our hut!

(*She starts to go.*)

ŚAKUNTALĀ: (*to herself*): My heart, even when your desire was within reach, you were bound by fear. Now you'll suffer the torment of separation and regret.

(*Stopping after a few steps, she speaks aloud.*)

Bower of creepers, refuge from my torment, I say goodbye until our joy can be renewed . . .

(*Sorrowfully, Śakuntalā exits with the other women.*)

KING (*coming out of hiding*): Fulfillment of desire is fraught with obstacles.

Why didn't I kiss her face
as it bent near my shoulder,
her fingers shielding lips
that stammered lovely warning? (22)

Should I go now? Or shall I stay here in this bower of creepers that my love enjoyed and then left?

I see the flowers her body pressed
on this bench of stone,
the letter her nails inscribed
on the faded lotus leaf,
the lotus-fiber bracelet
that slipped from her wrist—
my eyes are prisoners
in this empty house of reeds. (23)

VOICE IN THE AIR: King!

When the evening rituals begin,
shadows of flesh-eating demons swarm
like amber clouds of twilight,
raising terror at the altar of fire. (24)

KING: I am coming.
(*He exits.*)

END OF ACT THREE

ACT FOUR

(*The two friends enter, miming the gathering of flowers.*)

ANASŪYĀ: Priyaṁvadā, I'm delighted that Śakuntalā chose a suitable husband for herself, but I still feel anxious.

PRIYAṀVADĀ: Why?

ANASŪYĀ: When the king finished the sacrifice, the sages thanked him and he left. Now that he has returned to his palace women in the city, will he remember us here?

PRIYAṀVADĀ: Have faith! He's so handsome, he can't be evil. But I don't know what Father Kaṇva will think when he hears about what happened.

ANASŪYĀ: I predict that he'll give his approval.

PRIYAṀVADĀ: Why?

ANASŪYĀ: He's always planned to give his daughter to a worthy husband. If fate accomplished it so quickly, Father Kaṇva won't object.

PRIYAṀVADĀ (*looking at the basket of flowers*): We've gathered enough flowers for the offering ceremony.

ANASŪYĀ: Shouldn't we worship the goddess who guards Śakuntalā?

PRIYAṀVADĀ: I have just begun.

(*She begins the rite.*)

VOICE OFFSTAGE: I am here!

ANASŪYĀ (*listening*): Friend, a guest is announcing himself.

PRIYAṀVADĀ: Śakuntalā is in her hut nearby, but her heart is far away.

ANASŪYĀ: You're right! Enough of these flowers!

(*They begin to leave.*)

VOICE OFFSTAGE: So . . . you slight a guest . . .

> Since you blindly ignore
> a great sage like me,

the lover you worship
with mindless devotion
will not remember you,
even when awakened—
like a drunkard who forgets
a story he just composed! (1)

PRIYAṀVADĀ: Oh! What a terrible turn of events! Śakuntalā's distraction has offended someone she should have greeted.

(*Looking ahead.*)

Not just an ordinary person, but the angry sage Durvāsas himself cursed her and went away in a frenzy of quivering, mad gestures. What else but fire has such power to burn?

ANASŪYĀ: Go! Bow at his feet and make him return while I prepare the water for washing his feet!

PRIYAṀVADĀ: As you say.

(*She exits.*)

ANASŪYĀ (*after a few steps, she mimes stumbling*): Oh! The basket of flowers fell from my hand when I stumbled in my haste to go.

(*She mimes the gathering of flowers.*)

PRIYAṀVADĀ (*entering*): He's so terribly cruel! No one could pacify him! But I was able to soften him a little.

ANASŪYĀ: Even that is a great feat with him! Tell me more!

PRIYAṀVADĀ: When he refused to return, I begged him to forgive a daughter's first offense, since she didn't understand the power of his austerity.

ANASŪYĀ: Then? Then?

PRIYAṀVADĀ: He refused to change his word, but he promised that when the king sees the ring of recollection, the curse will end. Then he vanished.

ANASŪYĀ: Now we can breathe again. When he left, the king himself gave her the ring engraved with his name. Śakuntalā will have her own means of ending the curse.

PRIYAṀVADĀ: Come friend! We should finish the holy rite we're performing for her.

(*The two walk around, looking.*)

Anasūyā, look! With her face resting on her hand, our dear friend looks like a picture. She is thinking about her husband's leaving, with no thought for herself, much less for a guest.

ANASŪYĀ: Priyaṁvadā, we two must keep all this a secret between us. Our friend is fragile by nature; she needs our protection.

PRIYAṀVADĀ: Who would sprinkle a jasmine with scalding water?

(*They both exit; the interlude ends. Then a disciple of Kaṇva enters, just awakened from sleep.*)

DISCIPLE: Father Kaṇva has just returned from his pilgrimage and wants to know the exact time. I'll go into a clearing to see what remains of the night.

(*Walking around and looking.*)

It is dawn.

> The moon sets over the western mountain
> as the sun rises in dawn's red trail—
> rising and setting, these two bright powers
> portend the rise and fall of men. (2)
>
> When the moon disappears, night lotuses
> are but dull souvenirs of its beauty—
> when her lover disappears, the sorrow
> is too painful for a frail girl to bear. (3)

ANASŪYĀ (*throwing aside the curtain and entering*): Even a person withdrawn from worldly life knows that the king has treated Śakuntalā badly.

DISCIPLE: I'll inform Father Kaṇva that it's time for the fire oblation.

(*He exits.*)

ANASŪYĀ: Even when I'm awake, I'm useless. My hands and feet don't do their work. Love must be pleased to have made our innocent friend put her trust in a liar . . . but perhaps it was the curse of Durvāsas that changed him . . . otherwise, how could the king have made such promises and not sent even a message by now? Maybe we should send the ring to remind him. Which of these ascetics who practice austerities can we ask? Father Kaṇva has just returned from his pilgrimage. Since we feel that our friend was also at fault, we haven't told him that Śakuntalā is married to Duṣyanta and is pregnant. The problem is serious. What should we do?

PRIYAṀVADĀ (*entering, with delight*): Friend, hurry! We're to celebrate the festival of Śakuntalā's departure for her husband's house.

ANASŪYĀ: What's happened, friend?

PRIYAMVADĀ: Listen! I went to ask Śakuntalā how she had slept. Father Kaṇva embraced her and though her face was bowed in shame, he blessed her: "Though his eyes were filled with smoke, the priest's oblation luckily fell on the fire. My child, I shall not mourn for you . . . like knowledge given to a good student I shall send you to your husband today with an escort of sages."

ANASŪYĀ: Who told Father Kaṇva what happened?

PRIYAṀVADĀ: A bodiless voice was chanting when he entered the fire sanctuary.

(*Quoting in Sanskrit.*)

Priest, know that your daughter
carries Duṣyanta's potent seed
for the good of the earth—
like fire in mimosa wood. (4)

ANASŪYĀ: I'm joyful, friend. But I know that Śakuntalā must leave us today and sorrow shadows my happiness.

PRIYAṀVADĀ: Friend, we must chase away sorrow and make this hermit girl happy!

ANASŪYĀ: Friend, I've made a garland of mimosa flowers. It's in the coconut-shell box hanging on a branch of the mango tree. Get it for me! Meanwhile I'll prepare the special ointments of deer musk, sacred earth, and blades of dūrvā grass.

PRIYAṀVADĀ: Here it is!

(*Anasūyā exits; Priyaṁvadā gracefully mimes taking down the box.*)

VOICE OFFSTAGE: Gautamī! Śārṅgarava and some others have been appointed to escort Śakuntalā.

PRIYAṀVADĀ (*listening*): Hurry! Hurry! The sages are being called to go to Hastināpura.

ANASŪYĀ (*re-entering with pots of ointments in her hands*): Come, friend! Let's go!

PRIYAṀVADĀ (*looking around*): Śakuntalā stands at sunrise with freshly washed hair while the female ascetics bless her with handfuls of wild rice and auspicious words of farewell. Let's go to her together.

(*The two approach as Śakuntalā enters with Gautamī and other female ascetics, and strikes a posture as described. One after another, the female ascetics address her.*)

FIRST FEMALE ASCETIC: Child, win the title "Chief Queen" as a sign of your husband's high esteem!

SECOND FEMALE ASCETIC: Child, be a mother to heroes!

THIRD FEMALE ASCETIC: Child, be honored by your husband!

BOTH FRIENDS: This happy moment is no time for tears, friend.

(*Wiping away her tears, they calm her with dance gestures.*)

PRIYAṀVADĀ: Your beauty deserves jewels, not these humble things we've gathered in the hermitage.

(*Two boy ascetics enter with offerings in their hands.*)

BOTH BOYS: Here is an ornament for you!

(*Everyone looks amazed.*)

GAUTAMĪ: Nārada, my child, where did this come from?

FIRST BOY: From Father Kaṇva's power.

GAUTAMĪ: Was it his mind's magic?

SECOND BOY: Not at all! Listen! You ordered us to bring flowers from the forest trees for Śakuntalā.

> One tree produced this white silk cloth,
> another poured resinous lac to redden her feet—
> the tree nymphs produced jewels in hands
> that stretched from branches like young shoots. (5)

PRIYAṀVADĀ (*watching Śakuntalā*): This is a sign that royal fortune will come to you in your husband's house.

(*Śakuntalā mimes modesty.*)

FIRST BOY: Gautama, come quickly! Father Kaṇva is back from bathing. We'll tell him how the trees honor her.

SECOND BOY: As you say.

(*The two exit.*)

BOTH FRIENDS: We've never worn them ourselves, but we'll put these jewels on your limbs the way they look in pictures.

ŚAKUNTALĀ: I trust your skill.
(*Both friends mime ornamenting her. Then Kaṇva enters, fresh from his bath.*)
KAṆVA:

My heart is touched with sadness
since Śakuntalā must go today,
my throat is choked with sobs,
my eyes are dulled by worry—
if a disciplined ascetic
suffers so deeply from love,
how do fathers bear the pain
of each daughter's parting? (6)

(*He walks around.*)
BOTH FRIENDS: Śakuntalā, your jewels are in place; now put on the pair of silken cloths.
(*Standing, Śakuntalā wraps them.*)
GAUTAMĪ: Child, your father has come. His eyes filled with tears of joy embrace you. Greet him reverently!
ŚAKUNTALĀ (*modestly*): Father, I welcome you.
KAṆVA: Child,

May your husband honor you
the way Yayāti honored Śarmiṣṭhā.
As she bore her son Puru,
May you bear an imperial prince. (7)

GAUTAMĪ: Sir, this is a blessing, not just a prayer.
KAṆVA: Child, walk around the sacrificial fires!

(*All walk around; Kaṇva intoning a prayer in Vedic meter.*)

Perfectly placed around the main altar,
fed with fuel, strewn with holy grass,
destroying sin by incense from oblations,
may these sacred fires purify you! (8)

You must leave now!
(*Looking around.*)
Where are Śārṅgarava and the others?
DISCIPLE (*entering*): Here we are, sir!

KANVA: You show your sister the way!
ŚĀRṄGARAVA: Come this way!
(*They walk around.*)
KAṆVA: Listen, you trees that grow in our grove!

> Until you were well watered
> she could not bear to drink;
> she loved you too much
> to pluck your flowers for her hair;
> the first time your buds bloomed,
> she blossomed with joy—
> may you all bless Śakuntalā
> as she leaves for her husband's house. (9)

(*Miming that he hears a cuckoo's cry.*)

> The trees of her forest family
> have blessed Śakuntalā—
> the cuckoo's melodious song
> announces their response. (10)

VOICE IN THE AIR:

> May lakes colored by lotuses mark her path!
> May trees shade her from the sun's burning rays!
> May the dust be as soft as lotus pollen!
> May fragrant breezes cool her way! (11)

(*All listen astonished.*)
GAUTAMĪ: Child, the divinities of our grove love you like your family and bless you. We bow to you all!
ŚAKUNTALĀ (*bowing and walking around; speaking in a stage whisper*): Priyaṁvadā, though I long to see my husband, my feet move with sorrow as I start to leave the hermitage.
PRIYAṀVADĀ: You are not the only one who grieves. The whole hermitage feels this way as your departure from our grove draws near.

> Grazing deer
> drop grass,
> peacocks
> stop dancing,
> vines loose

pale leaves
falling
like tears. (12)

ŚAKUNTALĀ (*remembering*): Father, before I leave, I must see my sister, the vine Forestlight.

KAṆVA: I know that you feel a sister's love for her. She is right here.

ŚAKUNTALĀ: Forestlight, though you love your mango tree, turn to embrace me with your tendril arms! After today, I'll be so far away . . .

KAṆVA:

Your merits won you the husband
I always hoped you would have
and your jasmine has her mango tree—
my worries for you both are over. (13)

Start your journey here!

ŚAKUNTALĀ (*facing her two friends*): I entrust her care to you.

BOTH FRIENDS: But who will care for us?

(*They wipe away their tears.*)

KAṆVA: Anasūyā, enough crying! You should be giving Śakuntalā courage!

(*All walk around.*)

ŚAKUNTALĀ: Father, when the pregnant doe who grazes near my hut gives birth, please send someone to give me the good news.

KAṆVA: I shall not forget.

ŚAKUNTALĀ (*miming the interrupting of her gait*): Who is clinging to my skirt?

(*She turns around.*)

KAṆVA: Child,

The buck whose mouth you healed with oil
when it was pierced by a blade of kuśa grass
and whom you fed with grains of rice—
your adopted son will not leave the path. (14)

ŚAKUNTALĀ: Child, don't follow when I'm abandoning those I love! I raised you when you were orphaned soon after your birth, but now I'm deserting you too. Father will look after you.

Go back!

(*Weeping, she starts to go.*)

KAṆVA: Be strong!

> Hold back the tears that blind
> your long-lashed eyes—
> you will stumble if you cannot see
> the uneven ground on the path. (15)

ŚĀRṄGARAVA: Sir, the scriptures prescribe that loved ones be escorted only to the water's edge. We are at the shore of the lake. Give us your message and return!

ŚAKUNTALĀ: We shall rest in the shade of this fig tree.

(*All walk around and stop; Kaṇva speaks to himself.*)

What would be the right message to send to King Duṣyanta?

(*He ponders.*)

ŚAKUNTALĀ (*in a stage whisper*): Look! The wild goose cries in anguish when her mate is hidden by lotus leaves. What I'm suffering is much worse.

ANASŪYĀ: Friend, don't speak this way!

> This goose spends
> every long night
> in sorrow
> without her mate,
> but hope lets her
> survive
> the deep pain
> of loneliness. (16)

KAṆVA: Śārngarava, speak my words to the king after you present Śakuntalā!

ŚĀRṄGARAVA: As you command, sir!

KAṆVA:

> Considering our discipline,
> the nobility of your birth
> and that she fell in love with you
> before her kinsmen could act,
> acknowledge her with equal rank
> among your wives—

what more is destined for her,
the bride's family will not ask. (17)

ŚĀRṄGARAVA: I grasp your message.

KAṆVA: Child, now I must instruct you. We forest hermits know something about worldly matters.

ŚĀRṄGARAVA: Nothing is beyond the scope of wise men.

KAṆVA: When you enter your husband's family:

Obey your elders, be a friend to the other wives!
If your husband seems harsh, don't be impatient!
Be fair to your servants, humble in your happiness!
Women who act this way become noble wives;
Sullen girls only bring their families disgrace. (18)

But what does Gautamī think?

GAUTAMĪ: This is good advice for wives, child. Take it all to heart!

KAṆVA: Child, embrace me and your friends!

ŚAKUNTALĀ: Father, why must Priyaṁvadā and my other friends turn back here?

KAṆVA: They will also be given in marriage. It is not proper for them to go there now. Gautamī will go with you.

ŚAKUNTALĀ (*embracing her father*): How can I go on living in a strange place, torn from my father's side, like a vine torn from the side of a sandalwood tree growing on a mountain slope?

KAṆVA: Child, why are you so frightened?

When you are your husband's honored wife,
absorbed in royal duties and in your son,
born like the sun to the eastern dawn,
the sorrow of separation will fade. (19)

(*Śakuntalā falls at her father's feet.*)

Let my hopes for you be fulfilled!

ŚAKUNTALĀ (*approaching her two friends*): You two must embrace me together!

BOTH FRIENDS (*embracing her*): Friend, if the king seems slow to recognize you, show him the ring engraved with his name!

ŚAKUNTALĀ: Your suspicions make me tremble!

BOTH FRIENDS: Don't be afraid! It's our love that fears evil.

ŚĀRṄGARAVA: The sun is high in the afternoon sky. Hurry, please!
ŚAKUNTALĀ (*facing the sanctuary*): Father, will I ever see the grove again?
KAṆVA:

When you have lived for many years
as a queen equal to the earth
and raised Duṣyanta's son
to be a matchless warrior,
your husband will entrust him
with the burdens of the kingdom
and will return with you
to the calm of this hermitage (20)

GAUTAMĪ: Child, the time for our departure has passed. Let your father turn back! It would be better, sir, if you turn back yourself. She'll keep talking this way forever.
KAṆVA: Child, my ascetic practice has been interrupted.
ŚAKUNTALĀ: My father's body is already tortured by ascetic practices. He must not grieve too much for me!
KAṆVA (*sighing*):

When I see the grains of rice
sprout from offerings you made
at the door of your hut,
how shall I calm my sorrow! (21)

(*Śakuntalā exits with her escort.*)
BOTH FRIENDS (*watching Śakuntalā*): Śakuntalā is hidden by forest trees now.
KAṆVA: Anasūyā, your companion is following her duty. Restrain yourself and return with me!
BOTH FRIENDS: Father, the ascetics' grove seems empty without Śakuntalā. How can we enter?
KAṆVA: The strength of your love makes it seem so.
(*Walking around in meditation.*)
Good! Now that Śakuntalā is on her way to her husband's family, I feel calm.

A daughter belongs to another man—
by sending her to her husband today,

I feel the satisfaction
one has on repaying a loan. (22)

(*All exit.*)

END OF ACT FOUR

ACT FIVE

(*The king and the buffoon enter; both sit down.*)

BUFFOON: Pay attention to the music room, friend, and you'll hear the notes of a song strung into a delicious melody . . . the lady Haṁsapadikā is practicing her singing.
KING: Be quiet so I can hear her!
VOICE IN THE AIR (*singing*):

Craving sweet
new nectar,
you kissed
a mango bud once—
how could you forget her, bee,
to bury your joy
in a lotus? (1)

KING: The melody of the song is passionate.
BUFFOON: But did you get the meaning of the words?
KING: I once made love to her. Now she reproaches me for loving Queen Vasumatī. Friend Māḍhavya, tell Haṁsapadikā that her words rebuke me soundly.
BUFFOON: As you command!
(*He rises.*)
But if that woman grabs my hair tuft, it will be like a heavenly nymph grabbing some ascetic . . . there go my hopes of liberation!
KING: Go! Use your courtly charm to console her.
BUFFOON: What a fate!
(*He exits.*)
KING (*to himself*): Why did hearing the song's words fill me with such strong desire? I'm not parted from anyone I love . . .

Seeing rare beauty,
hearing lovely sounds,
even a happy man

becomes strangely uneasy . . .
perhaps he remembers,
without knowing why,
loves of another life
buried deep in his being. (2)

(*He stands bewildered. Then the king's chamberlain enters.*)

CHAMBERLAIN: At my age, look at me!

Since I took this ceremonial bamboo staff
as my badge of office in the king's chambers
many years have passed; now I use it
as a crutch to support my faltering steps. (3)

A king cannot neglect his duty. He has just risen from his seat of justice and though I am loath to keep him longer, Sage Kaṇva's pupils have just arrived. Authority to rule the world leaves no time for rest.

The sun's steeds were yoked before time began,
the fragrant wind blows night and day,
the cosmic serpent always bears earth's weight,
and a king who levies taxes has his duty. (4)

Therefore, I must perform my office.

(*Walking around and looking.*)

Weary from ruling them like children,
he seeks solitude far from his subjects,
like an elephant bull who seeks cool shade
after gathering his herd at midday. (5)

(*Approaching.*)

Victory to you, king! Some ascetics who dwell in the forest at the foothills of the Himālayas have come. They have women with them and bring a message from Sage Kaṇva. Listen, king, and judge!

KING (*respectfully*): Are they Sage Kaṇva's messengers?

CHAMBERLAIN: They are.

KING: Inform the teacher Somarāta that he should welcome the ascetics with the prescribed rites and then bring them to me himself. I'll wait in a place suitable for greeting them.

CHAMBERLAIN: As the king commands.
(*He exits.*)
KING (*rising*): Vetravatī, lead the way to the fire sanctuary.
DOORKEEPER: Come this way, king!
KING (*walking around, showing fatigue*): Every other creature is happy when the object of his desire is won, but for kings success contains a core of suffering.

High office only leads to greater greed;
just perfecting its rewards is wearisome—
a kingdom is more trouble than it's worth,
like a royal umbrella one holds alone. (6)

TWO BARDS OFFSTAGE: Victory to you, king!
FIRST BARD:

You sacrifice your pleasures every day
to labor for your subjects—
as a tree endures burning heat
to give shade from the summer sun. (7)

SECOND BARD:

You punish villains with your rod of justice,
you reconcile disputes, you grant protection—
most relatives are loyal only in hope of gain,
but you treat all your subjects like kinsmen. (8)

KING: My weary mind is revived.
(*He walks around.*)
DOORKEEPER: The terrace of the fire sanctuary is freshly washed and the cow is waiting to give milk for the oblation.
Let the king ascend!
KING: Vetravatī, why has Father Kaṇva sent these sages to me?

Does something hinder their ascetic life?
Or threaten creatures in the sacred forest?
Or do my sins stunt the flowering vines?
My mind is filled with conflicting doubts. (9)

DOORKEEPER: I would guess that these sages rejoice in your virtuous conduct and come to honor you.
(*The ascetics enter; Śakuntalā is in front with Gautamī; the chamberlain and the king's priest are in front of her.*)

CHAMBERLAIN: Come this way, sirs!
ŚĀRṄGARAVA: Śāradvata, my friend:

> I know that this renowned king is righteous
> and none of the social classes follows evil ways,
> but my mind is so accustomed to seclusion
> that the palace feels like a house in flames. (10)

ŚĀRADVATA: I've felt the same way ever since we entered the city.

> As if I were freshly bathed, seeing a filthy man,
> pure while he's defiled, awake while he's asleep,
> as if I were a free man watching a prisoner,
> I watch this city mired in pleasures. (11)

ŚAKUNTALĀ (*indicating she feels an omen*): Why is my right eye twitching?
GAUTAMĪ: Child, your husband's family gods turn bad fortune into blessings!
(*They walk around.*)
PRIEST (*indicating the king*): Ascetics, the guardian of sacred order has left the seat of justice and awaits you now. Behold him!
ŚĀRṄGARAVA: Great priest, he seems praiseworthy, but we expect no less.

> Boughs bend, heavy with ripened fruit,
> clouds descend with fresh rain,
> noble men are gracious with wealth—
> this is the nature of bountiful things. (12)

DOORKEEPER: King, their faces look calm. I'm sure that the sages have confidence in what they're doing.
KING (*seeing Śakuntalā*):

> Who is she? Carefully veiled
> to barely reveal her body's beauty,
> surrounded by the ascetics
> like a bud among withered leaves. (13)

DOORKEEPER: King, I feel curious and puzzled too. Surely her form deserves closer inspection.
KING: Let her be! One should not stare at another man's wife!

ŚAKUNTALĀ (*placing her hand on her chest, she speaks to herself*):
My heart, why are you quivering? Be quiet while I learn my noble husband's feelings.
PRIEST (*going forward*): These ascetics have been honored with due ceremony. They have a message from their teacher. The king should hear them!
KING: I am paying attention.
SAGES (*raising their hands in a gesture of greeting*): May you be victorious, king!
KING: I salute you all!
SAGES: May your desires be fulfilled!
KING: Do the sages perform austerities unhampered?
SAGES:

> Who would dare obstruct the rites
> of holy men whom you protect—
> how can darkness descend
> when the sun's rays shine? (14)

KING: My title 'king' is more meaningful now. Is the world blessed by Father Kaṇva's health?
SAGES: Saints control their own health. He asks about your welfare and sends this message . . .
KING: What does he command?
ŚĀRṄGARAVA: At the time you secretly met and married my daughter, affection made me pardon you both.

> We remember you to be a prince of honor;
> Śakuntalā is virtue incarnate—
> the creator cannot be condemned
> for mating the perfect bride and groom. (15)

And now that she is pregnant, receive her and perform your sacred duty together.
GAUTAMĪ: Sir, I have something to say, though I wasn't appointed to speak:

> She ignored her elders
> and you failed to ask her kinsmen—
> since you acted on your own,
> what can I say to you now? (16)

ŚAKUNTALĀ: What does my noble husband say?
KING: What has been proposed?
ŚAKUNTALĀ (*to herself*): The proposal is as clear as fire.
ŚĀRṄGARAVA: What's this? Your Majesty certainly knows the ways of the world!

> People suspect a married woman who stays
> with her kinsmen, even if she is chaste—
> a young wife should live with her husband,
> no matter how he despises her. (17)

KING: Did I ever marry you?
ŚAKUNTALĀ (*visibly dejected, speaking to herself*): Now your fears are real, my heart!
ŚĀRṄGARAVA:

> Does one turn away from duty in contempt
> because his own actions repulse him? (18a)

KING: Why ask this insulting question?
ŚĀRṄGARAVA:

> Such transformations take shape
> when men are drunk with power. (18b)

KING: This censure is clearly directed at me.
GAUTAMĪ: Child, this is no time to be modest. I'll remove your veil. Then your husband will recognize you.
(*She does so.*)
KING (*staring at Śakuntalā*):

> Must I judge whether I ever married
> the flawless beauty they offer me now?
> I cannot love her or leave her, like a bee
> near a jasmine filled with frost at dawn. (19)

(*He shows hesitation.*)
DOORKEEPER: Our king has a strong sense of justice. Who else would hesitate when beauty like this is handed to him?
ŚĀRṄGARAVA: King, why do you remain silent?
KING: Ascetics, even though I'm searching my mind, I don't remember marrying this lady. How can I accept a woman who is visibly pregnant when I doubt that I am the cause?

ŚAKUNTALĀ (*in a stage whisper*): My lord casts doubt on our marriage. Why were my hopes so high?
ŚĀRṄGARAVA: It can't be!

> Are you going to insult the sage
> who pardons the girl you seduced
> and bids you keep his stolen wealth,
> treating a thief like you with honor? (20)

ŚĀRADVATA: Śārṅgarava, stop now! Śakuntalā, we have delivered our message and the king has responded. He must be shown some proof.
ŚAKUNTALĀ (*in a stage whisper*): When passion can turn to this, what's the use of reminding him? But, it's up to me to prove my honor now.
(*Aloud.*)
My noble husband . . .
(*She breaks off when this is half-spoken.*)
Since our marriage is in doubt, this is no way to address him. Puru king, you do wrong to reject a simple-hearted person with such words after you deceived her in the hermitage.
KING (*covering his ears*): Stop this shameful talk!

> Are you trying to stain my name
> and drag me to ruin—
> like a river eroding her own banks,
> soiling water and uprooting trees? (21)

ŚAKUNTALĀ: Very well! If it's really true that fear of taking another man's wife turns you away, then this ring will revive your memory and remove your doubt.
KING: An excellent idea!
ŚAKUNTALĀ (*touching the place where the ring had been*): I'm lost! the ring is gone from my finger.
(*She looks despairingly at Gautamī.*)
GAUTAMĪ: The ring must have fallen off while you were bathing in the holy waters at the shrine of the goddess near Indra's grove.
KING (*smiling*): And so they say the female sex is cunning.
ŚAKUNTALĀ: Fate has shown its power. Yet, I will tell you something else.

KING: I am still obliged to listen.

ŚAKUNTALĀ: One day, in a jasmine bower, you held a lotus-leaf cup full of water in your hand.

KING: We hear you.

ŚAKUNTALĀ: At that moment the buck I treated as my son approached. You coaxed it with the water, saying that it should drink first. But he didn't trust you and wouldn't drink from your hand. When I took the water, his trust returned. Then you jested, 'Every creature trusts what its senses know. You both belong to the forest.'

KING: Thus do women further their own ends by attracting eager men with the honey of false words.

GAUTAMĪ: Great king, you are wrong to speak this way. This child raised in an ascetics' grove doesn't know deceit.

KING: Old woman,

> When naive female beasts show cunning,
> what can we expect of women who reason?
> Don't cuckoos let other birds nurture
> their eggs and teach the chicks to fly? (22)

ŚAKUNTALĀ (*angrily*): Evil man! you see everything distorted by your own ignoble heart. Who would want to imitate you now, hiding behind your show of justice, like a well over grown with weeds?

KING (*to himself*): Her anger does not seem feigned; it makes me doubt myself.

> When the absence of love's memory
> made me deny a secret affair with her,
> This fire-eyed beauty bent her angry brows
> and seemed to break the bow of love. (23)

(*Aloud.*)

Lady, Duṣyanta's conduct is renowned, so what you say is groundless.

ŚAKUNTALĀ: All right! I may be a self-willed wanton woman! But it was faith in the Puru dynasty that brought me into the power of a man with honey in his words and poison in his heart. (*She covers her face at the end of the speech and weeps.*)

ŚĀRṄGARAVA: A willful act unchecked always causes pain.

One should be cautious
in forming a secret union—
unless a lover's heart is clear,
affection turns to poison. (24)

KING: But sir, why do you demean me with such warnings? Do you trust the lady?

ŚĀRṄGARAVA (*scornfully*): You have learned everything backwards.

If you suspect the word of one
whose nature knows no guile,
then you can only trust
people who practice deception. (25)

KING: I presume you speak the truth. Let us assume so. But what could I gain by deceiving this woman?

ŚĀRṄGARAVA: Ruin.

KING: Ruin? A Puru king has no reason to want his own ruin!

ŚĀRADVATA: Śārṁgarava, this talk is pointless. We have delivered our master's message and should return.

Since you married her, abandon her or take her—
absolute is the power a husband has over his wife. (26)

GAUTAMĪ: You go ahead.

(*They start to go.*)

ŚAKUNTALĀ: What? Am I deceived by this cruel man and then abandoned by you?

(*She tries to follow them.*)

GAUTAMĪ (*stopping*): Śārngarava my son, Śakuntalā is following us, crying pitifully. What will my child do now that her husband has refused her?

ŚĀRṄGARAVA (*turning back angrily*): Bold woman, do you still insist on having your way?

(*Śakuntalā trembles in fear.*)

If you are what the king says you are,
you don't belong in Father Kaṇva's family—
if you know that your marriage vow is pure,
you can bear slavery in your husband's house. (27)

Stay! We must go on!

KING: Ascetic, why do you disappoint the lady too?

> The moon only makes lotuses open,
> the sun's light awakens lilies—
> a king's discipline forbids him
> to touch another man's wife. (28)

ŚĀRṄGARAVA: If you forget a past affair because of some present attachment, why do you fear injustice now?

KING (*to the priest*): Sir, I ask you to weigh the alternatives:

> Since it's unclear whether I'm deluded
> or she is speaking falsely—
> should I risk abandoning a wife
> or being tainted by another man'? (29)

PRIEST (*deliberating*): I recommend this . . .

KING: Instruct me! I'll do as you say.

PRIEST: Then let the lady stay in our house until her child is born. If you ask why: the wise men predict that your first son will be born with the marks of a king who turns the wheel of empire. If the child of the sage's daughter bears the marks, congratulate her and welcome her into your palace chambers. Otherwise, send her back to her father.

KING: Whatever the elders desire.

PRIEST: Child, follow me!

ŚAKUNTALĀ: Mother earth, open to receive me!

(*Weeping, Śakuntalā exits with the priest and the hermits. The king, his memory lost through the curse, thinks about her.*)

VOICE OFFSTAGE: Amazing! Amazing!

KING (*listening*): What could this be?

PRIEST (*re-entering, amazed*): King, something marvelous has occurred!

KING: What?

PRIEST: When Kaṇva's pupils had departed,

> The girl threw up her arms and wept,
> lamenting her misfortune . . . then . . . (30a)

KING: Then what?

PRIEST:

> Near the nymph's shrine a ray of light
> in the shape of a woman carried her away. (30b)

(*All mime amazement.*)

KING: We've already settled the matter. Why discuss it further?

PRIEST (*observing the king*): May you be victorious!

(*He exits.*)

KING: Vetravatī, I am bewildered. Lead the way to my chamber!

DOORKEEPER: Come this way, my lord!

(*She walks forward.*)

KING:

> I cannot remember marrying
> the sage's abandoned daughter,
> but the pain my heart feels
> makes me suspect that I did. (31)

(*All exit.*)

END OF ACT FIVE

ACT SIX

(*The king's wife's brother, who is city magistrate, enters with two policemen leading a man whose hands are tied behind his back.*)

BOTH POLICEMEN (*beating the man*): Speak, thief! Where'd you steal this handsome ring with the king's name engraved in the jewel?

MAN (*showing fear*): Peace, sirs! I wouldn't do a thing like that.

FIRST POLICEMAN: Don't tell us the king thought you were some famous priest and gave it to you as a gift!

MAN: Listen, I'm a humble fisherman who lives near Indra's grove.

SECOND POLICEMAN: Thief, did we ask you about your caste?

MAGISTRATE: Sūcaka, let him tell it all in order! Don't interrupt him!

BOTH POLICEMEN: Whatever you command, chief!

MAN: I feed my family by catching fish with nets and hooks.

MAGISTRATE (*mocking*): What a pure profession!

MAN:

> The work I do
> may be vile
> but I won't deny
> my birthright—
> a priest
> doing his holy rites
> pities the animals
> he kills. (1)

MAGISTRATE: Go on!

MAN: One day as I was cutting up a red carp, I saw the shining stone of this ring in its belly. When I tried to sell it, you grabbed me. Kill me or let me go! That's how I got it!

MAGISTRATE: Jānuka, I'm sure this ugly butcher's a fisherman by his stinking smell. We must investigate how he got the ring. We'll go straight to the palace.

BOTH POLICEMEN: Okay. Go in front, you pickpocket!

(*All walk around.*)

MAGISTRATE: Sūcaka, guard this villain at the palace gate! I'll report to the king how we found the ring, get his orders, and come back.

BOTH POLICEMEN: Chief, good luck with the king!

(*The magistrate exits.*)

FIRST POLICEMAN: Jānuka, the chief's been gone a long time.

SECOND POLICEMAN: Well, there are fixed times for seeing kings.

FIRST POLICEMAN: Jānuka, my hands are itching to tie on his execution garland.

(*He points to the man.*)

MAN: You shouldn't think about killing a man for no reason.

SECOND POLICEMAN (*looking*): I see our chief coming with a letter in his hand. It's probably an order from the king. You'll be thrown to the vultures or you'll see the face of death's dog again . . .

MAGISTRATE (*entering*): Sūcaka, release this fisherman! I'll tell you how he got the ring.

FIRST POLICEMAN: Whatever you say, chief!

SECOND POLICEMAN: The villain entered the house of death and came out again.

(*He unties the prisoner.*)

MAN (*bowing to the magistrate*): Master, how will I make my living now?

MAGISTRATE: The king sends you a sum equal to the ring. (*He gives the money to the man.*)

MAN (*bowing as he grabs it*): The king honors me.

FIRST POLICEMAN: This fellow's certainly honored. He was lowered from the execution stake and raised up on a royal elephant's back.

SECOND POLICEMAN: Chief, the reward tells me this ring was special to the king.

MAGISTRATE: I don't think the king valued the stone, but when he caught sight of the ring, he suddenly seemed to remember someone he loved, and he became deeply disturbed.

FIRST POLICEMAN: You served him well, chief!

SECOND POLICEMAN: I think you better served this king of fish. (*Looking at the fisherman with jealousy.*)

MAN: My lords, half of this is yours for your good will.

FIRST POLICEMAN: It's only fair!

MAGISTRATE: Fisherman, now that you are my greatest and dearest friend, we should pledge our love over kadamba-blossom wine. Let's go to the wine shop!

(*They all exit together; the interlude ends. Then a nymph named Sānumatī enters by the skyway.*)

SĀNUMATĪ: Now that I've performed my assigned duties at the nymph's shrine, I'll slip away to spy on King Duṣyanta while the worshippers are bathing. My friendship with Menakā makes me feel a bond with Śakuntalā. Besides, Menakā asked me to help her daughter.

(*Looking around.*)

Why don't I see preparations for the spring festival in the king's palace? I can learn everything by using my mental powers, but I must respect my friend's request. So be it! I'll make myself invisible and spy on these two girls who are guarding the pleasure garden.

(*Sānumatī mimes descending and stands waiting. Then a maid servant named Parabhṛtikā, "Little Cuckoo," enters, looking at a mango bud. A second maid, named Madhukarikā, "Little Bee," is following her.*)

FIRST MAID:

Your pale green stem
tinged with pink
is a true sign
that spring has come—
I see you,
mango-blossom bud,
and I pray
for a season of joy. (2)

SECOND MAID: What are you muttering to yourself?

FIRST MAID: A cuckoo goes mad when she sees a mango bud.

SECOND MAID (*joyfully rushing over*): Has the sweet month of spring come?

FIRST MAID: Now's the time to sing your songs of love.

SECOND MAID: Hold me while I pluck a mango bud and worship the god of love.

FIRST MAID: Only if you'll give me half the fruit of your worship.

SECOND MAID: That goes without saying . . . our bodies may be separate, but our lives are one . . .

(*Leaning on her friend, she stands and plucks a mango bud.*)
The mango flower is still closed, but this broken stem is fragrant.
(*She makes the dove gesture with her hands.*)

> Mango-blossom bud,
> I offer you to Love
> as he lifts
> his bow of passion.
> Be the first
> of his flower arrows
> aimed at lonely girls
> with lovers far away! (3)

(*She throws the mango bud.*)

CHAMBERLAIN (*angrily throwing aside the curtain and entering*): Not now, stupid girl! When the king has banned the festival of spring, how dare you pluck a mango bud!

BOTH MAIDS (*frightened*): Please forgive us, sir. We don't know what you mean.

CHAMBERLAIN: Did you not hear that even the spring trees and the nesting birds obey the king's order?

> The mango flowers bloom without spreading pollen,
> the red amaranth buds, but will not bloom,
> cries of cuckoo cocks freeze though frost is past,
> and out of fear, Love holds his arrow half-drawn. (4)

BOTH MAIDS: There is no doubt about the king's great power!

FIRST MAID: Sir, several days ago we were sent to wait on the queen by Mitrāvasu, the king's brother-in-law. We were assigned to guard the pleasure garden. Since we're newcomers, we've heard no news.

CHAMBERLAIN: Let it be! Be don't do it again!

BOTH MAIDS: Sir, we're curious. May we ask why the spring festival was banned?

SĀNUMATĪ: Mortals are fond of festivals. The reason must be serious.

CHAMBERLAIN: It is public knowledge. Why should I not tell them? Has the scandal of Śakuntalā's rejection not reached your ears?

BOTH MAIDS: We only heard from the king's brother-in-law that the ring was found.

CHAMBERLAIN (*to himself*): There is little more to tell.

(*Aloud.*)

When he saw the ring, the king remembered that he had married Śakuntalā in secret and had rejected her in his delusion. Since then the king has been tortured by remorse.

> Despising what he once enjoyed,
> he shuns his ministers every day
> and spends long sleepless nights
> tossing at the edge of his bed—
> when courtesy demands that
> he converse with palace women,
> he stumbles over their names,
> and then retreats in shame. (5)

SĀNUMATĪ: This news delights me.

CHAMBERLAIN: The festival is banned because of the king's melancholy.

BOTH MAIDS: It's only right.

VOICE OFFSTAGE: This way, sir!

CHAMBERLAIN (*listening*): The king is coming. Go about your business!

BOTH MAIDS: As you say.

(*Both maids exit. Then the king enters, costumed to show his grief, accompanied by the buffoon and the doorkeeper.*)

CHAMBERLAIN (*observing the king*): Extraordinary beauty is appealing under all conditions. Even in his lovesick state, the king is wonderful to see.

Rejecting his regal jewels,
he wears one golden bangle
above his left wrist;
his lips are pale with sighs,
his eyes wan from brooding at night—
like a gemstone ground in polishing,
the fiery beauty of his body
makes his wasted form seem strong. (6)

SĀNUMATĪ (*seeing the king*): I see why Śakuntalā pines for him though he rejected and disgraced her.

KING (*walking around slowly, deep in thought*):

This cursed heart slept
when my love came to wake it,
and now it stays awake
to suffer the pain of remorse. (7)

SĀNUMATĪ: The girl shares his fate.

BUFFOON (*in a stage whisper*): He's having another attack of his Śakuntalā disease. I doubt if there's any cure for that.

CHAMBERLAIN (*approaching*): Victory to the king! I have inspected the grounds of the pleasure garden. Let the king visit his favorite spots and divert himself.

KING: Vetravatī, deliver a message to my noble minister Piśuna: "After being awake all night, we cannot sit on the seat of justice today. Set in writing what your judgement tells you the citizens require and send it to us!"

DOORKEEPER: Whatever you command!

(*She exits.*)

KING: Vātāyana, attend to the rest of your business!

CHAMBERLAIN: As the king commands!

(*He exits.*)

BUFFOON: You've cleared out the flies. Now you can rest in some pretty spot. The garden is pleasant now in this break between morning cold and noonday heat.

KING: Dear friend, the saying "Misfortunes rush through any crack" is absolutely right:

Barely freed by the dark force

that made me forget Kaṇva's daughter,
my mind is threatened by an arrow
of mango buds fixed on Love's bow. (8)

BUFFOON: Wait, I'll destroy the love god's arrow with my wooden stick.
(*Raising his staff, he tries to strike a mango bud.*)
KING (*smiling*): Let it be! I see the majesty of brahman bravery. Friend, where may I sit to divert my eyes with vines that remind me of my love?
BUFFOON: Didn't you tell your maid Caturikā, "I'll pass the time in the jasmine bower. Bring me the drawing board on which I painted a picture of Śakuntalā with my own hand!"
KING: Such a place may soothe my heart. Show me the way!
BUFFOON: Come this way!
(*Both walk around; the nymph Sānumatī follows.*)
The marble seat and flower offerings in this jasmine bower are certainly trying to make us feel welcome. Come in and sit down!
(*Both enter the bower and sit.*)
SĀNUMATĪ: I'll hide behind these creepers to see the picture he's drawn of my friend. Then I'll report how great her husband's passion is.
(*She does as she says and stands waiting.*)
KING: Friend, now I remember everything. I told you about my first meeting with Śakuntalā. You weren't with me when I rejected her, but why didn't you say anything about her before? Did you suffer a loss of memory too?
BUFFOON: I didn't forget. You did tell me all about it once, but then you said, "It's all a joke without any truth." My wit is like a lump of clay, so I took you at your word . . . or it could be that fate is powerful . . .
SĀNUMATĪ: It is!
KING: Friend, help me!
BUFFOON: What's this? It doesn't become you! Noblemen never take grief to heart. Even in storms, mountains don't tremble.
KING: Dear friend, I'm defenseless when I remember the pain of my love's bewilderment when I rejected her.

When I cast her away, she followed her kinsmen,

but Kaṇva's disciple harshly shouted, "Stay!"
The tearful look my cruelty provoked
burns me like an arrow tipped with poison (9)

SĀNUMATĪ: The way he rehearses his actions makes me delight in his pain.

BUFFOON: Sir, I guess that the lady was carried off by some celestial creature or other.

KING: Who else would dare to touch a woman who worshipped her husband? I was told that Menakā is her mother. My heart suspects that her mother's companions carried her off.

SĀNUMATĪ: His delusion puzzled me, but not his reawakening.

BUFFOON: If that's the case, you'll meet her again in good time.

KING: How?

BUFFOON: No mother or father can bear to see a daughter parted from her husband.

KING:

Was it dream or illusion or mental confusion,
or the last meager fruit of my former good deeds?
It is gone now, and my heart's desires are
like riverbanks crumbling of their own weight. (10)

BUFFOON: Stop this! Isn't the ring evidence that an unexpected meeting is destined to take place?

KING (*looking at the ring*): I only pity it for falling from such a place.

Ring, your punishment is proof
that your fate is as flawed as mine—
you were placed in her lovely fingers,
glowing with crimson nails, and you fell. (11)

SĀNUMATĪ: The real pity would have been if it had fallen into some other hand.

BUFFOON: What prompted you to put the signet ring on her hand?

SĀNUMATĪ: I'm curious too.

KING: I did it when I left for the city. My love broke into tears and asked, "How long will it be before my noble husband sends news to me?"

BUFFOON: Then? What then?

KING: Then I placed the ring on her finger with this promise:

> One by one, day after day,
> count each syllable of my name!
> At the end, a messenger will come
> to bring you to my place. (12)

But in my cruel delusion, I never kept my word.

SĀNUMATĪ: Fate broke their charming agreement!

BUFFOON: How did it get into the belly of the carp the fisherman was cutting up?

KING: While she was worshipping at the shrine of Indra's wife, it fell from her hand into the Gaṅgā.

BUFFOON: It's obvious now!

SĀNUMATĪ: And the king, doubtful of his marriage to Śakuntalā, a female ascetic, was afraid to commit an act of injustice. But why should such passionate love need a ring to be remembered?

KING: I must reproach the ring for what it's done.

BUFFOON (*to himself*): He's gone the way of all madmen . . .

KING:

> Why did you leave her delicate finger
> and sink into the deep river? (13a)

Of course . . .

> A mindless ring can't recognize virtue,
> but why did I reject my love? (13b)

BUFFOON (*to himself again*): Why am I consumed by a craving for food?

KING: Oh, ring! Have pity on a man whose heart is tormented because he abandoned his love without cause! Let him see her again!

(*Throwing the curtain aside, the maid Caturikā enters with the drawing board in her hand.*)

CATURIKĀ: Here's the picture you painted of the lady.

(*She shows the drawing board.*)

BUFFOON: Dear friend, how well you've painted your feelings in this sweet scene! My eyes almost stumble over the hollows and hills.

SĀNUMATĪ: What skill the king has! I feel as if my friend were before me.

KING:

> The picture's imperfections are not hers,
> but this drawing does hint at her beauty. (14)

SĀNUMATĪ: Such words reveal that suffering has increased his modesty as much as his love.

BUFFOON: Sir, I see three ladies now and they're all lovely to look at. Which is your Śakuntalā?

SĀNUMATĪ: Only a dim-witted fool like this wouldn't know such beauty!

KING: You guess which one!

BUFFOON: I guess Śakuntalā is the one you've drawn with flowers falling from her loosened locks of hair, with drops of sweat on her face, with her arms hanging limp and tired as she stands at the side of a mango tree whose tender shoots are gleaming with the fresh water she poured. The other two are her friends.

KING: You are clever! Look at these signs of my passion!

> Smudges from my sweating fingers
> stain the edges of the picture
> and a tear fallen from my cheek
> has raised a wrinkle in the paint. (15)

Caturikā, the scenery is only half-drawn. Go and bring my paints!

CATURIKĀ: Noble Māḍhavya, hold the drawing board until I come back!

KING: I'll hold it myself.

(*He takes it, the maid exits.*)

> I rejected my love when she came to me,
> and now I worship her in a painted image—
> having passed by a river full of water,
> I'm longing now for an empty mirage. (16)

BUFFOON (*to himself*): He's too far gone for a river now! He's looking for a mirage!

(*Aloud.*)

Sir, what else do you plan to draw here?

SĀNUMATĪ: He'll want to draw every place my friend loved.

KING:

I'll draw the river Mālinī
flowing through Himālaya's foothills
where pairs of wild geese nest in the sand
and deer recline on both riverbanks,
where a doe is rubbing her left eye
on the horn of a black buck antelope
under a tree whose branches
have bark dresses hanging to dry. (17)

BUFFOON (*to himself*): Next he'll fill the drawing board with mobs of ascetics wearing long grassy beards.

KING: Dear friend, I've forgotten to draw an ornament that Śakuntalā wore.

BUFFOON: What is it?

SĀNUMATĪ: It will suit her forest life and her tender beauty.

KING:

I haven't drawn the mimosa flower on her ear,
its filaments resting on her cheek,
or the necklace of tender lotus stalks,
lying on her breasts like autumn moonbeams. (18)

BUFFOON: But why does the lady cover her face with her red lotus-bud fingertips and stand trembling in fear?

(*Looking closely.*)

That son-of-a-bee who steals nectar from flowers is attacking her face.

KING: Drive the impudent rogue away!

BUFFOON: You have the power to punish criminals. You drive him off!

KING: All right! Bee, favored guest of the flowering vines, why do you frustrate yourself by flying here?

A female bee waits on a flower,
thirsting for your love—
she refuses to drink
the sweet nectar without you. (19)

SĀNUMATĪ: How gallantly he's driving him away!

BUFFOON: When you try to drive it away, this creature becomes vicious.

KING: Why don't you stop when I command you?

> Bee, if you touch the lips of my love
> that lure you like a young tree's virgin buds,
> lips I gently kissed in festival of love,
> I'll hold you captive in a lotus flower cage. (20)

BUFFOON: Why isn't he afraid of your harsh punishment?
(*Laughing, he speaks to himself.*)
He's gone crazy and I'll be the same if I go on talking like this.
(*Aloud.*)
But sir, it's just a picture!

KING: A picture? How can that be?

SĀNUMATĪ: When I couldn't tell whether it was painted, how could he realize he was looking at a picture?

KING: Dear friend, are you envious of me?

> My heart's affection made me feel
> the joy of seeing her—
> but you reminded me again
> that my love is only a picture. (21)

(*He wipes away a tear.*)

SĀNUMATĪ: The effects of her absence make him quarrelsome.

KING: Dear friend, why do I suffer this endless pain?

> Sleepless nights prevent our meeting in dreams;
> her image in a picture is ruined by my tears. (22)

SĀNUMATĪ: You have clearly atoned for the suffering your rejection caused Śakuntalā.

CATURIKĀ (*entering*): Victory my lord! I found the paint box and started back right away . . . but I met Queen Vasumatī with her maid Taralikā on the path and she grabbed the box from my hand, saying, "I'll bring it to the noble lord myself!"

BUFFOON: You were lucky to get away!

CATURIKĀ: The queen's shawl got caught on a tree. While Taralikā was freeing it, I made my escape.

KING: Dear friend, the queen's pride can quickly turn to anger. Save this picture!

BUFFOON: You should say, "Save yourself!"
(*Taking the picture, he stands up.*)
If you escape the woman's deadly poison, then send word to me in the Palace of the Clouds.
(*He exits hastily.*)
SĀNUMATĪ: Even though another woman has taken his heart and he feels indifferent to the queen, he treats her with respect.
DOORKEEPER (*entering with a letter in her hand*): Victory, king!
KING: Vetravatī, did you meet the queen on the way?
DOORKEEPER: I did, but when she saw the letter in my hand, she turned back.
KING: She knows that this is official and would not interrupt my work.
DOORKEEPER: King, the minister requests that you examine the contents of this letter. He said that the enormous job of reckoning the revenue in this one citizen's case had taken all his time.
KING: Show me the letter!
(*The girl hands it to him and he reads barely aloud.*)
What is this? "A wealthy merchant sea captain named Dhanamitra has been lost in a shipwreck and the laws say that since the brave man was childless, his accumulated wealth all goes to the king." It's terrible to be childless! A man of such wealth probably had several wives. We must find out if any one of his wives is pregnant!
DOORKEEPER: King, it's said that one of his wives, the daughter of a merchant of Ayodhyā, has performed the rite to ensure the birth of a son.
KING: The child in her womb surely deserves his paternal wealth. Go! Report this to my minister!
DOORKEEPER: As the king commands!
(*She starts to go.*)
KING: Come here a moment!
DOORKEEPER: I am here.
KING: Is it his offspring or not?

> When his subjects lose a kinsman,
> Duṣyanta will preserve the estates—
> unless there is some crime.
> Let this be proclaimed. (23)

DOORKEEPER: It shall be proclaimed loudly.

(*She exits; reenters.*)

The king's order will be as welcome as rain in the right season.

KING (*sighing long and deeply*): Families without offspring whose lines of succession are cut off lose their wealth to strangers when the last male heir dies. When I die, this will. happen to the wealth of the Puru dynasty.

DOORKEEPER: Heaven forbid such a fate!

KING: I curse myself for despising the treasure I was offered.

SĀNUMATĪ: He surely has my friend in mind when he blames himself.

KING:

> I abandoned my lawful wife, the holy ground
> where I myself planted my family's glory,
> like earth sown with seed at the right time,
> ready to bear rich fruit in season. (24)

SĀNUMATĪ: But your family's line will not be broken.

CATURIKĀ (*in a stage whisper*): The king is upset by the story of the merchant. Go and bring noble Māḍhavya from the Palace of the Clouds to console him!

DOORKEEPER: A good idea!

(*She exits.*)

KING: Duṣyanta's ancestors are imperiled.

> Our fathers drink the yearly libation
> mixed with my childless tears,
> knowing that there is no other son
> to offer the sacred funeral waters. (25)

(*He falls into a faint.*)

CATURIKĀ (*looking at the bewildered king*): Calm yourself, my lord!

SĀNUMATĪ: Though a light shines, his separation from Śakuntalā keeps him in a state of dark depression. I could make him happy now, but I've heard Indra's consort consoling Śakuntalā with the news that the gods are hungry for their share of the ancestral oblations and will soon conspire to have her husband welcome his lawful wife. I'll have to wait for the auspicious time, but meanwhile I'll cheer my friend by reporting his condition. (*She exits, flying into the air.*)

VOICE OFFSTAGE: Help! Brahman-murder!

KING (*regaining consciousness, listening*): Is it Māḍhavya's cry of pain? Who's there?

DOORKEEPER: King, your friend is in danger. Help him!

KING: Who dares to threaten him?

DOORKEEPER: Some invisible spirit seized him and dragged him to the roof of the Palace of the Clouds.

KING (*getting up*): Not this! Even my house is haunted by spirits.

> When I don't even recognize
> the blunders I commit every day,
> how can I keep track
> of where my subjects stray? (26)

VOICE OFFSTAGE: Dear friend! Help! Help!

KING (*breaking into a run*): Friend, don't be afraid! I'm coming!

VOICE OFFSTAGE (*repeating the call for help*): Why shouldn't I be afraid? Someone is trying to split my neck in three, like a stalk of sugar cane.

KING (*casting a glance*): Quickly, my bow!

BOW-BEARER (*entering with a bow in hand*): Here are your bow and quiver.

(*The king takes his bow and arrows.*)

VOICE OFFSTAGE:

> I'll kill you as a tiger kills struggling prey!
> I'll drink fresh blood from your tender neck!
> Take refuge now in the bow Duṣyanta lifts
> to calm the fears of the oppressed! (27)

KING (*angrily*): How dare you abuse my name? Stop, carrion-eater! Or you will not live!

(*He strings his bow.*)

Vetravatī, lead the way to the stairs!

DOORKEEPER: This way, king.

(*All move forward in haste.*)

KING (*searching around*): There is no one here!

VOICE OFFSTAGE: Help! Help! I see you. Don't you see me? I'm like a mouse caught by a cat! My life is hopeless!

KING: Don't count on your powers of invisibility! My magical arrows will find you. I aim this arrow:

> It will strike its doomed target
> and spare the brahman it must save—
> a wild goose can extract the milk
> and leave the water untouched. (28)

(*He aims the arrow. Then Indra's charioteer Mātali enters, having released the buffoon.*)

MĀTALI: King!

> Indra sets demons as your targets;
> draw your bow against them!
> Send friends gracious glances
> rather than deadly arrows! (29)

KING (*withdrawing his arrow*): Mātali, welcome to great Indra's charioteer!

BUFFOON (*entering*): He tried to slaughter me like a sacrificial beast and this king is greeting him with honors!

MĀTALI (*smiling*): Your Majesty, hear why Indra has sent me to you!

KING: I am all attention.

MĀTALI: There is an army of demons descended from one-hundred-headed Kālanemi, known to be invincible . . .

KING: I have already heard it from Nārada, the gods' messenger.

MĀTALI:

> He is invulnerable to your friend Indra,
> so you are appointed to lead the charge—
> the moon dispels the darkness of night
> since the sun cannot drive it out. (30)

Take your weapon, mount Indra's chariot, and prepare for victory!

KING: Indra favors me with this honor. But why did you attack Māḍhavya?

MĀTALI: I'll tell you! From the signs of anguish Your Majesty showed, I knew that you were despondent. I attacked him to arouse your anger.

A fire. blazes when fuel is added;
a cobra provoked raises its hood—
men can regain lost courage
if their emotions are roused. (31)

KING (*in a stage whisper*): Dear friend, I cannot disobey a command from the lord of heaven. Inform my minister Piśuna of this and tell him this for me:

Concentrate your mind on guarding my subjects!
My bow is strung to accomplish other work. (32)

BUFFOON: Whatever you command!

(*He exits.*)

MĀTALI: Mount the chariot, Your Majesty!

(*The king mimes mounting the chariot; all exit.*)

END OF ACT SIX

ACT SEVEN

(*The king enters with Mātali by the skyway, mounted on a chariot.*)

KING: Mātali, though I carried out his command, I feel unworthy of the honors Indra gave me.

MĀTALI (*smiling*): Your Majesty, neither of you seems satisfied.

You belittle the aid you gave Indra
in face of the honors he conferred,
and he, amazed by your heroic acts,
deems his hospitality too slight. (1)

KING: No, not so! When I was taking leave, he honored me beyond my heart's desire and shared his throne with me in the presence of the gods:

Indra gave me a garland of coral flowers
tinged with sandalpowder from his chest,
while he smiled at his son Jayanta,
who stood there barely hiding his envy. (2)

MĀTALI: Don't you deserve whatever you want from Indra?

Indra's heaven of pleasures has twice
been saved by rooting out thorny demons—
your smooth-jointed arrows have now done
what Viṣṇu once did with his lion claws. (3)

KING: Here too Indra's might deserves the praise.

When servants succeed in great tasks,
they act in hope of their master's praise—
would dawn scatter the darkness
if he were not the sun's own charioteer? (4)

MĀTALI: This attitude suits you well!

(*He moves a little distance.*)

Look over there, Your Majesty! See how your own glorious fame has reached the vault of heaven!

Celestial artists are drawing your exploits
on leaves of the wish-granting creeper
with colors of the nymphs' cosmetic paints,
and bards are moved to sing of you in ballads. (5)

KING: Mātali, in my desire to do battle with the demons, I did not notice the path we took to heaven as we climbed through the sky yesterday. Which course of the winds are we traveling?

MĀTALI:

They call this path of the wind Parivaha—
freed from darkness by Viṣṇu's second stride,
it bears the Gaṅgā's three celestial streams
and turns stars in orbit, dividing their rays. (6)

KING: Mātali, this is why my soul, my senses, and my heart feel calm.

(*He looks at the chariot wheels.*)

We've descended to the level of the clouds.

MĀTALI: How do you know?

KING:

Crested cuckoos fly between the spokes,
lightning flashes glint off the horses' coats,
and a fine mist wets your chariot's wheel—
all signs that we go over rain-filled clouds. (7)

MĀTALI: In a moment, you'll be back in your own domain, Your Majesty.

KING (*looking down*): Our speeding chariot makes the mortal world appear fantastic. Look!

Mountain peaks emerge as the earth descends,
branches spread up from a sea of leaves,
fine lines become great rivers to behold—
the world seems to hurtle toward me. (8)

MĀTALI: You observe well! (*He looks with great reverence.*) The beauty of earth is sublime.

KING: Mātali, what mountain do I see stretching into the eastern and western seas, rippled with streams of liquid gold, like a gateway of twilight clouds?

MĀTALI: Your Majesty, it is called the "Golden Peak", the mountain of the demigods, a place where austerities are practiced to perfection.

> Mārīca, the descendant of Brahmā,
> a father of both demons and gods,
> lives the life of an ascetic here
> in the company of Aditi, his wife. (9)

KING: One must not ignore good fortune! I shall perform the rite of circumambulating the sage.

MĀTALI: An excellent idea!

(*The two mime descending.*)

KING (*smiling*):

> The chariot wheels make no sound,
> they raise no clouds of dust,
> they touch the ground unhindered—
> nothing marks the chariot's descent. (10)

MĀTALI: It is because of the extraordinary power that you and Indra both possess.

KING: Mātali, where is Mārīca's hermitage?

MĀTALI (*pointing with his hand*):

> Where the sage stands staring at the sun,
> as immobile as the trunk of a tree,
> his body half-buried in an anthill,
> with a snake-skin on his chest,
> his throat pricked by a necklace
> of withered thorny vines,
> wearing a coil of long matted hair
> filled with nests of śakunta birds. (11)

KING. I do homage to the sage for his severe austerity.

MĀTALI (*pulling hard on the chariot reins*): Great king, let us enter Mārīca's hermitage, where Aditi nurtures the celestial coral trees.

KING: This tranquil place surpasses heaven. I feel as if I'm bathing in a lake of nectar.

MĀTALI (*stopping the chariot*): Dismount, Your Majesty!

KING (*dismounting*): Mātali, what about you?

MĀTALI I have stopped the chariot. I'll dismount too.
(*He does so.*)
This way, Your Majesty!
(*He walks around.*)
You can see the grounds of the ascetics' grove ahead.
KING: I am amazed!

> In this forest of wish-fulfilling trees
> ascetics live on only the air they breathe
> and perform their ritual ablutions
> in water colored by golden lotus pollen.
> They sit in trance on jewelled marble slabs
> and stay chaste among celestial nymphs,
> practicing austerities in the place
> that others seek to win by penances. (12)

MĀTALI: Great men always aspire to rare heights!
(*He walks around, calling aloud.*)
O venerable Śākalya, what is the sage Mārīca doing now? What do you say? In response to Aditi's question about the duties of a devoted wife, he is talking in a gathering of great sages' wives.
KING (*listening*): We must wait our turn.
MĀTALI (*looking at the king*): Your Majesty, rest at the foot of this aśoka tree. Meanwhile, I'll look for a chance to announce you to Indra's father.
KING: As you advise . . .
(*He stops.*)
MĀTALI: Your Majesty, I'll attend to this.
(*He exits.*)
KING (*indicating he feels an omen*):

> I have no hope for my desire.
> Why does my arm throb in vain?
> Once good fortune is lost,
> it becomes constant pain. (13)

VOICE OFFSTAGE: Don't be so wild! Why is his nature so stubborn?
KING (*listening*): Unruly conduct is out of place here. Whom are they reprimanding?
(*Looking toward the sound, surprised.*)

Who is this child, guarded by two female ascetics? A boy who acts more like a man.

He has dragged this lion cub
from its mother's half-full teat
to play with it, and with his hand
he violently tugs its mane. (14)

(*The boy enters as described, with two female ascetics.*)

BOY: Open your mouth, lion! I want to count your teeth!

FIRST ASCETIC: Nasty boy, why do you torture creatures we love like our children? You're getting too headstrong! The sages gave you the right name when they called you "Sarvadamana, Tamer-of-everything."

KING: Why is my heart drawn to this child, as if he were my own flesh? I don't have a son. That is why I feel tender toward him . . . .

SECOND ASCETIC: The lioness will maul you if you don't let go of her cub!

BOY (*smiling*): Oh, I'm scared to death!

(*Pouting.*)

KING:

This child appears to be
the seed of hidden glory,
like a spark of fire
awaiting fuel to burn. (15)

FIRST ASCETIC: Child, let go of the lion cub and I'll give you another toy!

BOY: Where is it? Give it to me!

(*He reaches out his hand.*)

KING: Why does he bear the mark of a king who turns the wheel of empire?

A hand with fine webs connecting the fingers
open as he reaches for the object greedily,
like a single lotus with faint inner petals
spread open in the red glow of early dawn. (16)

SECOND ASCETIC: Suvratā, you can't stop him with words! The sage Mārkaṇḍeya's son left a brightly painted clay bird in my hut. Get it for him!

FIRST ASCETIC: I will!

(*She exits.*)

BOY: But until it comes I'll play with this cub.

KING: I am attracted to this pampered boy . . .

Lucky are fathers whose laps give refuge
to the muddy limbs of adoring little sons
when childish smiles show budding teeth
and jumbled sounds make charming words. (17)

SECOND ASCETIC: Well, he ignores me.

(*She looks back.*)

Is one of the sage's sons here?

(*Looking at the king.*)

Sir, please come here! Make him loosen his grip and let go of the lion cub! He's tormenting it in his cruel child's play.

KING (*approaching the boy, smiling*): Stop! You're a great sage's son!

When self-control is your duty by birth,
why do you violate the sanctuary laws
and ruin the animals' peaceful life,
like a young black snake in a sandal tree? (18)

SECOND ASCETIC: Sir, he's not a sage's son.

KING: His actions and his looks confirm it. I based my false assumption on his presence in this place.

(*He does what she asked; responding to the boy's touch, he speaks to himself.*)

Even my limbs feel delighted
from the touch of a stranger's son—
the father at whose side he grew
must feel pure joy in his heart. (19)

SECOND ASCETIC (*examining them both*): It's amazing! Amazing!

KING: What is it, madam?

SECOND ASCETIC: This boy looks surprisingly like you. He doesn't even know you, and he's acting naturally.

KING (*fondling the child*): If he's not the son of an ascetic, what lineage does he belong to?

SECOND ASCETIC: The family of Puru.

KING (*to himself*): What? His ancestry is the same as mine . . . so this lady thinks he resembles me. The family vow of Puru's descendants is to spend their last days in the forest.

As world protectors they first choose
palaces filled with sensuous pleasures,
but later, their homes are under trees
and one wife shares the ascetic vows. (20)

(*Aloud.*)
But mortals cannot enter this realm on their own.
SECOND ASCETIC: You're right sir. His mother is a nymph's child. She gave birth to him here in the hermitage of Mārīca.
KING (*in a stage whisper*) Here is a second ground for hope!
(*Aloud.*)
What famed royal sage claims her as his wife?
SECOND ASCETIC: Who would even think of speaking the name of a man who rejected his lawful wife?
KING (*to himself*): Perhaps this story points to me. What if I ask the name of the boy's mother? No, it is wrong to ask about another man's wife.
FIRST ASCETIC (*returning with a clay bird in her hand*): Look, Sarvadamana, a śakunta! Look! Isn't it lovely?
BOY: Where's my mother?
BOTH ASCETICS: He's tricked by the similarity of names. He wants his mother.
SECOND ASCETIC: Child, she told you to look at the lovely clay śakunta bird.
KING (*to himself*): What? Is his mother's name Śakuntalā? But names can be the same. Even a name is a mirage . . . a false hope to herald despair.
BOY: I like this bird!
(*He picks up the toy.*)
FIRST ASCETIC (looking frantically): Oh, I don't see the amulet-box on his wrist!
KING: Don't be alarmed! It broke off while he was tussling with the lion cub.
(*He goes to pick it up.*)

BOTH ASCETICS: Don't touch it! Oh, he's already picked it up! (*With their hands on their chests, they stare at each other in amazement.*)

KING: Why did you warn me against it?

FIRST ASCETIC: It contains the magical herb called Aparājitā, honored sir. Mārīca gave it to him at his birth ceremony. He said that if it fell to the ground no one but his parents or himself could pick it up.

KING: And if someone else does pick it up?

FIRST ASCETIC: Then it turns into a snake and strikes.

KING: Have you two seen it so transformed?

BOTH ASCETICS: Many times.

KING (*to himself, joyfully*): Why not rejoice in the fulfillment of my heart's desire?

(*He embraces the child.*)

SECOND ASCETIC: Suvratā, come, let's tell Śakuntalā that her penances are over.

(*Both ascetics exit*).

BOY: Let me go! I want my mother!

KING: Son, you will greet your mother with me.

BOY: My father is Duṣyanta, not you!

KING: This contradiction confirms the truth.

(*Śakuntalā enters, wearing the single braid of a woman in mourning.*)

ŚAKUNTALĀ: Even though Sarvadamana's amulet kept its natural form instead of changing into a snake, I can't hope that my destiny will be fulfilled. But maybe what my friend Sānumatī reports is right.

KING (*looking at Śakuntalā*): It is Śakuntalā!

> Wearing dusty gray garments,
> her face gaunt from penances,
> her bare braid hanging down—
> she bears with perfect virtue
> the trial of long separation
> my cruelty forced on her. (21)

ŚAKUNTALĀ (*seeing the king pale with suffering*): He doesn't resemble my noble husband. Whose touch defiles my son when the amulet is protecting him?

BOY (*going to his mother*): Mother, who is this stranger who calls me "son"?

KING: My dear, I see that you recognize me now. Even my cruelty to you is transformed by your grace.

ŚAKUNTALĀ (*to herself*): Heart, be consoled! My cruel fate has finally taken pity on me. It is my noble husband!

KING:

> Memory chanced to break my dark delusion
> and you stand before me in beauty,
> like the moon's wife Rohiṇī
> as she rejoins her lord after an eclipse. (22)

ŚAKUNTALĀ: Victory to my noble husband! Vic . . .

(*She stops when the word is half-spoken, her throat choked with tears.*)

KING: Beautiful Śakuntalā,

> Even choked by your tears,
> the word "victory" is my triumph
> on your bare pouting lips,
> pale-red flowers of your face. (23)

BOY: Mother, who is he?

ŚAKUNTALĀ: Child, ask the powers of fate!

KING (*falling at Śakuntalā's feet*):

> May the pain of my rejection
> vanish from you heart;
> delusion clouded my weak mind
> and darkness obscured good fortune—
> a blind man tears off a garland,
> fearing the bite of a snake. (24)

ŚAKUNTALĀ: Noble husband, rise! Some crime I had committed in a former life surely came to fruit and made my kind husband indifferent to me.

(*The king rises.*)

But how did my noble husband come to remember this woman who was doomed to pain?

KING: I shall tell you after I have removed the last barb of sorrow.

> In my delusion I once ignored
> a teardrop burning your lip—
> let me dry the tear on your lash
> to end the pain of remorse! (25)

(*He does so.*)

ŚAKUNTALĀ (*seeing the signet ring*): My noble husband, this is the ring!

KING: I regained my memory when the ring was recovered.

ŚAKUNTALĀ: When it was lost, I tried in vain to convince my noble husband who I was.

KING: Let the vine take back this flower as a sign of her union with spring.

ŚAKUNTALĀ: I don't trust it. Let my noble husband wear it!

(*Mātali enters.*)

MĀTALI: Good fortune! This meeting with your lawful wife and the sight of your son's face are reasons to rejoice.

KING: The sweet fruit of my desire! Mātali, didn't Indra know about all this?

MĀTALI: What is unknown to the gods? Come, Your Majesty! The sage Mārīca grants you an audience.

KING: Śakuntalā, hold our son's hand! We shall go to see Mārīca together.

ŚAKUNTALĀ: I feel shy about appearing before my elders in my husband's company.

KING: But it is customary at a joyous time like this. Come! Come!

(*They all walk around. Then Mārīca enters with Aditi; they sit.*)

MĀRĪCA (*looking at the king*):

> Aditi, this is king Duṣyanta,
> who leads Indra's armies in battle;
> his bow lets your son's thunderbolt
> lie ready with its tip unblunted. (26)

ADITI: He bears himself with dignity.

MĀTALI: Your Majesty, the parents of the gods look at you with affection reserved for a son. Approach them!

KING: Mātali, the sages so describe this pair:

Source of the sun's twelve potent forms,
parents of Indra, who rules the triple world,
birthplace of Viṣṇu's primordial form,
sired by Brahmā's sons, Marīci and Dakṣa. (27)

MĀTALI: Correct!

KING (*bowing*): Indra's servant, Duṣyanta, bows to you both.

MĀRĪCA: My son, live long and protect the earth!

ADITI: My son, be an invincible warrior!

ŚAKUNTALĀ: I worship at your feet with my son.

MĀRĪCA:

Child, with a husband like Indra
and a son like his son Jayanta,
you need no other blessing.
Be like Indra's wife Paulomī! (28)

ADITI: Child, may your husband honor you and may your child live long to give both families joy! Be seated!

(*All sit near Mārīca.*)

MĀRĪCA (*pointing to each one*):

By the turn of fortune,
virtuous Śakuntalā, her noble son,
and the king are reunited—
faith and wealth with order. (29)

KING: Sir, first came the success of my hopes, then the sight of you. Your kindness is unparalleled.

First flowers appear, then fruits,
first clouds rise, then rain falls,
but here the chain of events is reversed—
first came success, then your blessing. (30)

MĀTALI: This is the way the creator gods give blessings.

KING: Sir, I married your charge by secret marriage rites. When her relatives brought her to me after some time, my memory failed and I sinned against the sage Kaṇva, your kinsman. When I saw the ring, I remembered that I had married his daughter. This is all so strange!

Like one who doubts the existence
of an elephant who walks in front of him
but feels convinced by seeing footprints,
my mind had taken strange turns. (31)

MĀRĪCA: My son, you need not take the blame. Even your delusion has another cause. Listen!

KING: I am attentive.

MĀRĪCA: When Menakā took her bewildered daughter from the steps of the nymphs' shrine and brought her to my wife, I knew through meditation that you had rejected this girl as your lawful wife because of Durvāsa's curse, and that the curse would end when you saw the ring.

KING (*sighing*): So I am freed of blame.

ŚAKUNTALĀ (*to herself*): And I am happy to learn that I wasn't rejected by my husband without cause. But I don't remember being cursed. Maybe the empty heart of love's separation made me deaf to the curse . . . my friends did warn me to show the ring to my husband . . .

MĀRĪCA: My child, I have told you the truth. Don't be angry with your husband!

You were rejected when the curse
that clouded memory made him cruel,
but now darkness is lifted
and your power is restored—
a shadow has no shape
in a badly tarnished mirror,
but when the surface is clean
it can easily be seen. (32)

KING: Sir, here is the glory of my family!

(*He takes the child by the hand.*)

MĀRĪCA: Know that he is destined to turn the wheel of your empire!

His chariot will smoothly cross
the ocean's rough waves
and as a mighty warrior
he will conquer the seven continents.

Here he is called Sarvadamana,
Tamer-of-everything;
later when his burden is the world,
men will call him Bharata, Sustainer. (33)

KING: Since you performed his birth ceremonies, we can hope for all this.

ADITI: Sir, let Kaṇva be told that his daughter's hopes have been fulfilled. Menakā, who loves her daughter, is here in attendance.

ŚAKUNTALĀ (*to herself*): The lady expresses my own desire.

MĀRĪCA: He knows everything already through the power of his austerity.

KING: This is why the sage was not angry at me.

MĀRĪCA: Still, I want to hear his response to this joyful reunion. Who is there?

DISCIPLE (*entering*): Sir, it is I.

MĀRĪCA: Gālava, fly through the sky and report the joyous reunion to Kaṇva in my own words: "The curse is ended. Śakuntalā and her son are embraced by Duṣyanta now that his memory is restored."

DISCIPLE: As you command, sir!

(*He exits.*)

MĀRĪCA: My son, mount your friend Indra's chariot with your wife and son and return to your royal capital!

KING: As you command, sir!

MĀRĪCA: My son, what other joy can I give you?

KING: There is no greater joy, but if you will:

May the king serve nature's good!
May priests honor the goddess of speech!
And may Śiva's dazzling power
destroy my cycle of rebirths! (34)

(*All exit.*)

END OF ACT SEVEN AND OF THE PLAY

ŚAKUNTALĀ AND THE RING OF RECOLLECTION

Śakuntalā and Her Companions: three nineteenth century representations—Monier-Williams, Nalagarh miniature, and Raja Ravi Varma

4. Popular and high culture as historical parallels

It is sometimes said that one of the reasons for the invention or evolution of a high culture is that, when foreign conventions are introduced into an existing society, it has to create a high culture to either defend itself from, or determine the method of assimilating, the intrusions. Such an argument is also made to explain why the Sanskrit literary culture became so dominant in the early centuries A.D. The first use of Sanskrit for inscriptions is the innovation of rulers who had familial connections with the Iranian and Hellenistic world. Coincidentally, the language comes to be more extensively used from this period on and for a variety of texts relating to multiple aspects of social and personal life, many of which assume the status of high culture. However, it could equally well be argued that Sanskrit was used far earlier but not for political documents (as in inscriptions), its use being more frequent in ritual texts and texts of the diverse *śāstras*. The formulation of what was called Sanskrit in Pāṇini's grammar certainly predates the issuing of inscriptions in Sanskrit by a few centuries. What is significant is that its visibility increases in a larger range of texts dating from the early Christian era.

This is not to suggest that Sanskrit was confined to the highest levels of court culture. Those texts which had a socially less exalted audience also used Sanskrit, even if of a rather more popular variety. What is fascinating about the period from about the seventh century onwards, is the manner in which expressions of court culture and popular culture run parallel to each other, but often with characteristically different concerns. Yet, even here there is occasionally some interweaving, although this naturally takes place at the level of narrative and intention, whereas the more technical and complex considerations of literary style and form tend to cluster in court culture.

Subsequent to Kālidāsa there would have been two versions of the Śakuntalā story in circulation, that of the epic and that of the play. Those who were more at ease with the epic version are not likely to have been as familiar with the play, although those familiar with the latter may well have known the epic version. The *Mahābhārata* was better known as the literature of the oral tradition, drawing its inspiration from what were once elite clans which had now been superceded by a new elite of royal families and dynastic power. In this change the epic, at one level, became the literature of the lesser social groups, although at another level its conversion into a text of Vaiṣṇava propagation did make it approximate variant forms of the religion of the elites. As a compendium of lineage "histories" moreover, it could be drawn upon by those seeking *kṣatriya* origins. The didactic sections of the epic were also an attempt to incorporate world-views which would facilitate its appropriation by those now culturally dominant. This can perhaps be seen in, among other things, the variance relating to women as role models. The women of the *Mahābhārata* could be cited as role models and be appreciated by wider audiences. The new elites had their own courtly literature to provide them with ideal characters. The change in social attitudes reflected in the two types of literature is evident from the contradictions in the epic between the narrative and didactic sections, on how women were perceived. In the latter, they generally occupy a socially inferior and subordinate position.

Apart from epics, another category of texts intended for popular appeal were the *Purāṇas*, composed from around the Gupta period onwards. The Puranic stories were closer to the epic and were often referred to as *ākhyānas* or narratives. They were part of a mythology common to many, and of a believed ancestral history of various clans, providing links to the heroes of old. The epics and the *Purāṇas*, because they were recited to large gatherings, had some interaction with the culture of non-elites, but a play by Kālidāsa would have had a different audience, more appreciative of court literature. It would include urban elites and pockets of literati in the *agrahāras* of the rural areas. The popularity of the Śakuntalā story is evident from its being narrated, in brief, in a number of *Purāṇas*. Even where the story is not actually narrated, references to it suggest that it was well-known. Inspite of the *Purāṇas* often being somewhat later in date than Kālidāsa, it is the epic version which is generally their source, although there are exceptions.

In the *Matsya Purāṇa* a brief reference states that Duṣyanta became the father of a world conqueror through his wife Śakuntalā.[75] In the next verse we are told that a disembodied voice proclaimed the legitimacy of his son, comparing inexplicably, the mother to a pair of bellows. This was a variant on the more frequent description of the mother being simply a bag or a sack and the son belonging to the father alone, since the father is responsible for the seed/birth—an echo of the statement in the *Mahābhārata*.

Closer to the Kālidāsa version is the story in the *Padma Purāṇa* which has been quoted in the controversy regarding the date of both texts.[76] A longer narrative is given in the later *Bhāgavata Purāṇa*.[77] This story follows the usual pattern but there is a curious set of statements which is unique to this narrative and appropriate for a Vaiṣṇava text. We are told that Bharata is imbued with a ray of Vāsudeva, is friendly towards *brāhmaṇas*, keeps his promises, is virtuous, possessed of strength and anxious to wait upon his elders—all of which enhance the reputation of Duṣyanta. The ray of Vāsudeva/Viṣṇu is of course a new idea, and suggestive of the increasing association of kings with deities in the post-Gupta period, particularly the attempt to identify certain kings as incarnations of Viṣṇu. The narrative continues with the description of the many *aśvamedha*s conducted by Bharata, and is an elaboration of the passage in the *Śatapatha Brāhmaṇa*. Bharata was remembered for his largesse as he distributed many thousand cows to each *brāhmaṇa*, and also distributed lakhs of elephants each with gold-plated tusks—a wild exaggeration but in keeping with the ambience of a potlatch. The inclusion of elephants in the list is a departure from earlier texts, the elephant by now being valued not only as the animal on which royalty rode and hunted, but for effectiveness in battle and in gathering timber from the forests. For all the emphasis on lineage, Bharata was said to have been succeeded eventually by an adopted son. The constant repetition of the story of his own birth in the *Purāṇa*s was doubtless because he was perceived as an important node in the *vaṃśa* or succession list of the Candravaṃśa lineage, an importance underlined here by his having ruled for the fantasy figure of thrice twenty-seven thousand years.

*Bhāgavata Purāṇa**

You who are the descendent of Bharata, I shall now tell you the history of the lineage into which you are born. To this lineage belong many royal sages and *brāhmaṇas* . . .

Rājā Duṣyanta, out on a hunt, arrived at the *āśrama* of Kaṇva. There he saw a beautiful young woman whose beauty added lustre to the surroundings, like the magic of a deity. He was infatuated by her.

This encouraged him to address her in gentle words.

"Lovely lady with lotus-petal eyes, what keeps you here in an unpeopled forest? You with your enticing waist, you have the bearings of a young woman from a royal family. Belonging as I

**Bhāgavata Purāṇa*, 9, 20, 7-32. (trans. R. Thapar)

do to the Puru lineage, I would recognise this in you and not make an unrighteous request."

Śakuntalā replied,

"As is known to the holy sage Kaṇva, I am the daughter of Viśvāmitra and was abandoned in the forest by my mother Menakā. Please be seated and accept the hospitality of the hermitage . . . eat of our wild rice and stay here if it should please you."

Duṣyanta replied,

"Lady with the arching eyebrows, it is proper for you to offer hospitality since you are a descendent of Kuśika. Young women of royal families are free to select their own husbands." [Would you select me?]

She consented to marry him by *gāndharva* rites. As a king, he knew the right time and place for the right act, in accordance with *dharma*.

The royal sage of predictable procreativity, placed his semen in the queen. He returned to his capital the next morning. In time she gave birth to a son.

The appropriate rituals were performed at the boy's birth by Kaṇva. He grew to be a child so strong that he could catch lion cubs and play with them.

The good woman sought her royal husband. She took with her the boy who showed great prowess. In him was incorporated a part of Hari.

The *rājā* rejected his wife and his son, although both were blameless and irreproachable. At this point a disembodied voice spoke and made a statement to all assembled who were listening,

"The mother is only a pouch. It is from the father alone that the son is born. Accept your son Duṣyanta and do not reject Śakuntalā.

The son releases the father from the abode of Yama/Death, by continuing the lineage. You had deposited Bharata in the womb of Śakuntalā and she is stating the truth."

On the death of Duṣyanta, Bharata became a ruler of great renown, incorporating in himself a ray of Hari.

The symbol of the discus could be seen on his right palm and the lotus on the soles of his feet. He performed the *mahābhiṣeka* and many other sacrifices.

With over a hundred horses and with Dīrghatamas officiating as his priest, he performed *aśvamedhas* along the Gaṅgā.

With seventy-eight horses he performed *aśvamedhas* along the Yamunā, liberally gifting wealth. A thousand *brāhmaṇas* each received over a thousand cows as their *dakṣinā*.

And he performed a further number of *aṣvamedhas*. He was superior even to the gods in wealth.

At Maṣnāra he donated many black elephants each with gold-plated tusks.

There was none to compare with the eminence and the affluence of Bharata. He conquered the Kirātas, Hūnas, Yavanas, Āndhras, Kaṅkas, Khaśas, Śakas and destroyed the *mlecchas* who opposed the *brāhmaṇas* . . .

As long as he ruled the desires of his subjects were fulfilled. His rule, which extended over the world, lasted for thrice twenty-seven thousand years.

It is interesting that the Kālidāsa version, which would be roughly contemporary with the composing of the early *Purāṇas*, is either not reflected in most of these *Purāṇas* or only marginally so, and that the epic story remained current in the recitations by *pauranikas* and *kathākāras*. Such recitations and narrations were common among audiences who kept the oral tradition alive. The association with the *Purāṇas* allowed elements of the popular culture to be incorporated and to that extent, the epics and the Purāṇas were appropriated by the not-so-high culture. The inclusion of the story in the *Purāṇas* however added a religious undertone to what was originally a fragment of the story of a lineage.

In narrative form and devoid of sectarian trappings, it inspired a story in Somadeva's *Kathāsarītasāgara*, in the eleventh century.[78] There are echoes in this story of the earlier narratives, some deviations and perhaps a hint of caricature.

*Kathāsaritsāgara**

Story of Kadalīgarbhā

There is in this land a city named Ikshumatī, and by the side of it there runs a river called by the same name; both were created by Viśvāmitra. And near it there is a great forest, and in it a hermit of the name of Mankaṇaka had made himself a hermitage and performed penance with his heels upwards. And while he was performing austerities, he saw an Apsaras of the name of Menakā coming through the air, with her clothes floating on the breeze. Then his mind was bewildered by Cupid, who had found his opportunity, and there was born to him a daughter named Kadalīgarbhā, beautiful in every limb. And since she was born in the interior of a plantain, her father, the hermit Mankaṇaka, gave her the name of Kadalīgarbhā. She grew up in his hermitage like Kṛipī the wife of Droṇa, who was born to Gautama on his beholding Rambhā. And once on a time Driḍhavarman, a king born in Madhyadeśa, who in the excitement of the chase was carried away by his horse, entered that hermitage. He beheld Kadalīgarbhā clothed in garments of bark, having her beauty exceedingly set off by the dress appropriate to the daughter of an ascetic. And she, when seen, captivated the heart of that king so completely, that she left no room in it for the women of his harem. While thinking to himself—"Shall I be able to obtain as a wife this daughter of some hermit or other, as Dushyanta obtained Śakuntalā the daughter of the hermit Kanva?"—the king beheld that hermit Mankaṇaka coming with fuel and *kuśa*-grass. And leaving his horse, he approached him and worshipped at his feet, and when questioned, discovered himself to that hermit. Then the hermit gave the following order to Kadalīgarbhā—"My dear child, prepare the *arghya* for this king our guest." She said—"I will do

*Story from *Kathāsarītasāgara* from C.H.Tawney (ed. and trans.), *The Kathāsarītasāgara*, Munshiram Manoharlal, Delhi 1968 (reprint, Chapter XXXII, pp. 286-90).

so"—and bowing, prepared the hospitable offering, and then the king said to the hermit—"Whence did you obtain this maiden who is so beautiful?"—Then the hermit told the king the story of her birth, and her name Kadalīgarbhā, which indicated the manner of it. Then the king, considering the maiden born from the hermit's thinking on Menakā to be an Apsaras, earnestly craved her hand of her father. And the sage gave him that daughter named Kadalīgarbhā, for the actions of the sages of old time, guided by divine insight, were without hesitation. And the nymphs of heaven, discovering the fact by their divine power, came there out of love for Menakā, and adorned her for the wedding. And on that very occasion they put mustard-seeds into her hand and said to her,—"As you are going along the path, sow them, in order that you may know it again. If, daughter, at any time your husband should scorn you, and you should wish to return here, then you will be able, as you come along, to recognise the path by these, which will have sprung up." When they had said this to her, and her marriage had been celebrated, the king Driḍhavarman placed Kadalīgarbhā on his horse, and departed thence. His army came up and escorted him, and in company with that bride of his, who sowed the mustard-seeds all along the path, he reached his own palace. There he became averse to the society of his other wives, and dwelt with that Kadalīgarbhā, after telling her story to his ministers.

Then his principal wife, being exceedingly afflicted, said to his minister in secret, after reminding him of the benefits she had conferred upon him: "The king is now exclusively attached to his new wife and has deserted me, so take steps to make this rival of mine depart." When that minister heard that, he said—"Queen, it is not appropriate for people like me to destroy or banish their masters' wives. This is the business of the wives of wandering religious mendicants, addicted to jugglery and such practices, associating with men like themselves. For those hypocritical female ascetics, creeping unforbidden into houses, skilled in deception, will stick at no deed whatever." When he said this to her, the queen, as if abashed, said to him in affected shame—"Then I will have nothing to do with this proceeding disapproved of by the virtuous." But she laid up his speech in her heart, and dismissing that minister, she summoned by the mouth of her maid a certain wandering female ascetic. And she told her all that desire of hers from the beginning, and promised to give her great wealth if the business were successfully accomplished. And the wicked female ascetic, from desire of gain, said to the afflicted queen—"Queen, this is an easy matter, I will accomplish it for you, for I know very many expedients of various kinds." Having thus consoled the queen, that female ascetic departed; and after reaching her house, she reflected as one afraid, "Alas! whom will not excessive desire of gain delude, since I rashly made such a promise before the queen? But the fact is, I know no device of the kind, and it is not possible to carry on any deception in the palace, as I do in other places, for the authorities might perhaps find it out and punish me. There may be one resource in this difficulty, for I have a friend, a barber, and as he is skilled in devices of the kind, all may yet go well, if he exert himself in the matter." After thus reflecting, she went to the barber, and told him all her plan that was to bring her prosperity. Then the barber, who was old and cunning, reflected—"This is good luck, that an opportunity of making something has now presented itself to me. So we must not kill the king's new wife, but we must preserve her alive, for her father has divine insight, and would reveal the whole transaction. But by separating her from the king we will now batten upon the queen, for great people become servants to a servant who shares their criminal secrets. And in due time I will re-unite her to the king, and tell him the whole story, in order that he and the sage's daughter may become a source of subsistence to me. And thus I shall not have done anything very wrong, and I shall have a livelihood for a long time." Having thus reflected, the barber said to the hypocritical female ascetic—"Mother, I will do all this, but it would not be proper to slay that new wife of the king's by means of magic, for the king might some day find it out, and then he would destroy us all: besides we should incur the sin of woman-murder, and her father the sage would curse us. Therefore it is far better that she should be separated from the king by means of our ingenuity, in order that the queen may be happy, and we may obtain wealth. And this is an easy matter to me, for what can I not accomplish by force of intellect? Hear my ingenuity, I will relate a story which illustrates it."

Story of the king and the barber's wife

This king Dridhavarman had an immoral father. And I was then his servant, being engaged in the duties which belong to me. He, one day, as he was roaming about here, cast eyes on my wife; and as she was young and beautiful, his mind became attached to her. And when he asked his attendants who she was, they said—"The barber's wife." He thought—"What can the barber do?" So the wicked king entered my house, and after enjoying at will the society of my wife, departed. But, as it happened, I was away from my house that day, being absent somewhere or other. And the next day, when I entered, I saw that my wife's manner had altered, and when I asked her the reason, she told me the whole story, being full of pride at what had occurred. And in that way the king went on puffing up my wife by continual visits, which I was powerless to prevent. A prince distracted by unholy passion makes no distinction between what is lawful and what is illicit. The forest is like straw to a sylvan fire fanned by the wind. So, not being in possession of any other expedient for restraining my sovereign, I reduced myself with spare diet, and took refuge in feigned sickness. And in this state I went into the presence of that king to perform my duties, sighing deeply, pale and emaciated. Then the king, seeing that I seemed to be ill, asked me meaningly the following question—"Hola! tell me why you have become thus?" And after he had questioned me persistently, I answered the king in private, after imploring immunity from punishment—"King, my wife is a witch. And when I am asleep she extracts my entrails and sucks them, and then replaces them as before—This is how I have become lean. So how can continual refreshment and eating nourish me?" When I said this to the king, he became anxious and reflected—"Can she really be a witch? Why was I captivated by her? I wonder whether she will suck my entrails also, since I am well nourished with food. So I will myself contrive to test her this very night." Having thus reflected, the king caused food to be given me on the spot. Then I went home and shed tears in the presence of my wife, and when she questioned me, I said to her—"My beloved, you must not reveal to any one what I am about to tell you. Listen! That king has teeth as sharp as the edge of a thunderbolt, where teeth are not usually found, and they broke my razor to-day while I was performing my duties. And in this way I shall break a razor every time. So how am I to be continually procuring fresh razors? This is why I weep, for the means of supporting myself in my home are destroyed." When I had said this to my wife, she made up her mind to investigate the marvel of the concealed teeth while the king was asleep, since he was to visit her at night. But she did not perceive that such a thing had never been seen since the world was, and could not be true. Even clever women are deceived by the tales of an impostor.

So the king came at night and visited my wife at will, and as if fatigued, pretended to go to sleep, remembering what I had said. Then my wife, thinking he was asleep, slowly stretched out her hand to find his concealed teeth. And as soon as her hand reached him, the king exclaimed—"A witch! A witch!" and left the house in terror. Henceforth my wife, having been abandoned by the king out of fear, became satisfied with me and devoted to me exclusively. In this way I saved my wife on a former occasion from the king by my intelligence.

Having told this story to the female ascetic, the barber went on to say—"So, my good lady, this desire of yours must be accomplished by wisdom; and I will tell you, mother, how it is to be done, listen to me. Some old servant of the harem must be won over to say to this king in secret every day, 'Your wife Kadalīgarbhā is a witch.' For she, being a forest maiden, has no attendants of her own, and what will not all alien servants do for gain, being easily corrupted? Accordingly, when the king becomes apprehensive on hearing what the old servant says, you must contrive to place at night hands and feet and other limbs in the chamber of Kadalīgarbhā. Then the king will see them in the morning, and concluding that what the old man says is true, will be afraid of Kadalīgarbhā and desert her of his own accord. So the queen will be delighted at getting rid of a rival wife, and entertain a favourable opinion of you, and we shall gain some advantage." When the barber said this to the female ascetic, she consented and went and told the whole matter to the king's head queen. And the queen carried out her suggestions, and the king, who had been warned, saw the hands and feet in the morning with his own eyes, and abandoned Kadalīgarbhā, thinking her to be wicked. So the female ascetic, together with the barber, enjoyed to the full the presents which the queen secretly gave to her, being pleased with her aid.

So Kadalīgarbhā, being abandoned by Driḍhavarman, went out from the palace, grieved because the king would be cursed. And she returned to the hermitage of her father by the same path by which she came, which she was able to recognise by the mustard-seeds she had sown, which had sprung up. Her father, the hermit Mankaṇaka, when he saw her suddenly arrived there, remained for some time suspecting immorality on her part. And then he perceived the whole occurrence by the power of contemplation, and after lovingly comforting her, departed thence with her. And he went and told the king, who bowed before him, the whole treacherous drama, which the head queen had got up out of hatred for her rival. At that moment the barber himself arrived, and related the whole occurrence to the king, and then proceeded to say this to him: "In this way, my sovereign, I sent away the lady Kadalīgarbhā, and so delivered her from the danger of the incantations which would have been practised against her, since I satisfied the head queen by an artifice." When the king heard that, he saw that the speech of the great hermit was certainly true, and he took back Kadalīgarbhā, recovering his confidence in her. And after respectfully accompanying the departing hermit, he rewarded the barber with wealth, thinking that he was attached to his person: kings are the appointed prey of rogues. Then the king, being averse to the society of his queen, lived in great comfort with Kadalīgarbhā.

What would be described as stereotypes from the tradition of popular literature are not only visible but crucial in this narrative: the heroine is named after the pith of the plantain tree, mustard seeds are used to mark the path, the barber is the one who plots and counterplots with those in power—a stock character said to be wily and shrewd. The accusation against Kadalīgarbhā of being a witch, and the placing of incriminating objects in her room is not unknown to folk literature.

These were some of the popular representations of the story. That the play was familiar to those claiming to be sophisticated poets is apparent from either the use of similar language and imagery in other compositions, such as in inscriptions, or by reference to Kālidāsa as a renowned poet, as in an inscription at Aihole.[79] Appreciation from *Bānabhaṭṭa*, the seventh century author of the Harṣacarita, is fulsome. *Bānabhaṭṭa* borrows the theme of the curse and the ring while fantasising on his own ancestry at the beginning of the *Harṣacarita*. Encroachments into forests, which by now were being carried out more frequently, are described with greater realism in the *Harṣacarita*, whereas in the play they are romanticised.[80]

Verses from Kālidāsa are included in anthologies of Sanskrit poetry such as Vidyākara's *Subhāṣitaratnakośa*, compiled in A.D. 1100;[81] in the eleventh century work of Bhoja, the *Sarasvatīkaṇṭhābharaṇa;* and many more in the fourteenth century *Sāhityadarpaṇa*.[82] Even more central to culture was the assessment of his plays in current literary theories. Initially the enthusiasm for the plays seems to have been muted, but by the end of the millennium the drama on Śakuntalā was not only rated as the finest exemplar of the *nāṭaka*, it was also praised for illustrating the much discussed theory of *rasa*. The discussions initially remained within the confines of Sanskritic culture, although by the end of the first millennium A.D., this culture had a wide geographical reach.

Familiarity with the play was enhanced by its featuring in discussions on literary criticism and aesthetics in texts from about the ninth century onwards, many of which were commentaries in part on the authoritative *Nāṭyaśāstra*, composed at an earlier date. It discussed virtually every aspect of drama—from the construction of the theatre to the subtleties of mime and acting, including categories of plays and varieties of heroes and heroines.[83] Apart from the quality of its verse and the structure of its plot, the reputation of Kālidāsa's play was also based on the fact that the hero and heroine exemplified the qualities mentioned in the *Nāṭyaśāstra* as characteristic of the ideal.

Works of the early Christian era, those such as of Bhāmaha, had begun to classify and discuss the genres of literature, but it was only towards the end of the first millennium A.D. that there appears to have been an efflorесence of interest in literature, its meaning and form. This was in part sparked off by the commentaries and treatises on the *Nāṭyaśāstra,* and by a growing interest in theories of aesthetics. Among the more important of these were Ānandavardhana's *Dhvanyāloka* of the ninth century where, discussing both dramaturgy and poetics, he argued extensively on the nature of meanings.[84] The *Daśarūpaka* of Dhanañjaya attempted to summarise the *Nāṭyaśāstra* and make it more accessible. The *Abhinavabhārati* of Abhinavagupta in the eleventh century carried the discussion further as did the later *Sāhitya Darpaṇa* of Viśvanātha Kavirāja, and the more didactic *Nāṭaka Candrikā* of Rūpa Gosvāmi.[85] Of the commentaries on the play itself there were quite a few, among which the better known were those of a later period by Śaṅkara, Candraśekhara, Kaṭayavema and Rāghavabhaṭṭa. Among these, the commentary of Rāghavabhaṭṭa is regarded as analytic and incisive and is the most quoted. It was presumably also at the time of these commentaries that the anonymous adage, variously rendered, began to be cited, placing Kālidāsa as among the best of poets, praising the play and judging the fourth act as the epitome of Sanskrit literature.[86]

The period from about the tenth to the sixteenth centuries witnessed many commentaries on a variety of texts, some of which were quite routine, while others were pertinent to an active intellectualism. Perhaps the gradual change to the more extensive use of regional languages required that the existing texts in Sanskrit be subjected to detailed explanation for, with the evolution of literary forms in the regional languages, they were now seen as the source for much contemporary discussion. At the more mundane level the proliferation of *agrahāras* and *maṭhas* emerging as financially independent, comfortable centres of scholasticism and Sanskrit learning, permitted an active study and discussion of earlier texts. This was not carried out as an exercise in dilettantism, but was central to the changes of the times which often contested earlier traditions or at least demanded new explanations for them. Commentarial literature which both explored and froze what came to be viewed as the classical past, has yet to be analysed in terms of its historical context and the intellectual requirements of the time.

Literary criticism in the post-Gupta period and particularly at the turn of the millennium, A.D. 1000, saw major exegeses on the earlier theory of *rasas*. Briefly, the theory deals with the depiction or even suggestion of emotions and moods believed to be the more sensitive articulation in literature, transmitted to one or more reader or viewer. It assumes that a literary form produces an intended reaction in the reader, expressed as an emotional state, and that the individual emotion is transmuted into a recognised human experience as captured in literature and, more so, poetry. In terms of relating the *Abhijñāna-śākuntalam* to the *rasa* theory, to questions concerning the *śṛṅgāra-rasa* or the *vīra-rasa*, the play was a departure from the intentions of the epic poet who underlines neither.

Much of the discussion in the commentaries focused on the question of the dominant mood in a play, on the construction of the plot and the characterisation of the protagonists. These were important to differentiating the genre of dramatic literature. Mood was subsumed in the term *rasa,* with meaning ranging over essence, emotions, sentiment and even the psychic state produced in the spectator. Of the *rasas* known by convention—initially eight and eventually nine—only one or two were dominant in each play. Styles of course varied as did the embellishment of plot and character. Of the categories of drama listed, perhaps heroic comedy was the most popular (if plays such as the one under discussion can be labelled "heroic comedy"). The plot proceeded through five successive stages from a germinal beginning—the *bīja*—through the continuity of the *bindu* spreading like a drop of oil in water, to the denouement—the *kārya.* The plot could be analysed in terms of the five *saṃdhis*—the articulations or junctures, which did not have to coincide with the Acts of the play, as is argued in the commentary of Rāghavabhaṭṭa. This allowed for a freer interpretation of the meaning of plot and mood. Each *saṁdhi* had a dozen or more *aṅgas,* literally limbs, not all of which were used in every drama, but theoretically, there was much scope for a nuanced playing on emotions and moods.

The universalisation of *rasa* was viewed by some as transcending meaning in poetry, for *rasa* is the essence of poetry. The closeness of drama and poetry, discussed by Ānandavardhana and Abhinavagupta, lay not merely in poetry being a part of dramatic dialogue, but in the centrality of *rasa* which brought them into proximity. Such views however were debated in the discussion on both *rasa* and *dhvani.* In poetry, *dhvani* was used both in the sense of that which is expressed, and that which is implied. In drama, *rasa* was created through *abhinaya,* and this was said to be a combination of bodily movements, speech, dress and the acting out of the emotions. In the context of such discussions, the commentaries on this play were more than just a recounting of the plot and a description of the characters. Thus Abhinavagupta explores Kālidāsa's use of memory; Barbara Stoler Miller reads this not as a discursive recollection of past events, but as an intuiting of the past which transcends personal experience, and introduces us into the universe of imagination evoked by beauty.

Rāghavabhaṭṭa's commentary analyses the structure of the plot on the basis of preceding discussions. The tension of the play is derived from the interaction between *śṛṅgāra-rasa* and *vīra-rasa*, where the former has been interpreted as the love between the hero and the heroine as well as the universal love embodied in the ideals of the *āśrama*; and the latter as the notion not only of the heroic but of social obligation and duty, looking to the wider world of *dharma*.[87] The two moods of the play therefore demand incidents such as the curse of Durvāsas and Duṣyanta's amnesia. The resolution of the tension requires a reciprocity between love and the fulfilment of social obligations.

The analysis of the plot in terms of the five *saṁdhis* does not necessarily conform to earlier views. These are neither attempts to reiterate the divisions required by the performance since they do not coincide with the divisions according to the Acts, nor are they just a series of incidents, since they have to follow the phases of the *saṁdhis* and be causally linked. This involves a detailed discussion of the existence of the two predominant *rasas* and their interplay. Whether the play is dominated by one or the other, or whether the author intended the two to be balanced, remains something of an open question. Although it is said that the separation of the two *rasas* has eventually to be reconciled, there is no indication that any action was thought to be overly erotic and therefore meriting disapproval. This is worth keeping in mind when considering the rather different Orientalist interpretation of the play, where discussion on the erotic is in the forefront.

The centrality of *rasa* in the play is enhanced by the earlier controversy in Sanskrit literary theory regarding erotic elements in the poetry of Kālidāsa.[88] Was nature being used to evoke the sensuous? The objection was to the description in the *Kumārasambhava* of the dalliance between Śiva and Pārvatī after their marriage, a description which few attribute to Kālidāsa, anyway. The objection is not to the erotic *per se*, but to the depiction of deities in a heightened erotic mode, which was thought to be inappropriate. The introduction of the erotic into poetry may also have been encouraged by the prevalence of texts such as the *Kāmasūtra* which, like parallel texts in other cultures prior to the impact of Judaeo-Christian attitudes, had considerable currency not as pornography but as a legitimate exploration of one of the pleasures of life. For the literary theorists, eroticism was acceptable as it remained within the confines of a poetry intended for pleasure, and was not part of a religious idiom. The plays of Kālidāsa were framed in a narrative derived from epic themes and using characters believed to be, at most, quasi-historical, and therefore not centrally concerned with deities.

Major texts often had more than one recension and the Kālidāsa play is no exception. This is a reflection of the extensive use of written texts by now, of variations in the copying of manuscripts and the existence of multiple centres of Sanskritic learning. The latter resulted in the recognition of two traditions, the *mārga* or mainstream Sanskritic culture and texts, and the *deśī,* which was the regional and local tradition. Nevertheless the two were not completely separate, and the fact that Sanskrit texts gradually came to be written in the script used for the regional language indicates some overlap between the two. This could also result in variant readings.

There are four major recensions of the *Abhijñāna-śākuntalam,* listed as Bengali, Devanāgari, Kashmiri and Dravidian, largely on the basis of the scripts used. Of these the first two are the most important.[89] The Bengali recension is a little longer than the Devanāgari and this has led to speculation about which might be the more authentic. The extra length consists of minor additions in most places; however, in Act III, the dialogue between Śakuntalā and Duṣyanta is more drawn out, with a further underlining of the erotic mood.

It has recently been argued that the shorter recension was the literary version, and the somewhat longer, a performance version which therefore had some additions, although it also came to be treated as a literary text.[90] If this is so, then it is interesting that the inflation was mainly of the erotic mood, seen as a legitimate expression of *śṛṅgāra-rasa* with no association of disapproval attached to it. Possibly it also had to do with the debate on which of the moods—*śṛṅgāra-rasa* or *vīra-rasa,* the erotic romantic or the heroic—was being emphasised in the play. This may have led to a version from Bengal trying to tilt the balance in the direction of the former. A manuscript of the Bengali recension goes back to the sixteenth century when the commentaries were also known, but significantly the commentary by Rāghavabhaṭṭa uses the Devanāgari recension.[91]

In the period after A.D. 1300 many courts of the Sultans and the Mughals were using Turkish and Persian and some, the regional languages. Yet this was also the period when theatrical activity was particularly evident. There was enough patronage of Sanskrit to encourage commentaries and discussions on literature, but theatrical activity also fed into, and was in turn enriched by, the popular tradition of drama, poetry and dance. Sanskrit drama has also been examined more recently in a comparison with the continuous theatrical tradition of the *kūṭiyāṭṭam* theatre in Kerala, associated with some of the temples.[92] To assume that the Sanskrit theatrical tradition or discourse on theory relating to literature and the arts collapsed in this period, would be quite incorrect.

5. Adaptations: another popular tradition and its role in another court

Up till now, the main theoretical analyses of the play consisted of commentaries. Subsequently, the major new forms were adaptations and translations into a variety of languages. These insert yet another dimension—other than historical change—into the narrative since the rendering of the text now takes on the characteristics of, both, the language of the adaptation and translation, and of its literary forms. This is even more evident when the adaptation is from a literary form to a visual image, although it is also present within languages. The reader and the original text were in communication, but the adaptation and translation of the narrative into various other languages complicated this communication with new genres and the cultural contexts of other languages.

Given this, the innovations, and what is introduced into the text as a result of language change, need to be observed.[93] Plot changes are more easily perceived whereas character changes are more blurred. How then is Śakuntalā depicted in the new forms, and what comments do these new texts elicit? The pre-eminence of the play in the Sanskritic literary tradition meant that choosing it for other genres and languages both acknowledged widespread familiarity with it, and demonstrated that only the best had been selected for adaptation. Some of these forms enjoyed the patronage of the major courts, others would have had humbler patrons. Further commentaries became more extensive than before, for exegesis breeds exegesis, but commentary and translation also keep the text alive and ensure a return to the original from time to time.[94] Nevertheless adaptations and translations assume a cultural divergence and are means of communication between these divergences.

Interest in pre-Mughal literature among members of the Mughal court is evident from the patronage extended to those writing in Sanskrit, and the production of manuscripts, often illustrated, on themes from texts in Sanskrit and the regional languages.[95] In the reign of Akbar, Abul Fazl ordered a translation of the *Mahābhārata* into Persian. This may have included the Śakuntalā episode, although there is no specific reference to it or to the play. The continuing popularity of the story can however be seen in the early eighteenth century when it was translated into the language of everyday speech.

In 1716, the Mughal Emperor, Farrukh Siyar, bestowed a title on a nobleman returning victorious from a campaign.[96] The recipient decided to celebrate this event and asked the poet laureate, Nawāz Kaveśvara, to render the text of the Kālidāsa play on Śakuntalā into what he called "Braj-ki-boli". This the poet did in the form of a narrative, *Śakuntalā*, calling it a *kathā*, and composed it in the current poetic metres of Braj poetry interspersed with brief passages of prose. This was not a translation but a retelling of the story in a new genre. It is also thought that the retelling may have borrowed the general ambience from the epic version, although the narrative itself follows the Kālidāsa version. Judging by the way it is set out and the occasion for which it was composed, it may have been the basis for a dance or a mime, performed to the accompaniment of the verses and perhaps some music as well—not unfamiliar even in performances of the original play. The composition was intended for a felicitation, and its theme of the triumph of love after many vicissitudes may have attracted the poets and patrons of the time. The genre of *nāṭaka,* even in the past, was frequently associated with festivals. Doubtless, a rendering in Braj-*bhāṣā* would also have evoked the imagery of the many-faceted love as portrayed in the *Kṛṣṇa* cycles, and the equally extensive *bārahmāsā* poetry. But at the same time, it introduces elements of the Indo-Persian cultural tradition into the narrative.

The Braj version begins with an invocation to *Rādhā-Kṛṣṇa* and describes the *kathā-kāvya* which follows as based on the theme of the *gāndharva* marriage of Śakuntalā and Duṣyanta.[97] This underlines a particular form of marriage, by now a thing of the past. Unlike the earlier versions, the story opens with the seduction of Viśvāmitra by Menakā, and reads almost like a premonition of the main event of the narrative, except that the gender roles are reversed. The verses are pithy and pointed, such as the one referring to this first seduction:

ek muhurata ke sukh kāraṇa
khoyo tapu kari varṣa hajāran

(page 3, verse 5)

Śakuntalā is abandoned and Kaṇva takes the foundling whom he chances upon, to his *āśrama*. The subsequent story follows the Kālidāsa narrative and relies on comfortable versification, but essentially the story is told as that of Śakuntalā and concerns only what affects her directly. The *vidūṣaka* is therefore deleted—an unfortunate choice since the *vidūṣaka* in this idiom would have been an effective commentator. The colloquial form of the language bereft of the elegance of Kālidāsa's Sanskrit, may account for its folk-tale quality.

Duṣyanta agrees to defend the *āśrama* against the *rākṣasas* but frequently wanders through the *vana*/forest looking for Śakuntalā; the forest takes on the appearance of a series of informal gardens, allowing the inclusion of much of the usual imagery of Braj poetry and the repeated mention of *viraha*/separation, so central to some of this poetry. There is much embellishment on the theme of love. Duṣyanta's rejection of Śakuntalā and his calling her a *raṇḍi*/whore, arouses her anger and she retorts in the same vein as the epic Śakuntalā: that he is acting in a way which is devoid of *dharma* and that he has no right to abuse her: *kyon bin kāj kalinka lagāvata*? Later, Duṣyanta stops off on his way to fight the *asuras* and hears the story of Bharata from one of the women ascetics in the *āśrama*. The ring having been found, he is full of remorse at having lost Śakuntalā, so when she appears, he places his head at her feet and asks for forgiveness:

rājahin aur na kacchu kahi āyo
Śakuntalā ke paga shīra nāyo
(page 81, verse 58)

The story assumes that the Mughal court is sensitive to the earlier tradition. Thus when the ascetics appeal to the king to defend their *yajñas*/sacrificial rituals from desecration by the *rākṣasas*, this protection is accepted as a normal part of the function of kingship. Even though the story is set in what, by now, was the remote past, interest in this past is evinced by reviving the story as part of a contemporary celebration.

The sentiment associated with the separation, *viraha*, of lovers or of husbands and wives is prominent. *Viraha* is central to *bārahmāsā* poetry, a form generally regarded as originating in popular culture, but which took on sophisticated forms in the compositions of poets at various courts and elsewhere from the fourteenth century onwards.[98] The description of nature changing through the seasons is deeply embedded in this poetry, where winter is poignantly the time of separation, and spring, of love. This is not the preferred theme in Sanskrit poetry although there are many poems on the seasons, Kālidāsa's *Ṛtusamhāram* being a particularly fine example. His *Meghadūtam* has something of the mood of a *bārahmāsā*.[99] The link with the seasons may have to do with this poetry being popular among those whose occupation required long periods of travel, leaving behind a wife or a beloved who was the subject of the poem.[100] The connection with the cult of Rādhā and

Kṛṣṇa, and with epics in the idiom of the regional languages, is so close that it is difficult to determine a priority of influence; it was probably mutual. Sometimes epics were close to the *viraha bārahmāsā* form as in the *Cāndāyan* of Mullā Dāūd, the *Mṛgāvatī* of Sheikh Qutban and the *Padmāvat* of Malik Muhammad Jayasī.[101] These were also inspired by Persian literary forms—the *qasīdah*, the *masnavī* and the *dāstān*—rich in symbolic meaning. They were admired and adapted into the literature of the regional languages close to the contemporary court tradition, especially Hindi and Urdu. The mix of believed historical memory, legend and myth, permitting multiple meanings, found a receptive audience.

The importance of *viraha* was also evident in the literature of the regional languages; it made its entry through perspectives derived from *bhakti*, where the separation of the worshipper from her deity was a form of *viraha*. In the poetry of Avadh *viraha* evoked more than just human love. The symbolism of separation and longing with the anticipation of an eventual union, enters Sufi thought and that of the Kṛṣṇa *bhaktas*, where the soul in search of the beloved/the deity was regarded as the most perfect form of love. In Sufi poetry *viraha* signified the intense desire for the Divine, often requiring descriptions of the torment which such a search entailed; whereas much of *bārahmāsā* poetry frequently speaks of the tormented woman, the *virahinī*. The Gorakhanātha tradition also composed poetry in this genre, such as the *Gorakṣavijaya* of Sheikh Fayzulla.

This is not to suggest that the Braj version of the Śakuntalā narrative was a *bārahmāsā;* rather, to see in its composition some elements from the prevailing style of local poetry which, to some extent, would alter the ambience of the Braj version. The latter has an element of a return to the popular tradition even though it was commemorating a court celebration. It mediates between the epic version and the play of Kālidāsa, between the past and the present, and between the Sanskritic and the Indo-Persian culture. In a sense the mediations are the coming together of the *mārga* and the *deśī* traditions on each occasion. The curse and the ring become a substitute for the seasons, the cause of a long separation as well as of the ultimate coming together of husband and wife. There was also the poetry of the *rītikāla* which highlighted the love of the *nāyaka* and the *nāyikā*, without the intrusion of the seasons. Since the Braj version of the Śakuntalā narrative was intended for a festive celebration it may have drawn from this category of poetry as well.

The composing of *bārahmāsās* continues into the late eighteenth and early nineteenth centuries. Among these, one is mentioned in contemporary sources as the *Bārahmāsā* of Mirza Qasim Ali whose pen-name was Jawan. This provides a link to Jawan's other enterprise involving the narrative of Śakuntalā. In 1801 Mirza Qasim Ali, a recognised Urdu poet, was appointed to teach Urdu at Fort William College in Calcutta. He was asked to translate the Braj *Śakuntalā* into Urdu, which was published in 1806 as *Śakuntalā*. Jawan was probably helped by Lalluji Lal, teaching Hindi at the same college, and perhaps by Munshi Beni Narayan from Lahore, another colleague. Lalluji Lal had as his patron, Gilchrist, who was encouraging officers of the East India Company to learn Hindi and Urdu; by the end of the eighteenth century Urdu had almost become a required language. The translation was doubtless seen as an attempt to provide a text for teaching the language, which would also tie in with some notion of local literary traditions. The narration is in prose with occasional verses scattered in between, and the language is what Jawan calls the *zaban-i-rekhta* or the common tongue. The verses veer towards doggerel at times and the dialogue has a homely use of folk proverbs. That the attempt was not to translate the Sanskrit play but the Braj adaptation, was possibly because Jawan did not have an adequate knowledge of Sanskrit—or that the Braj version had superceded the

Sanskrit in popularity, at least in some of the north Indian court circles, the attraction being the accessibility of language and a familiar literary form. Nevertheless the narrative moves out of the narrow frame of a court play and takes on greater universality.

Jawan's version has some noticeable differences when compared to earlier ones.[102] Conversations in it tend to be down-to-earth, and without courtly frills; and the narrative is set in the framework of the Persian *dāstān*, the fable and fantasy, where love and emotions can be exaggerated in the manner of the Majnus and the Farhads. The sight of the beloved frequently causes the king to faint. Thus:

hosh jātā rahā nighāh ke sāth
sabr rukhsat huā ek āha ke sāth

It is interesting that the notion of an *apsarā* is now replaced and Menakā is referred to as the *pari* or fairy, more familiar from the Persian tradition. Menakā's seduction of the *ṛṣi* is described at some length, with the poignant statement that all his *punji*/capital was lost in one breath. The story then proceeds in much the same way as in the Braj version. The *vidūṣaka* is again omitted. Was the concept feared by the courts of the time? Or was there a sensitivity and hesitation about making fun of a *brāhmaṇa*? Śakuntalā seems constantly to hide behind her *ghunghat* in embarassment at realising that she is in love.

The story tends to meander and the language is intended for a popular audience. Thus Śakuntalā's anger at the king's rejection is rendered, in Jawan's version, as a frontal accusation of deceipt: "*Are be-insāf. Tu kyā kehtā hai. Tune mujjh se ki ṭhaggi* . . ." When she cannot find the ring, the king abuses her and, again echoing the epic, calls her a liar and a wanton woman. The *āśrama* of Kaśyapa/Mārīca is reminiscent of descriptions of gardens in paradise from Persian literature, with its myriad flowers of bright and beautiful hue, its well-laid-out fountains, trees laden with luscious fruit and singing birds—quite the opposite of the ascetic hermitage in the play, but very close in style to the gardens of miniature paintings. There are many features in this translation which would date it to the eighteenth century.

Interestingly, it was republished with the title, *Śakuntalā nāṭaka.* The collophon was expanded to include a statement that the play had been written by the famous poet, Kālidāsa, who lived in the time of King Vikramāditya, and that the play in Sanskrit had been rendered into Braj in the time of Farrukh Siyar. Was it the interest of the Orientalists in the play that gave it added status, or was its popularity in the smaller princely courts of the nineteenth century a continuing feature?

6. Translations: Orientalism, German romanticism and the image of Śakuntalā

POPULAR culture has a continuing tension with dominant culture; this tension is suggested within Sanskrit literature through the variant forms of the narrative of Śakuntalā as well as in adaptations in related languages. This takes on another dimension when one form is singled out as representative, translated into languages not directly related to the original, and interpreted in idioms distant from it. Frequently the new idiom carries the endorsement of those who give shape to the dominant culture and whose power is accepted by the dominated in order to be seen as legitimate.

Upto this point the various versions of the story of Śakuntalā which have been discussed were formulated within varying genres of literature; in languages which were related—Sanskrit, Braj-*bhāṣā* and Urdu—and at different points of Indian history. The historical context provided a frame and some degree of continuity. Even where there was a change, this did not take the form of a disjuncture as it did with the translations which became part of the colonial experience. With translations there is a change of tack. Where a text is translated into another language, the context expands to include the cultural concerns of the society whose language is used in the translation. The form remains the same—in that the translations retain the form of Kālidāsa's work—but it is assessed at one remove, as it were. The earliest translations are in various European languages and the interest they evoke leads to a renewed interest in the Kālidāsa play, which is also translated into various Indian regional languages. But the reading of the play by Orientalist scholarship and by European literary opinion colours the understanding of the play and of the narrative. The epic and the Braj version recede and the Kālidāsa play is virtually the sole representation of the story. And translation, as is well known, changes the cultural role of the narrative. In this case it shifts attention away from variants of the narrative to an interpretation of Śakuntalā whose role as an icon changes with each interpretation.

At the end of the eighteenth century, Sir William Jones and other officers of the East India Company at Calcutta were translating texts relating to law and religion from Sanskrit, Persian and other Indian languages, in an effort to understand the high culture of the colony which they were governing, to enable better control over it. Asserting power required a knowledge of the history and culture of those now in a subservient position. Such translations were partly a response to intellectual curiosity, and partly an aspect of the practical function of East India Company officials in India. Jones was evidently much taken with Sanskrit literature and Hindu mythology, as is evident from his poems, such as the "Hymn to Camdeo", the "Hymn to Narayan", and "The Enchanted Fruit" composed in 1784-85. They grew out of his readings in the *Purāṇas* and his attempt to find parallels with Graeco-Roman religions and Biblical chronology.[103] Jones' poetry and essays came to be reflected in the imagination of the poets of the Romantic Movement. Jones' writing touched many chords in Europe: the supposedly primitive and spontaneous poetry of the Orient, its origins in emotion and imagination, and the emphasis on the lyric form.[104] Translating a Sanskrit text, however, was more ambitious.

One may also ask whether William Jones was not subconsciously influenced by what has been called the "hunt for the Welsh past", with its revival of bards, Druids and nature worship.[105] The involvement of his family with Welsh nationalism would have familiarised him with such pursuits. Welsh was supposed to hold the secrets to man's primitive language—consequently links were sought between Noah and the Welsh. This was an ambience in which myths, far from being dismissed as fantasy, were instead believed to incorporate statements about the past.

Jones heard about the genre of *nāṭaka* and thought it was a kind of history but Pandit Radhakanta, who advised him on such matters, clarified the meaning of a *nāṭaka* as being similar to the plays performed by the English in the cool season in Calcutta—a very perceptive observation! When asked to suggest a *nāṭaka*, Radhakanta referred to what was regarded as the best in the tradition, Kālidāsa's *Abhijñāna-śākuntalam*. Jones' other adviser was a *vaidya* from Nadia who also helped with this translation. The Bengali version was given to Jones perhaps because, by now, the Devanāgari version had little currency in Bengal. Jones was enthused on reading it and decided to translate it. He saw it as demonstrating the high quality of Indian civilisation and thought it all the more remarkable as it was written at a time ". . . when Britons were as unlettered and unpolished as the army of Hanumat . . ." and he described Kālidāsa as "the Indian Shakespeare".[106] The latter description ties in with the comment frequently made that the language of Jones' translation is reminiscent of Shakespearean English.

His first translation was into Latin since he felt that the structural similarities of the two languages would facilitate a Latin translation. From Latin he translated it into English and published it in 1789 as *Sacontalá or The Fatal Ring*.[107] He explains that he faced two problems; one, translating it into a foreign idiom although the translation was not the most felicitous; and second, his wish to convince readers of the greatness of Indian civilisation. The latter led him to tone down some of what he thought were the more erotic passages, which he assumed would unnecessarily result in

English hostility towards the Sanskrit classics. The Bengali recension was a little more provocative than the others and he was anticipating possible criticism from the more timid European views on erotica in literature.[108] That it was an initial venture in translating Sanskrit literature into English is evident from the additional phrases here and there, which Jones incorporates in order to clarify the meaning.

William Jones was not averse to literary Romanticism, as is evident from his own poetry, particularly the poems composed on Indian themes, and doubtless one of the play's attractions for him was its evocation of nature. This was the period when the debate on Nature and Culture had begun to convulse the literary scene in Europe. But perhaps his personal inclination was even more towards neo-Classicism and he saw Śakuntalā as a "rustic girl", a term he frequently uses, rather than as a "child of nature", the phrase that the German Romantic poets would use. Although embarrassed by the eroticism of some of the verses in the play, he does not use this to make a moral evaluation of its characters.

In assessing the play for performance he felt that a great part of the courtship in the hermitage could be omitted, as also the dialogue between the king and the *vidūṣaka*. Jones seems not have understood the relationship between the latter two and the necessity for its inclusion in the projection of the hero. Incidentally, both these sections of the play draw attention to the passion of the lovers. It would seem that Jones was anxious that the play not be performed in its entirety to a Calcutta audience of the East India Company officials and their wives, nor that the expanded version be read in England.

What were viewed as erotic passages had been perceived differently by Indian audiences in the past, and indeed the nineteenth century European view of erotica seems somewhat absurd to us today. A reference is made to the *jaghanagauravāt*, the heavy hips of Śakuntalā, followed by a verse explaining that their weight caused a deep imprint of her heels on the sand where she walked.[109] This was thought to be erotic, and Jones translated it as "elegant limbs"; later translators referred to the "graceful undulation of her gait" (Monier Williams) or the "weight of rounded hips" (Edgren), and some omitted it altogether. "Drooping breasts" became "drooping neck" and so on.[110] Yet such descriptions had not only been acceptable to Indian audiences but regarded as essential to the creation of the *śṛṅgāra-rasa.* Such embarrassment with the erotic affected many European translations, and Jones' reluctance is echoed by A.L. de Chezy when he translated the play into French. Orientalism was trying to define and comprehend the culture of the colonised in European terms. Thus the colonised are viewed as civilised, but their civilisation may take some unpalatable forms, and these can be corrected or deleted.

*Preface to Sacontalá or The Fatal Ring**

In one of the letters which bear the title of edifying, though most of them swarm with ridiculous errours, and all must be consulted with extreme diffidence, I met, some years ago, with the following passage: "In the north of India there are many books, called Nátac, which, as the Bráhmens assert, contain a large portion of ancient history without any mixture of fable;" and having an eager desire to know the real state of this empire before the conquest of it by the Savages of the North, I was very solicitous, on my arrival in Bengal, to procure access to those books, either by the help of translations, if they had been translated, or by learning the language in which they were originally composed, and which I had yet a stronger inducement

*The *Preface* by William Jones.

to learn from its connection with the administration of justice to the Hindûs; but when I was able to converse with the Bráhmens, they assured me that the Nátacs were not histories, and abounded with fables; that they were extremely popular works, and consisted of conversations in prose and verse, held before ancient Rájás in their publick assemblies, on an infinite variety of subjects, and in various dialects of India: this definition gave me no very distinct idea; but I concluded that they were dialogues on moral or literary topicks; whilst other Europeans, whom I consulted, had understood from the natives that they were discourses on dancing, musick, or poetry. At length a very sensible Bráhmen, named Rádhácánt, who had long been attentive to English manners, removed all my doubts, and gave me no less delight than surprise, by telling me that our nation had compositions of the same sort, which were publickly represented at Calcutta in the cold season, and bore the name, as he had been informed, of plays. Resolving at my leisure to read the best of them, I asked which of their Nátacs was most universally esteemed; and he answered without hesitation, Sacontalá, supporting his opinion, as usual among the Pandits, by a couplet to this effect: "The ring of Sacontalá, in which the fourth act, and four stanzas of the act, are eminently brilliant, displays all the rich exuberance of Cálidása's genius." I soon procured a correct copy of it; and, assisted by my teacher Rámalóchan, began with translating it verbally into Latin, which bears so great a resemblance to Sanscrit, that it is more convenient than any modern language for a scrupulous interlineary version: I then turned it word for word into English, and afterwards, without adding or suppressing any material sentence, disengaged it from the stiffness of a foreign idiom, and prepared the faithful translation of the Indian drama, which I now present to the publick as a most pleasing and authentick picture of old Hindû manners, and one of the greatest curiosities that the literature of Asia has yet brought to light.

Dramatick poetry must have been immemorially ancient in the Indian empire: the invention of it is commonly ascribed to Bheret, a sage believed to have been inspired, who invented also a system of musick which bears his name; but this opinion of its origin is rendered very doubtful by the universal belief, that the first Sanscrit verse ever heard by mortals was pronounced in a burst of resentment by the great Válmic, who flourished in the silver age of the world, and was author of an Epick Poem on the war of his contemporary, Ráma, king of Ayódhyà; so that no drama in verse could have been represented before his time; and the Indians have a wild story, that the first regular play, on the same subject with the Rámáyana, was composed by Hanumat or Pávan, who commanded an army of Satyrs or Mountaineers in Ráma's expedition against Lancà: they add, that he engraved it on a smooth rock, which, being dissatisfied with his composition, he hurled into the sea; and that, many years after, a learned prince ordered expert divers to take impressions of the poem on wax, by which means the drama was in great measure restored; and my Pandit assures me that he is in possession of it. By whomsoever or in whatever age this species of entertainment was invented, it is very certain, that it was carried to great perfection in its kind, when Vicramáditya, who reigned in the first century before Christ, gave encouragement to poets, philologers, and mathematicians, at a time when the Britons were as unlettered and unpolished as the army of Hanumat: nine men of genius, commonly called the nine gems, attended his court, and were splendidly supported by his bounty; and Cálidás is unanimously allowed to have been the brightest of them. A modern epigram was lately reported to me, which does so much honour to the author of Sacontalá, that I cannot forbear exhibiting a literal version of it: "Poetry was the sportful daughter of Válmic, and, having been educated by Vyása, she chose Cálidás for her bridegroom after the manner of Viderbha: she was the mother of Amara, Sundar, Sanc'ha, Dhanic; but now, old and decrepit, her beauty faded and her unadorned feet slipping as she walks, in whose cottage does she disdain to take shelter?"

All the other works of our illustrious poet, the Shakespeare of India, that have yet come to my knowledge, are a second play, in five acts, entitled Urvasí; an heroic poem, or rather a series of poems in one book, on the Children of the Sun; another, with perfect unity of action, on the Birth of Cumára, god of war; two or three love tales in verse; and an excellent little work on Sanscrit Metre, precisely in the manner of Terentianus; but he is believed by some to have revised the works of Válmic and Vyása, and to have corrected the perfect editions of them which are now current: this at least is admitted by all, that he stands next in reputation to those venerable bards; and we must regret, that he has left only two dramatick poems, especially as the stories in his Raghuvansa would have supplied him with a number of excellent subjects. Some of his contemporaries, and other Hindû poets even to our own times, have composed so many tragedies, comedies, farces, and musical pieces, that the Indian theatre would fill as many volumes as that of any nation in ancient or modern Europe: all the Pandits assert that their plays are innumerable; and, on my first inquiries concerning them, I had notice of more than thirty, which they consider as the flower of their Nátacs, among which the Malignant Child, the Rape of Ushá, the Taming of Durvásas, the Seizure of the Lock, Málati and Mádhava, with five or six dramas on the adventures of their incarnate gods, are the most admired after those of Cálidás. They are all in verse, where the dialogue is elevated; and in prose, where it is familiar: the men of rank and learning are represented speaking pure Sanscrit, and the women Prácrit, which is little more than the language of the Bráhmens melted down by a delicate articulation to the softness of Italian; while the low persons of the drama speak the vulgar dialects of the several provinces which they are supposed to inhabit.

The play of Sacontalá must have been very popular when it was first represented; for the Indian empire was then in full vigour, and the national vanity must have been highly flattered by the magnificent introduction of those kings and heroes in whom the Hindûs gloried; the scenery must have been splendid and beautiful; and there is good reason to believe, that the court at Avanti was equal in brilliancy during the reign of Vicramáditya, to that of any monarch in any age or country. Dushmanta, the hero of the piece, appears in the chronological tables of the Bráhmens among the Children of the Moon, and in the twenty-first generation after the flood; so that, if we can at all rely on the chronology of the Hindûs, he was nearly contemporary with Obed, or Jesse; and Puru, his most celebrated ancestor, was the fifth in descent from Budha, or Mercury, who married, they say, a daughter of the pious king, whom Vishnu preserved in an ark from the universal deluge: his eldest son Bheret was the illustrious progenitor of Curu, from whom Pándu was lineally descended, and in whose family the Indian Apollo became incarnate; whence the poem, next in fame to the Rámáyan, is called Mahábhárat.

As to the machinery of the drama, it is taken from the system of mythology, which prevails to this day, and which it would require a large volume to explain; but we cannot help remarking, that the deities introduced in the Fatal Ring are clearly allegorical personages. Maríchi, the first production of Brahmá, or the Creative Power, signifies light, that subtil fluid which was created before its reservoir, the sun, as water was created before the sea; Casyap, the offspring of Maríchi, seems to be a personification of infinite space, comprehending innumerable worlds; and his children by Aditi, or his active power (unless Aditi means the primeval day, and Diti, his other wife, the night), are Indra, or the visible firmament, and the twelve Adityas, or suns, presiding over as many months.

On the characters and conduct of the play I shall offer no criticism; because I am convinced that the tastes of men differ as much as their sentiments and passions, and that, in feeling the beauties of art, as in smelling flowers, tasting fruits, viewing prospects, and hearing melody, every individual must be guided by his own sensations and the incommunicable associations of his own ideas. This only I may add, that if Sacontalá should ever be acted in India, where alone it could be acted with perfect knowledge of Indian dresses, manners, and scenery, the piece might easily be reduced to five acts of a moderate length, by throwing the third act into the second, and the sixth into the fifth; for it must be confessed that the whole of Dushmanta's conversation with his buffoon, and great part of his courtship in the hermitage, might be omitted without any injury to the drama.

It is my anxious wish that others may take the pains to learn Sanscrit, and may be persuaded to translate the works of Cálidás: I shall hardly again employ my leisure in a task so foreign to my professional (which are, in truth, my favourite) studies; and have no intention of translating any other book from any language except the Law Tract of Menu, and the new Digest of Indian and Arabian laws; but, to show, that the Bráhmens, at least, do not think polite literature incompatible with jurisprudence, I cannot avoid mentioning, that the venerable compiler of the Hindû Digest, who is now in his eighty-sixth year, has the whole play of Sacontalá by heart; as he proved when I last conversed with him, to my entire conviction. Lest however, I should hereafter seem to have changed a resolution which I mean to keep inviolate, I think it proper to say, that I have already translated four or five other books, and among them the Hitópadésa, which I undertook, merely as an exercise in learning Sanscrit, three years before I knew that Mr. Wilkins, without whose aid I should never have learnt it, had any thought of giving the same work to the publick.

Jones' translation took Europe by storm. It was in turn translated into virtually all the European languages including Icelandic, in some more than once during the nineteenth century, and some at fourth remove: from Latin to English to French to Italian. This enthusiastic acclamation for the play was also due to Georg Forster, who in 1791 published a German translation of the text by Jones. Forster had been interested in Tahiti, and his reading of Jones' translation led him to believe that there might have been a link between Tahitians and Indians. His fascination with the play arose from: " . . . the fact that the tenderest emotions of which the human heart is capable could have been as well expressed on the Ganges by dark-skinned people, as on the Rhine, the Tyber or the Ilissus by our white race."[111] Forster maintains that the child-like and unspoilt relationship, which the Hindu has with nature has been lost to the modern European who has to be reminded of it through Indian literature.[112]

Forster sent his translation to Goethe who praised it almost to excess, in spite of his otherwise contemptuous comments on the many-armed deities of Indian religion. His well-weathered verse on the play, an instant reaction, hardly bears repeating:

> Would'st thou the young year's blossoms and the fruits of its decline,
> And all by which the soul is charmed, enraptured, feasted, fed,
> Would'st thou the Earth and Heaven itself in one sole name combine?
> I name thee, O Sakuntala! and all at once is said.

Yet even later his comments, born of reflection in tranquillity, support his earlier enthusiasm, an enthusiasm which doubtless encouraged the play being highlighted by German Romanticism. In a letter to A.L. de Chezy in 1830, he wrote:

> . . . Only now do I grasp the extravagant impression that this work excited in me. Here the poet appears to us in his highest role, as a representative of the natural state, of the finest way of life, of the finest moral striving, of the most dignified majesty and the most earnest contemplation of God: at the same time however he remains lord and master of his creation; he can dare common and ridiculous opposites which nevertheless must be considered as necessary links in the whole organism . . .[113]

In each decade of the nineteenth century there was yet another translation in yet another language.[114] Not only was the play read and occasionally performed, but it also provided the story for a number of minor operas and ballets such as Theophile Gautier's ballet pantomime, *Sacountala,* with music by Ernest Reyer in 1858, or the opera by Franco Alfano in 1921. Franz Schubert's opera of 1820 remained incomplete and is now lost. Camille Claudel is said to have been deeply moved by the play. Both in France and in Russia it was taken up by the Symbolists, and it had a magnetic attraction for the poets of the European Romantic movement. If the English Romantic poets drew inspiration from the writings of William Jones, German Romanticism of the nineteenth century saw a new vision in this play. Translations of the *Mahābhārata* version of the narrative were also known through the publication of these in 1794 by Charles Wilkins in English, and by Friedrich Schlegel in German, in 1808. But these may have been viewed as too plain in comparison with the play.

Romanticism was predominant in European literature and the arts during the late eighteenth and nineteenth centuries. It was in part a reaction to the neo-classicism of the previous period, which had enthused over the discovery of the Graeco-Roman tradition and had submitted to the dictates of Aristotle and Horace, in particular in literary theory. It was also a response to the "discovery" of the Orient, described as the Oriental Renaiassance. The Śakuntalā of the play became the ideal Indian woman encapsulating the beauty of womankind, but more than that, her portrayal as the child of nature was what attracted German Romanticism most. The identification of the heroine with nature was an appropriate counter to the crafted women of neo-classicism.

Interest in Greek drama had preceded this new enthusiasm. Part of the earlier Greek Renaissance, it was avidly discussed in literary and philosophical studies by the nineteenth century. Goethe, for example, was reading Greek tragedy and was much taken, as were others, with the *Antigone* of Sophocles, at the same time that he was ecstatic about Śakuntalā. Quite how a romantic comedy was juxtaposed with a tragedy of the dimensions of *Antigone*, and both treated with enthusiastic admiration, is rather puzzling. That they encapsulated two opposite moods may be part of the explanation. Holderlin, Hegel and Schelling wrote extensively on *Antigone,* and for A.W. von Schlegel it epitomised high morality and absolute purity.[115]

Romanticism preferred the less orderly aspect of the Graeco-Roman past and looked for the exotic, the unusual, the irrational, the emotional and the imaginative as against the typical, the rational and the real. The availability of literature from the "Orient" revealed another world. It was a move away from the known European civilisation to the imagined fantasies of societies outside Europe, and from a time long past. Folk tales, fairy tales, poetry from various parts of the world and mythology contributed to its perception of what literature is about. Novalis sums it up in his statement:

> The world must be romanticised. In giving the usual a noble sense, the ordinary a mysterious experience, the well-known the dignity of the unknown, the temporal a perennial aura, I am romanticising.[116]

The creation of what has been called the ideal of India in German Romanticism was also conditioned by a simmering of ideas rooted in early Greek views of India, and drawn upon in European writings on India of the fifteenth century and after.[117] Throughout the earlier centuries, Greek and Latin authors had nurtured stories of the supposed conversations between Alexander of Macedon and the "gymnosophists" of India—by which was meant *brāhmaṇas,* Buddhists, ascetics, philosophers and a variety of religious teachers. They were thought to have explained the essentials of Indian philosophy—metempsychosis, non-duality, the unity of man and nature, and the meaning of renunciation—to Alexander or to later Greek visitors. They became central to the ideas of the neo-Platonists, who believed that much that was essentially an alternative to Judaeo-Christian and mainstream European thought, was derived from Indian sources. The articles of William Jones gave some support to the identity of *Vedānta* with

Pythagorian and Platonic philosophies, and endorsed its importance in Indian philosophy, encouraging comparative studies of language and religion. These theories now interested the Romantics. The departure from dependence on such views for knowledge about Indian thought, came with the possibility of studying Sanskrit texts in the original in Europe, rather than relying on the hearsay of earlier writers. That such readings would be coloured by European perceptions of the texts was not recognised.

Romanticism therefore was not merely a reaction to neo-classicism; it was also a part of the parallel tradition which continued to question ideas and perspectives based on Judaeo-Christian thought and the Enlightenment. One ancestral strand in Romanticism, apart from many others, was perhaps the persistence of neo-Platonism. This can be seen in the earlier fascination for Roman culture giving way to the Greek, which was thought to be closer to the ideals of Romanticism. Familiarity with Greek culture inevitably encouraged a further investigation of the debates around Pythagoras and Plato and their possible indebtedness to Indian thought, a debate which is also apparent among the English Romantic poets.

J.G. von Herder referred to the Kālidāsa play as a rare masterpiece, which challenged Aristotle's theories and could be used to question the hold of the classical literary canon in European writing. For him it was beyond history and pointed to a new vision. Śakuntalā to his mind represented the fairy-tale atmosphere of the child-like Indian . . . the flower fantasy which (like the Indians themselves) breathes the blissful peace of paradise. Śakuntalā is compared to a flower unfolding its innocence in a holy retreat.[118] He adds that the play has yielded more insight into the true and living concepts of the Indians' way of thought than have all the Upanekats (*Upaniṣads*) and Bhagavȧdams.[119] Herder, in his Foreword to the second edition of the Forster translation published in 1803, defines the image of India as a contact of spirits, where everything is touched gently and tenderly, and perhaps to that extent is an illusion.[120]

The brothers Frederick and August Wilhelm von Schlegel were initially both enthusiasts of Sanskrit and of things Indian. This is apparent from their statements in setting forth the principles of German Romanticism in 1798-1800. The unity of poetry and mythology so central to Romanticism was said to be characteristic of Sanskrit literature which, they maintained, embedded the childhood of mankind in its sensuality. The hermitage of Kaṇva is the idyllic settlement, even as Kashmir is the earthly paradise. However, Frederick Schlegel's enthusiasm for the play gradually receded and he later thought the characters flat, and the dialogue and plot, slow and dull. He intended to translate the epic version of the story even though, in comparing it to the play, he described it as "an Egyptian pyramid to a small elegant miniature".[121] Nevertheless, even for him there was a child-like innocence of the golden age associated with Indians, the noblest people of antiquity.

A major figure of German Romanticism, F. von Hardenberg, or Novalis, was important to the early phase of the movement when the return to antiquity and its values was regarded as essential to the construction of culture. For him, Sanskrit held the secrets of the universe, and among the mysteries he invoked was the symbolism of the Blaue Blume—the Blue Flower, which drew into itself many ideas and was associated with India.[122] Possibly, somewhere, he linked it to the blue lotus, the *nīla kamala*, which is referred to in passing in the play. Endorsing the image of Śakuntalā as an icon of German Romanticism, led him to call his fiancée, Sakontala!

By contrast, the English Romantic poets were less overtly enthusiastic about Kālidāsa and the literature of the Sanskrit classics, although they drew in varying degrees from Orientalist scholarship, and occasionally from reading some Indian literature in translation. Most were familiar with what William Jones had written, and admired him for revealing a new civilisation which gave direction to some of the ideas they were formulating. Jones' hymns to various

Hindu deities were part of this revelation. It is thought that Coleridge's references to the god who floats upon the lotus in "The Triumph of Loyalty", were to Viṣṇu. "Kublai Khan" may also have been influenced by Jones' essay on Tartary.[123] The debate on whether Pythagoras received his ideas from Indian philosophers, and the close parallels between neo-Platonism and *Vedānta* were frequently discussed. Shelley was reading Jones, among others, on India and the impact of this reading has been traced in "Prometheus Unbound" as also in "Queen Mab". The Indian background to Robert Southey's poem, "The Curse of Kehama" reflects the same source.[124] These poets may well have read the translation of the play but do not refer to it directly.

A review of the later translation of the play (by Monier Williams) which appeared in *The Edinburgh Review* of July 1858, touches on many of these perceptions.[125] The author of the review describes dramatic poetry as the peculiar glory of the Indo-Teutonic race. He goes on to say that India was a nation of dreaming mystics, such as those met by Alexander's companions, and Kaṇva's *āśrama* is the kind of grove where Alexander discovered the gymnosophists. The seventh Act of the play, he writes, can be compared to Southey's poem on Kehama. The enterprising reviewer was attempting to give some historicity to the play, a small departure from the purely Romanticist reaction.

Blackwoods Edinburgh Magazine, although reflecting Victorian England, speaks of the play with a greater Romanticism:

> . . . It is delightful to sink away into those green and noiseless sanctuaries, to look on the brahmins as they pass their whole lives in silent and reverential adoration—to observe virgins playing with the antelopes and bright-plumaged birds among those gorgeous woods—and, as the scene shifts, to find ourselves amid the old

> magnificence of oriental cities, or wafted on the chariot of some deity up to the palaces of the sky . . .

The reference to virgins playing with antelopes is of course very evocative of medieval European Romance literature, where such well-known themes as the virgin with a unicorn run through it like a thread, sometimes even becoming the central theme, as in the magnificent tapestries associated with the monastery at Cluny. There was a search for parallels from the European past, the argument being that manifestations of Indian culture are reminiscent of the infancy of Europe.

Acclamation for the play by German Romanticism has other, perhaps not so tangential, aspects. The projection of Śakuntalā as nature's child would have been reminiscent of other children of nature, such as the nymphs of Greek literature, water spirits and fertility spirits who inhabited springs, woodlands and hills, and had loving, although never permanent relationships with men. Seeing nymphs in *apsarās* made the *apsarās* less alien. Where the original text mentions *ākāśe*/a voice from the air, it gets translated as invisible wood-nymphs and sylvan goddesses. The departure of Śakuntalā for the court is a farewell to the innocent joys of a life in nature, and the arrival of years of incomprehensible tribulations associated with the mores of life at the court.

It has been said that the Oriental Renaissance in its initial phase, was the check-mating of Cartesian absolutism, although the western image of India altered from incredulous amazement to condescending veneration.[126] It can be argued that the insistence on seeing a Sanskrit classic as a eulogy on nature also carries some racist undertones in the nineteenth century. Those close to nature were the primitive peoples—primitive in the nineteenth century sense of being at the start of the evolutionary scale, a notion which has in it an element of contempt. The reference to child-like Indians was not entirely complimentary. Max Müller's description of India consisting of idyllic village communities, where people were gentle and passive and spent their time meditating,[127] evokes the *āśrama* of Kaṇva. Supplementing this was the eroticism of the play, where eroticism was also linked to the primitive. The language was beautiful, but the erotic thoughts which it expressed were less noble. This reflected the weakness of Indian civilisation. It was more appropriate therefore to delete such passages. If Indian society, in its closeness to Nature, represented the infancy of human society as many thought it did, then there would also be support for the idea that the present of India was similar to the lost, utopian past of Europe.

The Romanticist celebrations of human creativity have, in various ways, set up an oppositional parallel to positivist, materialist, teleological and other universalist schemes.[128] Where the first was attempting to understand the world, the second was concerned with explaining it. But there were points of overlap—even Enlightenment rationalism was neither unified nor uncontested—conditioned partly by the way in which culture, language and society were linked.

For Herder and Schlegel, the interlocking of language and culture was crucial to the human being, for language endows humans with consciousness. This combination is best seen in the dynamic interaction of language and culture as in Sanskrit, German and Celtic, all vibrant languages. The mechanical, non-dynamic languages were English and Latin.[129] This made the Indian image important to the argument. Such ideas also fell happily into place in the racial theories of the nineteenth century. Herder argued for the concept of the *volk*/the people, and the uniqueness of each *volkgeist*/spirit of the people which, like fundamental truths, could not be analysed through rational enquiry. The concept of the *volk*, with its roots in primitive beginnings and a closeness to nature remained vague, but could be borrowed by a variety of later movements searching for identity and descent. German Romanticism is thus believed to have provided some germinal ideas to later theories of cultural nationalism.[130]

Such views coincided with a search for a new experience, different from that of Europe, and the hope that the Oriental Renaissance would reveal other dimensions as yet not experienced, as had the earlier Greek Renaissance.[131] The Oriental Renaissance was viewed from two different perspectives. The first was the belief that it would reveal connections with the ancient past of Europe. The sons of Noah were said to have migrated in diverse directions, including the Orient, and the theory of such migrations was sought to be strengthened by the idea of a monogenesis of languages, duly encouraged by the new-found theories of an ancestral Indo-European language. There was in this argument a hint of arrogance, that all cultures could ultimately be traced back to the Bible. The second was the understanding that this Renaissance would lead to new experiences of mind and emotion, vastly different from those familiar to Europe—a hope which still surfaces periodically in western societies. The intensity of this expectation signified an escape from what was perceived as the degeneration in the quality of life in Europe, largely because of industrialisation.

This can be seen in the interest which the play evoked in Russia. Given the cultural proximity of Russia to France and Germany in the nineteenth century, it was expected that the wave of enthusiasm for Śakuntalā in Europe would reach Russia, even if it took its own course there. As early as 1792, N.M.Karamzin translated sections of the play from German into Russian, declaring Kālidāsa to be as great a poet as Homer. Innumerable poems in Russian, praising Śakuntalā, were based on European translations of the text, and in 1858, M. Petipa, one of the founders of Russian ballet, wrote a libretto for an opera on the theme. Of the many translations in the late nineteenth century, that of K. Balmont was performed in the new experimental theatre of A. Tairov in 1914, and was so well-received that

Balmont was called upon to lecture widely on Kālidāsa. The Indological connection was that Balmont had spent time with Sylvain Levi in Paris, the French Indologist who had written a major work on the theatre in India, and with the Russian Indologist, S.F. Oldenberg, who had endorsed the translations. Tairov's experimental theatre was associated with new methods of presentation and acting, such as those of Stanislavsky, and it is interesting that the Kālidāsa play was among its initial ventures.

These are the bare bones of an activity which was deeply interlinked with the poets of Romanticism and Symbolism. For the latter, sound in language was primary and had layers of meaning, thus unknowingly evoking some of the ideas discussed in earlier Indian literary theory. These were also the circles interested in theosophy. Balmont not only translated plays, but some of his own poetry was on *māyā* and *nirvāṇa* —themes from Indian thought and fashionable at the time. He also translated poems by Yeats who, in his early years, was attracted to theosophical ideas. There were therefore a number of links between Indian and European writers and thinkers in the early twentieth century, and Śakuntalā is not unimportant as a part of these.

The play as drama was taken more seriously in Europe than in England, the intervention of a colonial relationship perhaps preventing enthusiasm. In 1919, an abridged version was performed by the Indian Art and Dramatic Society at the Winter Garden Theatre in London for two matinee shows, and the lead role was taken by Sybil Thorndike. This must have been something of a momentous, if momentary, event for the London stage. In 1920 this abridged and adapted version by Laurence Binyon and K.N. Dasgupta was published, but had few major performances.[132]

Enthusiastic translations of the play into various European languages did not preclude an inability to grasp the perspective of Sanskrit *kāvya* and of Kālidāsa.[133]

Aristotelian poetics were debated, but there was no interest in investigating theories of poetics relating to classical Sanskrit literature. The translations amended the text in accordance with literary norms in the languages of translation. Humour is of course notoriously difficult to translate and therefore tends to be ignored. The Indian concept of drama was very different from that of Aristotle. The erotic becomes a barrier and moral homilies, both spoken and unspoken, enter the language of the translation. The mysterious bond between pleasure and suffering was part of the inheritence of Romantic and Decadent sensitivities. This should have resulted in unquestioning approval of the play but it is possible that its erotic sensibility, coming from an alien culture, reduced its acceptability. This would have placed it outside what has been seen as a trend in nineteenth century European literature—introducing an erotic sensibility which becomes, according to one view, the mainspring of works of the imagination.[134]

The projection of the Indian world as one which could host the fantasies of Europe declined in the late nineteenth century, with the more aggressive European relationship with the world in the form of Imperialism, and of theories of race and Social Darwinism. But the image created by the Romantics, with all its ambiguities, remained an undertone, nurtured on memories of the earlier reception. In a sense, the Kālidāsa play had performed its function and now, in the post-Romantic period had been relegated to a curiosity of European Romanticism. It was at this point, however, that it became important to the emergent Indian middle-class in the latter half of the nineteenth century in India.

7. Translation: colonial views

To return to the British, and India. Jones' enthusiasm was of course not shared by the English Utilitarians who had always found him too sympathetic to Indian culture. James Mill, whose endorsement of Utilitarian philosophy led him to being extremely critical of the Indian past, was one of those for whom Sanskrit literature was the literature of a self-indulgent society.[135] It is only nations in their infancy that produce literature in praise of the pastoral, for such societies are fettered by despots; they can only indulge in light romances, rather than analyse their condition. The *gāndharva* marriage, the curse of Durvāsas and the authority of the *brāhmaṇas* were all signs of Indian degradation.[136] Irrationality was, for Mill, a characteristic of Indian civilisation. Such a perception was far removed from the enthusiastic reading of Śakuntalā as the child of nature. On the contrary, it was a statement of culture having superceded nature, if it is viewed in terms of their juxtaposition.

More ambiguous than Mill were the attitudes of other scholars working as administrators in India. It was necessary, they felt, for those who governed India to be familiar with Indian culture as, indeed, it had been the policy of earlier scholar-administrators to educate Europe about India. It was also the policy to rediscover the Indian past for the Indian and to revive Indian culture as defined by Orientalist scholarship. The object was to not only make the emergent middle-class Indian aware of this culture, but to imprint on his mind the interpretation given to it by Orientalist scholarship. This was another strategy of control.[137] While the pastoral beauty and lyrical charm of the play were appreciated, the unabridged play was not approved of as a text for teaching Sanskrit in schools and colleges, because it was said to support immorality and impurity.[138]

This is demonstrated in the next major translation of the play into English, that of Monier-Williams published in 1855, entitled *Śakoontalá or The Lost Ring*. Monier-Williams was later associated with the Boden Chair at Oxford and was Professor of Sanskrit at Haileybury College, where those who were to be posted out to administer India were being trained. His was clearly an influential point of view. Jones' translation, according to Monier-Williams, was based on the only available manuscript at the time, but it was a corrupt manuscript and the translation was lacking in accuracy. Monier-Williams used the Devanāgari manuscript instead of Bengali, since he thought it was older and less tampered with, and the erotic passages were fewer. His motivation for a new translation was the thought that the greatness of Britain, now ruling an Indian empire, required that the British be conversant with literature which epitomised Hindu custom and culture—such as this play by Kālidāsa.

Apart from the fact that this was good copy for his own translation, one wonders whether he really thought that most Indians in the past lived either in *āśramas* or in royal courts. The play was seen as a vignette on Indian or rather, Hindu, life. That there was a gap of at least fifteen hundred years between the time of the original writing and these translations did not seem to matter, for it was believed that Indian society was static and had not registered much change since early times.

Introduction to Śakoontalá or The Lost Ring

Only seventy years have elapsed since the great English Orientalist, Sir William Jones, astonished the learned world

Monier-Williams, *Śakoontalá*, London: 1856, Introduction.

by the discovery of a Sanskṛit Dramatic Literature. He has himself given us the history of this discovery. It appears that, on his arrival in Bengal, he was very solicitous to procure access to certain books called Nāṭaks, of which he had read in one of the 'Lettres Édifiantes et Curieuses,' written by the Jesuit Missionaries of China. But, although he sought information by consulting both Bráhmans and Europeans, he was wholly unable for some time to satisfy his curiosity as to the nature of these books. It was reported to him that they were not histories, as he had hoped, but that they abounded with fables, and consisted of conversations in prose and verse held before ancient Rájás, in their public assemblies. Others, again, asserted that they were discourses on dancing, music, and poetry. At length, a sensible Bràhman, conversant with European manners, removed all his doubts, and gave him no less delight than surprise, by telling him that the English nation had compositions of the same sort, which were publicly represented at Calcutta in the cold season, and bore the name of Plays. The same Bráhman, when asked which of these Nāṭaks was most universally esteemed, answered without hesitation, 'Śakoontalá.'

It may readily be imagined with what interest the keen Orientalist received this communication; with what rapidity he followed up the clue; and, when at length his zeal was rewarded by actual possession of a MS. copy of one of these dramas, with what avidity he proceeded to explore the treasures which, for eighteen hundred years, had remained as unknown to the European world as the gold-fields of Australia. Indeed, it has now been ascertained that the antiquity of some of the Sanskṛit dramas thus brought to light, extends back to a still more remote period than the commencement of the Christian era.

The earliest with which we are acquainted, the 'Toy-cart,' translated by Professor H.H. Wilson, is attributed to a regal author, King Śúdraka, whose reign is generally fixed in the second century B.C., and it is not improbable that others, the names of which only have been preserved, may belong to a previous century. Considering that the nations of Europe can scarcely be said to have possessed a dramatic literature before the fourteenth or fifteenth century of the present era, the great age of the Hindú plays would of itself be a most interesting and attractive circumstance, even if their poetical merit were not of a very high order. But when to the antiquity of these productions is added their extreme beauty and excellence as literary compositions, and when we also take into account their value as representations of the early condition of Hindú society—which, notwithstanding the lapse of two thousand years, has in many particulars obeyed the law of unchangeableness ever stamped on the manners and customs of the East—we are led to wonder that the study of the Indian drama has not commended itself in a greater degree to the attention of Europeans, and especially of Englishmen. The English student, at least, is bound by considerations of duty, as well as curiosity, to make himself acquainted with a subject which illustrates and explains the condition of the millions of Hindús who owe allegiance to his own Sovereign and are governed by English laws.

Of all Indian dramatists, and indeed of all Indian poets, the most celebrated is Kálidása, the writer of the present play. He comes next in date to the author of the 'Toy-cart'; and although little is known of the circumstances of his life, yet there is satisfactory evidence to prove that he lived in the time of King Vikramáditya I., whose capital was Ujjayiní, now Oujein (a sacred and very ancient city situated to the north-east of Gujarát), and who flourished in the middle of the century preceding the commencement of our era.

From the absence of historical literature in India, our knowledge of the state of Hindústán between the incursion of Alexander and the Muhammadan conquest is very slight. But it is ascertained with tolerable accuracy that, after the invasion of the kingdoms of Bactria and Afghánistán, the Tartars or Scythians (called by the Hindús 'Śakas') overran the north-western provinces of India, and retained possession of them till the reign of Vikramáditya. This great monarch succeeded in driving back the barbaric hordes beyond the Indus, and so consolidated his empire that his dominion extended over the whole of Northern Hindústán. His name is even now cherished among the Hindús with pride and affection, and the date of his victory over the

Scythians, B.C. 56, is the starting point of the Samvat era, from which they still continue to count. There is good authority for affirming that the reign of Vikramáditya I. was equal in brilliancy to that of any monarch in any age or country. He was a liberal patron of science and literature, and gave the most splendid encouragement to poets, philologists, astronomers, and mathematicians. Nine illustrious men of genius adorned his court, and were supported by his bounty. They were called the 'Nine Gems'; and Kálidása is by general consent allowed to have been the brightest of the nine. To him (as to another celebrated Indian Dramatist, Bhavabhúti, who flourished in the eighth century) only three plays are attributed; and of these the 'Śakoontalá' (here translated) has acquired the greatest celebrity.

Indeed, the popularity of this play with the natives of India exceeds that of any other dramatic, and probably of any other poetical composition. But it is not in India alone that the 'Śakoontalá' is known and admired. Its excellence is now recognized in every literary circle throughout the continent of Europe; and its beauties, if not yet universally known and appreciated, are at least acknowledged by many learned men in every country of the civilized world. The four well-known lines of Goethe, so often quoted in relation to the Indian drama, may here be repeated:

> *"Willst du die Blüthe des frühen, die Früchte des spateren Jahres,*
> *Willst du was reizt und etzückt, willst du was sättigt und nahrt,*
> *Willst du den Himmel, die Erde, mit einem Namen begreifen:*
> *Nenn' ich Sakontàlà, Dich, und so ist Alles gesagt."*

> Wouldst thou the young year's blossoms and the fruits of its decline,
> And all by which the soul is charmed, enraptured, feasted, fed?
> Wouldst thou the earth and heaven itself in one sole name combine?
> I name thee, O Śakoontalá! and all at once is said.

Augustus William von Schlegel, in his first Lecture on Dramatic Literature, says: "Among the Indians, the people from whom perhaps all the cultivation of the human race has been derived, plays were known long before they could have experienced any foreign influence. It has lately been made known in Europe that they have a rich dramatic literature, which ascends back for more than two thousand years. The only specimen of their plays (Náṭaks) hitherto known to us is the delightful 'Śakoontalá,' which, notwithstanding the colouring of a foreign clime, bears in its general structure a striking resemblance to our romantic drama."

Alexander von Humboldt, in treating of Indian poetry, observes: "Kálidása, the celebrated author of the 'Śakoontalá,' is a masterly describer of the influence which Nature exercises upon the minds of lovers. This great poet flourished at the splendid court of Vikramáditya, and was, therefore, contemporary with Virgil and Horace. Tenderness in the expression of feeling, and richness of creative fancy, have assigned to him his lofty place among the poets of all nations."

These considerations induced me, in 1853, to compile and publish a correct edition of the text of the 'Śakoontalá' from various original MSS., with English translations of the metrical passages, and explanatory notes, being in fact the only edition ever published in this country. To the notes of that edition I must refer all students of Sanskrit literature who desire a close and literal translation of the present drama. In the preface I pledged myself at some future time to present the English public with a *free* translation of the whole play. That pledge is here redeemed, and the following pages contain the first English translation, in prose and verse, of the true and pure version of the most celebrated drama of the Shakspere of India.

The need felt by the British public for some such translation as I have here offered can scarcely be questioned. A great people, who, through their empire in India, command the destinies of the Eastern world, ought surely to be conversant with the most popular of Indian dramas, in which the customs of the Hindús, their opinions, prejudices, and fables, their religious rites, daily occupations and amusements, are reflected as in a mirror. Nor is the prose translation of Sir W. Jones (excellent though it be) adapted to meet the requirements of the Englishman who, unacquainted with Sanskṛit, desires an accurate representation of the original text, and notes to explain unintelligible allusions. That translation was unfortunately made from modern and corrupt manuscripts (the best that could then be procured), in which the bold and nervous phraseology of Kálidása has been weakened, his delicate expressions of refined love clothed in a meretricious dress, and his ideas, grand in their simplicity, diluted by repetition or amplification. It is, moreover, altogether unfurnished with explanatory annotations. The text of my edition, on the contrary, represents the old and pure version of the drama, and from that text the present translation has been made; while abundant notes have been added, sufficient to answer the exigencies of the non-oriental scholar. Moreover, the metrical portions of the play have, for the first time, been rendered into verse.

It may be remarked that in every Sanskṛit play the women and inferior characters speak a kind of provincial Sanskṛit or *patois* called Prákṛit—bearing the same relation to Sanskṛit that Italian bears to Latin, or that the spoken Latin of the age of Cicero bore to the highly polished Latin in which he delivered his Orations. Even the heroine of the drama is made to speak in the vulgar dialect. The hero, on the other hand, and all the higher male characters, speak in Sanskṛit; and, as if to invest them with greater dignity, half of what they say is in verse. Indeed the prose part of their speeches is often very commonplace, being only introductory to the lofty sentiment of the poetry that follows. Thus, if the whole composition be compared to a web, the prose will correspond to the warp, or that part which is extended lengthwise in the loom, while the metrical portion will answer to the cross-threads which constitute the woof. The original verses are written in a great variety of Sanskṛit metres. For example, the first thirty-four verses of 'Śakoontalá' exhibit eleven different varieties of metre. No metrical system in English could give any idea of the almost infinite resources of the Sanskṛit in this respect. Blank verse has therefore been employed, as more in unison with the character of our own dramatic writings, and rhyming stanzas have only been admitted when the subject-matter seemed to call for such a change. Perhaps the chief consideration that induced me to adopt this mode of metrical translation was, that the free and unfettered character of the verse enabled me to preserve more of the freshness and vigour of the original. If the poetical ideas of Kálidása have not been expressed in language as musical as his own, I have at least done my best to avoid diluting them by paraphrastic circumlocutions or additions. If the English verses are prosaic, I have the satisfaction of knowing that by resisting the allurements of rhyme, I have done all in my power to avoid substituting a fictitious and meagre poem of my own for the grand, yet simple and chaste creation of Kálidása. The unrestricted liberty of employing hypermetrical lines of eleven syllables, sanctioned by the highest authority in dramatic composition, has, I think, facilitated the attainment of this object. One of our own poets has said in relation to such lines, 'Let it be remembered that they supply us with another cadence; that they add, as it were, a string to the instrument; and—by enabling the poet to relax at pleasure, to rise and fall with his subject—contribute what is most wanted, compass and variety. They are nearest to the flow of an unstudied eloquence, and should therefore be used in the drama.' Shakspere does not scruple to avail himself of this license four or five times in succession, as in the well-known passage beginning—

"To be or not to be, that is the question;"

and even Milton uses the same freedom once or twice in every page.

The poetical merit of Kálidása's 'Śakoontalá' is so universally admitted that any remarks on this head would be superfluous. I will merely observe that, in the opinion of learned natives, the Fourth Act, which describes the departure of Śakoontalá from the hermitage, contains the most obvious beauties; and that no one can read this act, nor indeed any part of the play, without being struck with the richness and elevation of its author's genius, the exuberance and glow of his fancy, his ardent love of the beautiful, his deep sympathy with Nature and Nature's loveliest scenes, his profound knowledge of the human heart, his delicate appreciation of its most refined feelings, his familiarity with its conflicting sentiments and emotions. But in proportion to the acknowledged excellence of Kálidása's composition, and in proportion to my own increasing admiration of its beauties, is the diffidence I feel lest I may have failed to infuse any of the poetry of the original into the present version. Translation of poetry must, at the best, resemble the process of pouring a highly volatile and evanescent spirit from one receptacle into another. The original fluid will always suffer a certain amount of waste and evaporation.

The English reader, remembering that the author of the 'Śakoontalá' lived in the century preceding the Christian era, will at least be inclined to wonder at the analogies which it offers to our own dramatic composition of fifteen or sixteen centuries later. The dexterity with which the plot is arranged and conducted, the ingenuity with which the incidents are connected, the skill with which the characters are delineated and contrasted with each other, the boldness and felicity of the diction; would scarcely be unworthy of the great dramatists of modern times. Nor does the parallel fail in the management of the business of the stage, in minute directions to the actors, and various scenic artifices. The asides and aparts, the exits and the entrances, the manner, attitude, and gait of the speakers, the tone of voice with which they are to deliver themselves, the tears, the smiles, and the laughter, are as regularly indicated as in a modern drama.

In reference to the constitution and structure of the play here translated, a few general remarks on the dramatic system of the Hindús may not be inappropriate.

Dramatic poetry is said to have been invented by the sage Bharata, who lived at a very remote period of Indian history, and was the author of a system of music. The drama of these early times was probably nothing more than a species of rude pantomime, in which music and dancing were accompanied by mute gesticulation. There is little trace of real dramatic dialogue until the second century B.C., and the art of theatrical representation was not brought to perfection till the era of Vikramáditya. In India, as in Greece, scenic entertainments took place at religious festivals, and on solemn public occasions. Kálidása's 'Śakoontalá' seems to have been acted at the commencement of the summer season—a period peculiarly sacred to Káma-deva, the Indian god of Love. We are told that it was enacted before an audience 'consisting chiefly of men of education and discernment.' As the greater part of every play was written in Sanskṛit, which, although spoken in some portion of India at a remote period, was certainly not the vernacular language of the country at the time when the Hindú dramas were performed, few spectators would be present who were not of the learned and educated classes. This circumstance is in accordance with the constitution of Hindú society, whereby the productions of literature, as well as the offices of state, were reserved for the privileged castes.

Every play opens with a prologue, or, to speak more correctly, an introduction, designed to prepare the way for the entrance of the *dramatis personae.* The prologue commences with a benediction or prayer (pronounced by a Bráhman, or if the stage-manager happened to be of the Bráhmanical caste, by the manager himself), in which the poet invokes the favour of the national deity in behalf of the audience. The blessing is generally followed by a dialogue between the manager and one or two of the actors, in which an account is given of the author of the drama, a complimentary tribute is paid to the critical acumen of the spectators, and such a reference is made to past occurrences or present circumstances as may be necessary for the elucidation of the plot. At the conclusion of the prologue; the manager, by some abrupt exclamation, adroitly introduces one of the dramatic personages, and the real performance commences.

The play, being thus opened, is carried forward in scenes and acts; each scene being marked by the entrance of one character and the exit of another, as in the French drama. The *dramatis personae* were divided into three classes—the inferior characters (*nicha*), who were said to speak Prákṛit in a monotonous unemphatic tone of voice (*anudáttoktyá*); the middling (*madhyama*), and the superior (*pradhàna*), who were said to speak Sanskṛit with accent, emphasis, and expression (*udáttoktyá*). In general, the stage is never left vacant till the end of an act, nor does any change of locality take place until then. The commencement of a new act is often marked, like the commencement of the piece, by an introductory monologue or dialogue spoken by one or more of the *dramatis personae,* and called Vishkambha or Praveśaka. In this scene, allusion is frequently made to events supposed to have occurred in the interval of the acts, and the audience is the better prepared to take up the thread of the story, which is then skilfully carried on to the concluding scene. The piece closes, as it began, with a prayer for national plenty and prosperity, addressed to the favourite deity, and spoken by one of the principal personages of the drama.

Although, in the conduct of the plot, and the delineation of character, the Hindú dramatists show considerable skill, yet they do not appear to have been remarkable for much fertility of invention. Love, according to Hindú notions, is the subject of most of their dramas. The hero, who is generally a king, and already the husband of a wife or wives (for a wife or two more or less is no incumbrance in Indian plays), is suddenly smitten with the charms of a lovely woman, sometimes a nymph, or, as in the case of Śakoontalá, the daughter of a nymph by a mortal father. The heroine is required to be equally impressible, and the first tender glance from the hero's eye reaches her heart. With true feminine delicacy, however, she locks the secret of her passion in her own breast, and by her coyness and reserve keeps her lover for a long period in the agonies of suspense. The hero, being reduced to a proper state of desperation, is harassed by other difficulties. Either the celestial nature of the nymph is in the way of their union, or he doubts the legality of the match, or he fears his own unworthiness, or he is hampered, by the angry jealousy of a previous wife. In short, doubts, obstacles and delays make great havoc of both hero and heroine. They give way to melancholy, indulge in amorous rhapsodies, and become very emaciated. So far, it must be confessed, the story is decidedly dull, and its pathos, notwithstanding the occasional grandeur and beauty of the imagery, often verges on the ridiculous. But, by way of relief, an element of life is generally introduced in the character of the Vidúshaka, or Jester, who is the constant companion of the hero; and in the young maidens, who are the confidential friends of the heroine, and soon become possessed of her secret. By a curious regulation, the Jester is always a Bráhman, and therefore of a caste superior to the king himself; yet his business is to excite mirth by being ridiculous in person, age, and attire. He is represented as grey-haired, hump-backed, lame, and hideously ugly. In fact, he is a species of buffoon, who is allowed full liberty of speech, being himself a universal butt. His attempts at wit, which are rarely very successful, and his allusions to the pleasures of the table, of which he is a confessed votary, are absurdly contrasted with the sententious solemnity of the despairing hero, crossed in the prosecution of his love-suit. His clumsy interference in the intrigues of his friend only serves to augment his difficulties, and occasions many an awkward dilemma. On the other hand, the shrewdness of the heroine's confidantes never seems to fail them under the most trying circumstances; while their sly jokes and innuendos, their love of fun, their girlish sympathy with the progress of the love-affair, their warm affection for their friend, heighten the interest of the plot, and contribute not a little to vary its monotony.

Fortunately, in the 'Śakoontalá,' the story is diversified and the interest well sustained by a chain of stirring incidents. The first link of the chain, however, does not commence until the Fourth Act, when the union of the heroine with King Dushyanta, and her acceptance of the marriage ring as a token of recognition, are supposed to have taken place. Then follows the King's departure and temporary desertion of his bride; the curse pronounced on Śakoontalá by the choleric Sage; the monarch's consequent loss of memory; the bride's journey to the palace of her husband; the mysterious disappearance of the marriage token; the public repudiation of Śakoontalá; her miraculous assumption to a celestial asylum; the unexpected discovery of the ring by a poor fisherman; the King's agony on recovering his recollection; his aërial voyage in the car of Indra; his strange meeting with the refractory child in the groves of Kaśyapa; the boy's battle with the young lion; the search for the amulet, by which the King is proved to be his father; the return of Śakoontalá, and the happy re-union of the lovers;—all these form a connected series of moving and interesting incidents. The feelings of the audience are wrought up to a pitch of great intensity; and whatever emotions of terror, grief, or pity, may have been excited, are properly tranquilized by the happy termination of the story. Indeed, if a calamitous conclusion be necessary to constitute a tragedy, the Hindú dramas are never tragedies. They are mixed compositions, in which joy and sorrow, happiness and misery, are woven in a mingled web,—tragicomic representations, in which good and evil, right and wrong, truth and falsehood, are allowed to blend in confusion during the first acts of the drama. But, in the last act, harmony is always restored, order succeeds to disorder, tranquility to agitation; and the mind of the spectator, no longer perplexed by the apparent ascendancy of evil, is soothed, and purified, and made to acquiesce in the moral lesson deducible from the plot.

The play of 'Śakoontalá,' as Sir W. Jones observes, must have been very popular when it was first performed. The Indian empire was then in its palmy days, and the vanity of the natives would be highly flattered by the introduction of those kings and heroes who were supposed to have laid the foundation of its greatness and magnificence, and whose names were connected with all that was sacred and holy in their religion. Dushyanta, the hero of the drama, according to Indian legends, was one of the descendants of the Moon, or, in other words, belonged to the Lunar dynasty of Indian princes; and, if any dependence may be placed on Hindú chronology, he must have lived in the twenty-first or twenty-second generation after the Flood. Puru, his most celebrated ancestor, was the sixth in descent from the Moon's son Budha, who married a daughter of the good King Satya-vrata, preserved by Vishṇu in the Ark at the time of the Deluge. The son of Dushyanta, by Śakoontalá, was Bharata, from whom India is still called by the natives Bharata-varsha. After him came Samvaraṇa, Kuru, Śántanu, Bhíshma, and Vyása. The latter was the father of Dhṛitaráshṭra and Páṇḍu, the quarrels of whose sons form the subject of the great Sanskṛit epic poem called Mahábhárata, a poem with which the audience would be quite familiar, and in which they would feel the greatest pride.

The pedigree of Śakoontalá, the heroine of the drama, was no less interesting, and calculated to awaken the religious sympathies of Indian spectators. She was the daughter of the celebrated Viśwámitra, a name associated with many remarkable circumstances in Hindú mythology and history. His genealogy and the principal events of his life are narrated in the Rámáyaṇa, the first of the two epic poems which were to the Hindús what the Iliad and the Odyssey were to the Greeks. He was originally of the regal caste; and, having raised himself to the rank of a Bráhman by the length and rigour of his penance, he became the preceptor of Rámachandra, who was the hero of the Rámáyaṇa, and one of the incarnations of the god Vishṇu. With such antecedents, the audience could not fail to bring a sharpened appetite, and a self-satisfied frame of mind, to the performance of the play.

Although in the following translation it has been thought expedient to conform to modern usage, by indicating at the head of each Act the scene in which it is laid, yet it is proper to apprize the English reader that in scenery and scenic apparatus the Hindú drama must have been very defective. No directions as to changes of scene are given in the original text of the play. This is the more curious, as there are numerous stage directions which prove that in respect of dresses and decoration the resources of the Indian theatre were sufficiently ample.

It is probable that a curtain suspended across the stage, and divided in the centre, answered all the purposes of scenes. Behind the curtain was the space or room called *nepathya*, where the decorations were kept, where the actors attired themselves, and remained in readiness before entering the stage, and whither they withdrew on leaving it. When an actor was to enter hurriedly, he was directed to do so 'with a toss of the curtain.'

The machinery and paraphernalia of the Indian theatre were also very limited, contrasting in this respect unfavourably with the ancient Greek theatre, which appears to have comprehended nearly all that modern ingenuity has devised. Nevertheless, seats, thrones, weapons, and chariots, were certainly introduced, and as the intercourse between the inhabitants of heaven and earth was very frequent, it is not improbable that there may have been aërial contrivances to represent the chariots of celestial beings, as on the Greek stage. It is plain, however, from the frequent occurrence of the word *náṭayitwá*, 'gesticulating,' 'acting,' that much had to be supplied by the imagination of the spectator, assisted by the gesticulations of the actors.

For further information relative to the dramatic system of the Hindús, the reader is referred to the notes appended to the present translation. It is hoped that they will be found sufficient to explain every allusion that might otherwise be unintelligible to the English reader.

M.W.

East-India College, Haileybury,
January, 1856.

The reading of the play was beginning to shift: from Śakuntalā being the child of nature or the "rustic maiden" of Monier-Williams, to her innocence being subverted by the passion of the lovers. Nature and culture were no longer in oppositional juxtaposition, for nature had receded and the mores of culture were triumphant, and would gradually become essential to assessing the actions of Śakuntalā. The nineteenth century concern with the morality of the woman was in itself a critique of nature, that is, of those beyond the confines of settled society. The subject of morality is now conceptualised in a variety of ways, each underlining the importance of this issue.

By way of an aside, the illustrations in the first edition of this translation carry their own message, and are described by the reviewer in *The Edinburgh Review* of 1858 as "the most sumptuous specimen of decorative Oriental printing that has ever issued from the English press". Scattered through the book are prints in the current nineteenth century style, but framed like Mughal miniatures with a decorated margin or *hāshia*. The landscapes are distinctly south Indian, and those of the last few scenes have south Indian style temples with *gopurams*. The king's palace however has domes and minarets, and Duṣyanta himself looks like a nawab. Yet according to Monier-Williams, "... no expense or trouble has been spared to ensure accuracy and correctness in the delineation of the landscapes and figures; and to adapt the costumes, as far as possible, to the usages of the age in which the drama was performed." It is curious that these discrepancies in style did not strike the author who was certainly a knowledgeable Sanskritist. All that seemed to matter was conveying an impression of the Orient, even if confused and unhistorical.

Monier-Williams' translation soon became standard and was extremely popular. Its publication gave it a huge audience and doubtless encouraged translations of the play from Sanskrit into Indian regional languages. If the Introduction of the 1856 edition reads like the appraisal of the play by an Orientalist scholar, the 1898 edition positions the play in more clearly colonial terms. Monier-Williams reiterates the two-way policy of acquainting Europe with Oriental ideas, and reviving Indian culture for its own people in an Orientalist format.

He states:

"... a literal translation ... might have commended itself to Oriental students, but would not have given a true idea of the beauty of India's most cherished drama to general readers, whose minds are cast in a European mould and who require a translator to clothe Oriental ideas, as far as practicable, in a dress comfortable to European canons of taste ... "

He adds:

"... The English student at least, is bound by considerations of duty, as well as curiosity to make himself acquainted with a subject which elucidates and explains the conditions of the millions of Hindus who owe allegiance to his own soverign, and are governed by English laws ... "

Sketches illustrating the translation by Monier-Williams

K.K. Datta Gupta

Duṣyanta and his courtiers (Nalagarh miniature)

K.K. Datta Gupta

Duṣyanta in Kaṇva's hermitage, relinquishing arms (Nalagarh miniature)

This is followed by a little self-congratulation:

> ... youthful English-speaking Indians—cultured young men educated at the Universities of Calcutta, Madras and Bombay—have acted the Sakoontala in the very words of my translations ... "[139]

As proof of this last point, he includes in the book, a letter from V. Padmanabha Aiyer of Trivandrum dated 1893 referring to such a performance. The letter states:

> The Hindus have a great liking for this play and not one of the enlightened Hindu community will fail to acknowledge your translation to be a very perfect one. Our object in acting Hindu plays is to bring home to the Hindus the good lessons that our ancient authors are able to teach us.

Evidently the Indian middle class in some areas was reading the play in English translation and performing it likewise. Was this to encourage the British in India to also attend the performances and be educated in "Hindu culture"? By now there were just a few left who still had the enthusiasm of William Jones. Such performances were advertised in *The Bombay Times* of 1855 and a short summary of the story was included. Or was there already in the larger towns, a cross-section of the Indian middle class speaking different regional languages and therefore attending performances in English? The Parsi Elphinstone Dramatic Society, founded in 1861 in Bombay, staged plays in English. There were also the Kalidasa Elphinstone Dramatic Society and the Victoria Natak Mandali, both performing the plays of Shakespeare and Kālidāsa, the latter either in Sanskrit or in translations into Marathi, Gujarati and Hindi; and in 1867, the Monier-Williams' translation was staged.

Among the presentations of local theatre were the performances of female impersonators. Bal Gandharva's impersonation of Śakuntalā is said to have been particularly striking.[140] Such impersonation was encouraged where women were permitted to be part of a sequestered audience, but not encouraged to perform. Like cross-dressing, emotions associated with women and treated almost as cross-emotions, became central to the performance of female impersonators. This was another world, distanced from that of the colonial interpreters of Indian culture.

Monier-Williams' approach to the play is substantially different from that of Jones. His perspective reflects much that was current in the relationship between the coloniser and the colonised in India. The coloniser is less curious about the culture of the colonised, and more concerned about asserting what he believes to be the appropriate culture for them. This is both a reflection of changed colonial attitudes towards the culture of the colonised, incorporating some of the biases of Mill and Macaulay, as well as a change in colonial policy where curiosity has given way to control. Romance can be viewed as adultery, expressing the current Victorian insistence that women be kept under supervision. That the colonised had a civilisation is conceded, but much is made of what is seen as warts. In spite of his enthusiasm for the play the condescension of Monier-Williams is apparent. There is also, for a Sanskritist, curiously little interest in the views of earlier literary theorists. The appreciation of poetry takes second place to practical ways of making society more functional. A controlled culture was a safe area where the coloniser and the colonised could meet—controlling the culture of the colonised was a form of inventing a new way of perceiving and using that culture.

Translations from Sanskrit into the regional languages of India were published in the latter part of the nineteenth century. Prior to that, presumably, the Sanskrit version was better known, and translations into other Indian languages would have remained in manuscript form. The nineteenth century translations were received with enthusiasm, and the narrative came to be incorporated into dance forms as well. The play was assessed as a gem from what was now being called "the classical age of Indian culture", or "the Golden Age" of Indian history, and the fact that it had been so widely appreciated in Europe added to its prestige in Indian eyes.

What is most noticeable in these comments and the reception of the play at this time, is the shift towards seeing the play as an icon of Hindu culture—according to Monier-Williams it provided a glimpse of the Hindu subjects of the British empire. This was a somewhat different argument from that of William Jones, although it had the same result. For Jones the Hindus of earlier times represented the condition of human society prior to its dispersal, therefore they were part of its prehistory. For him Indian culture was Hindu and he warned against following "the muddy rivulets of Musalman writing in India instead of drinking from the pure fountain of Hindu learning",[141] although he does not explain why. Inevitably from this period, texts such as the play came to be viewed as Hindu texts per se. This was a new perspective on the narrative. The Braj version does not make it specifically Hindu, nor does the translation of Jawan. In emphasising it as Hindu, Jawan's attempt at universalising the story began to fade.

Ishwarachandra Vidyasagar, who taught at Fort William College in the latter part of the nineteenth century, published the play on the basis of the Devanāgari manuscript and the commentary of Rāghavabhaṭṭa. This became the standard text[142] for students learning Sanskrit. Therefore, that which was thought to be indelicate was deleted or glossed over. This new fastidiousness, both imposed on and expressive of the Indian middle class, was a radical change from earlier times when audiences read the play or saw it performed without embarrassment. Vidyasagar advocated education for girls and widow remarriage, but a liberal view of the role of women in society was now influenced by colonial attitudes to gender issues. This "moral" tone was partly borrowed from more recent Orientalist scholarship and from the impress of Victorian views. In terms of Victorian values, virtue for women was largely a question of sexual chastity. Where British Orientalists may even, on occasion, have conceded erotic freedom, their Indian counterparts would by now have become fearful of embarrassment and ensuing denigration. The imprint of what is believed to be virtuous can be indelible.

The moral tone was also partly derived from family life requiring the subordination of women. This is not to suggest that in earlier periods the daughter, the wife and the mother were free to take their own decisions, but concessions to human relationships could at least be made in the fantasy world of literature. The change in tone would also have had to do with the fact that these texts were now published, taught in schools and colleges, and read by young men and women. The censoring of the text avoided situations and relationships which were thought to transgress nineteenth century codes of social behaviour. This was when the pressure to construct a homogenous, national culture also began to be seen as necessary.

8. Śakuntalā from the perspective of middle-class nationalism

INITIALLY, the prominence of the Kālidāsa play coincided with the period when some change was sought in the more oppressive customs required to be observed by women in what is called the period of social reform. Rammohun Roy was vocal in demanding the abolition of *satī;* for some Indians, the insistence on widow immolation was outrageous, for others it was embarrassing, but for many more it was acceptable as part of "tradition". The gradual emergence of nationalism inevitably brought with it a selection from the past of what was regarded as the traditional role of women. This was sieved through the perspective of a nationalist response to both the Orientalist and the Utilitarian and Evangelical interpretations of an Indian past.[143] Nineteenth century nationalism fostered a conservative attitude towards social practices inspite of the movements for social reform, and to question tradition could be seen as a concession to western ideas.[144] Pre-colonial Indian society had been projected by the British as oppressive of women. One reaction was to idealise such practices and see them as part of the spiritual, inner life of traditional India, unlikely to be appreciated by the materialist, outgoing west. The other reaction was to argue for a change in these attitudes. The forging of the more wide-ranging middle-class norms drew both from European codes and those regarded as traditionally Indian, where inevitably the codes of the upper castes were incorporated. Gradually the definition of womanly virtue focused on modesty as the prime quality, followed by chastity, self-sacrifice, submission, devotion and patience. These would have been familiar to the Śakuntalā of Kālidāsa, but would not have come easily to the epic Śakuntalā.

Nationalist reactions, some confrontational and some acquiescent, denied an inherent oppression of women in pre-colonial India, and interpreted the classical tradition in positive terms, postulating a past utopia. Some argued enthusiastically that the spirituality of India was invested in its women. Thus whereas Indian men could adopt western attitudes and appearance, women had to conform to a tradition dictated by men who read the past in a manner which was suited to the present. Education was intended to inculcate the realisation in women that they were the guardians of spiritual virtues. Women, therefore, were subjected to a new kind of patriarchy.[145]

This view was supported by some European women who arrived in India, sympathetic to Indian nationalism. Some were theosophists, and for them the defence of a particular kind of Hinduism was an essential part of Indian nationalism. Annie Besant was articulate in defining an "ancient ideal" for women's education in India based on supposed Aryan prototypes. Such views failed to question either existing patriarchy or caste hierarchies.[146] Even those who were not theosophists, such as Sister Nivedita, idealised the Hindu family and the Hindu woman, an idealisation which questioned the need for equality between men and women. It was even argued that where women could attain the blessedness of being worshipped as mothers and goddesses, the demand for equality seemed almost retrogressive.

There was also the other white woman, the colonial wife, anxious to subordinate herself to gender specific sexual sanction and conventions of respectability, which came to characterise the middle class of the colonising power.[147] For the latter the sexual domination of the male was a metaphor for European supremacy. This then reinforced the attitude of some among the indigenous elite who imitated the colonisers. In a situation of racial confrontation, the white woman became an object to be protected by the colonisers, whereby protection was interpreted as preventing sexual mixing, even voluntary. This again became an attitude appropriated by sections of the indigenous elite who were experiencing the process of acquiring bourgeois respectability, and their women were expected to display feminine virtues of spirituality—self-sacrifice, benevolence, devotion and religiosity—which would enable them to be mothers and be looked upon as goddesses. Nationalist ideology, in its earlier phase, assumed that a woman's sole importance was in the domestic sphere as wife and mother. Qualities emphasised as feminine were patience and complete selflessness, qualities which Śakuntalā displays in the *āśrama* of Mārīca. Whereas for German Romanticism, Śakuntalā in Kaṇva's *āśrama* was the child of nature, for Indian nationalism it was Śakuntalā of Mārīca's *āśrama* who epitomised the virtues of a good Hindu woman. Viewed from the perspective of nationalism, some women from the epics were quoted as models.[148] To express sexuality came to be associated with the socially inferior; therefore the sexuality in the relationship of Śakuntalā and Duṣyanta had to be underplayed.

With the Kālidāsa play, there was also the problem of not understanding with sufficient sensitivity, the attitudes to men and women as articulated in Sanskrit literature. The implications of Sanskrit as a living tradition, sharing a frame of reference in intellectual activity, and the weakening of this role with English becoming the language of middle-class thought were not adequately recognised.[149] This may not have been a primary disjuncture in the social change of the nineteenth century, but in the interaction of literature and social attitudes it was an evident factor. Such a change also meant judging the classical tradition from a different perspective. This is not to suggest that there is a known perspective which we can return to now, but rather to insist that the awareness of other perspectives prevalent in the past should be apparent in interpreting literature.

Nationalism of a later period and in the early twentieth century witnessed a gradual change, in which it was the participation of women in nationalist and related activities which introduced the notion of some emancipation for them. But when it came to the perspective of women in society, it was western conservatism, especially in relation to sexual matters, which influenced middle class norms. There appears to have been a quiet appropriation of some of the attitudes of the Judaeo-Christian tradition and of Victorian morals with regard to sexual behaviour, quite apart from the male fear of female sexuality, apparent in some aspects of what was now being called Hinduism. Social reform did not radically alter the conservatism of the time. The idealisation of the past was based less on comprehending an Indian reality and more on what was considered appropriate from a twentieth century perspective.

Participation in the demand for reform and, later, in the national movement, was not intended to free women but to encourage a sense of partnership; although with rare exceptions, the woman remained the subordinate partner. Nevertheless, this change from nineteenth century attitudes may have been viewed with apprehension by some. Women became participants in the national movement, rather than using the movement to create possibilities for their own emancipation. From this perspective, Śakuntalā's initial modesty would have been acclaimed; but she was also seen as having allowed a transgression of this modesty and, what was even more unacceptable, exercised a free choice in making the transgression. The concern with the erotic introduced the question of morality. This was not the morality of Duṣyanta's rejection of Śakuntalā, however, but that of Śakuntalā responding to sexual desire and agreeing to a *gāndharva* marriage.

It was only a matter of time, therefore, before someone would declare Śakuntalā's action as a "fall". An essay written by Rabindranath Tagore in Bengali and published in *Prācīna Sāhitya* in 1907, was translated into English by

Jadunath Sarkar for publication in the *Modern Review*, under the title, "Sakuntala—Its Inner Meaning". Tagore compares the change in Śakuntalā from what he regards as the dross in Act III, to its luminosity in Act VII, a comparison which leads him to speak of her fall in the earlier Act. The essay uses the words *patana* and *patita*, which it has been suggested could be better translated as "surrender", particularly as the word *parābhava* has been used in an intervening paragraph, which may be translated as "defeat".[150] In effect, however, the meaning of "fall" may be preferable, in that it is this sentiment which hovers in Tagore's discussion. The implication is that Śakuntalā has acted in a manner which has degraded her and she is then required to rehabilitate herself. This would have been a judgemental assessment. It was, in any case, a representative statement on the play by a modern Indian.[151]

Sakuntala
*Its Inner Meaning**

BY RABINDRANATH TAGORE

Would'st thou the young year's blossoms
and the fruits of its decline,
And all by which the soul is charmed,
enraptured; feasted, fed,
Would'st thou the Earth and Heaven itself
in one sole name combine?
I name thee, O Śakuntala! and all at
once is said.

Goethe

Goethe, the master-poet of Europe, has summed up his criticism of *Sakuntala* in a single quatrain; he has not taken the poem to pieces. This quatrain seems to be a small thing like the flame of

*In K.N. Das Gupta and Laurence Binyon (eds.), *Sakuntala, Its Inner Meaning*, Macmillan and Co. Ltd., Calcutta: 1920, pages v-xiii.

a candle, but it lights up the whole drama in an instant, and reveals its inner nature. In Goethe's words, *Sakuntala* blends together the young year's blossoms and the fruits of maturity; it combines heaven and earth in one.

We are apt to pass over this eulogy lightly as a mere poetical outburst. We are apt to consider that it only means in effect that Goethe regarded *Sakuntala* as fine poetry. But it is not really so. His stanza breathes not the exaggeration of rapture, but the deliberate judgement of a true critic. There is a special point in his words. Goethe says expressly that *Sakuntala* contains the history of a development—the development of flower into fruit, of earth into heaven, of matter into spirit.

In truth there are two unions in *Sakuntala*; and the *motif* of the play is the progress from the earlier union of the First Act, with its earthly unstable beauty and romance, to the higher union in the heavenly hermitage of eternal bliss described in the last Act. This drama was meant not for dealing with a particular passion, not for developing a particular character, but for translating the whole subject from one world to another—to elevate love from the sphere of physical beauty to the eternal heaven of moral beauty.

With the greatest ease Kalidas has effected this junction of earth with heaven. His earth so naturally passes into heaven that we do not mark the boundary-line between the two. In the First Act the poet has not concealed the gross earthiness of the fall of Sakuntala; he has clearly shown, in the conduct of the hero and heroine alike, how much desire contributed to that fall. He has fully painted all the blandishments, playfulness, and fluttering of the intoxicating sense of youth, the struggle between deep bashfulness and strong self-expression. This is a proof of the simplicity of Sakuntala; she was not prepared beforehand for the outburst of passion which the occasion of Dushyanta's visit called forth. Hence she had not learned how to restrain herself, how to hide her feelings. Sakuntala had not known Cupid before; hence her heart was bare of armour, and she could not distrust either the sentiment of love or the character of the lover. The daughter of the hermitage was off her guard, just as the deer there knew not fear.

Dushyanta's conquest of Sakuntala has been very naturally

drawn. With equal ease has the poet shown the deeper purity of her character in spite of her fall—her unimpaired innate chastity. This is another proof of her simplicity.

The flower of the forest needs no servant to brush the dust of her petals. She stands bare; dust settles on her; but in spite of it she easily retains her own beautiful cleanliness. Dust did settle on Sakuntala, but she was not even conscious of it. Like the simple wild deer, like the mountain spring, she stood forth pure in spite of mud.

Kalidas has let his hermitage-bred youthful heroine follow the unsuspecting path of Nature; nowhere has he restrained her. And yet he has developed her into the model of a devoted wife, with her reserve, endurance of sorrow, and life of rigid spiritual discipline. At the beginning, we see her self-forgetful and obedient to Nature's impulses like the plants and flowers; at the end we see her deeper feminine soul—sober, patient under ill, intent on austerities, strictly regulated by the sacred laws of piety. With matchless art Kalidas has placed his heroine at the meeting-point of action and calmness, of Nature and Law, of river and ocean, as it were. Her father was a hermit, but her mother was a nymph. Her birth was the outcome of interrupted austerities, but her nurture was in a hermitage, which is just the spot where nature and austerities, beauty and restraint are harmonised. There is none of the conventional bonds of society there, yet we have the harder regulations of religion. Her *gandharva* marriage, too, was of the same type; it had the wildness of nature joined to the social tie of wedlock. The drama *Sakuntala* stands alone and unrivalled in all literature, because it depicts how Restraint can be harmonised with Freedom. All its joys and sorrows, unions and partings, proceed from the conflict of these two forces.

Sakuntala's simplicity is natural, that of Miranda is unnatural. The different circumstances under which the two were brought up account for this difference. Sakuntala's simplicity was not girt round with ignorance, as was the case with Miranda. We see in the First Act that Sakuntala's two companions did not let her remain unaware of the fact that she was in the first bloom of youth. She had learnt to be bashful. But all these things are external. Her simplicity, on the other hand, is more deeply seated, and so also is her purity. To the very end the poet shows that she had no experience of the outside world. Her simplicity is innate. True, she knew something of the world, because the hermitage did not stand altogether outside society; the rules of home life were observed here too. She was inexperienced though not ignorant of the outside world; but trustfulness was firmly enthroned in her heart. The simplicity which springs from such trustfulness had for a moment caused her fall, but it also redeemed her for ever. This trustfulness kept her constant to patience, forgiveness, and loving kindness, in spite of the cruellest breach of her confidence. Miranda's simplicity was never subjected to such a fiery ordeal; it never clashed with knowledge of the world.

Our rebellious passions raise storms. In this drama Kalidas has extinguished the volcanic ire of tumultuous passion by means of the tears of the penitent heart. But he has not dwelt too long on the disease—he has just given a glimpse of it and then dropped the veil. The desertion of Sakuntala by the amorous Dushyanta, which in real life would have happened as the natural consequence of his character, is here brought about by the curse of Durvasa. Otherwise, the desertion would have been so extremely cruel and pathetic as to destroy the peace and harmony of the whole play. But the poet has left a small rent in the veil through which we can get an idea of the royal sin. It is in the Fifth Act. Just before Sakuntala arrives at court and is repudiated by her husband, the poet momentarily draws aside the curtain from the King's love affairs. A woman's voice is heard singing behind the scene:

O honey-bee! having sucked the mango-blossoms in your search for new honey, you have forgotten the recent loving welcome by the lotus!

This tear-stained song of a stricken heart in the royal household gives us a rude shock, especially as our heart was hitherto filled with Dushyanta's love-passages with Sakuntala. Only in the preceding Act we saw Sakuntala setting out for her husband's home in a very holy, sweet, and tender mood, carrying with herself the blessings of the hoary sage Kanwa and the good wishes of the whole forest world. And now a stain falls on the picture we had so hopefully formed of the home of love to which she was going.

When the jester asked, "What means this song?" Dushyanta smiled and said, "We desert our loves after a short spell of love-making, and therefore I have deserved this strong rebuke from Queen Hansapadika." This indication of the fickleness of royal love is not purposeless at the beginning of the Fifth Act. With masterly skill the poet here shows that what Durvasa's curse had brought about had its seeds in human nature.

In passing from the Fourth Act to the Fifth we suddenly enter a new atmosphere; from the ideal world of the hermitage we go forth to the royal court with its hard hearts, crooked ways of love-making, difficulties of union. The beauteous dream of the hermitage is about to be broken. The two young hermits who are escorting Sakuntala, at once feel that they have entered an altogether different world, "a house encircled by fire!" By such touches at the beginning of the Fifth Act, the poet prepares us for the repudiation of Sakuntala at its end, lest the blow should be too severe for us.

Then comes the repudiation. Sakuntala feels as if she had been suddenly struck with a thunderbolt. Like a deer stricken by a trusted hand, this daughter of the forest looks on in blank surprise, terror, and anguish. At one blow she is hurled away from the hermitage, both literal and metaphorical, in which she has so long lived. She loses her connection with the loving friends, the birds, beasts, and plants and the beauty, peace, and purity of her former life. She now stands alone, shelterless. In one moment the music of the first four Acts is stilled!

O the deep silence and loneliness that then surround her! She whose tender heart has made the whole world of the hermitage her own folk, to-day stands absolutely alone. She fills this vast vacuity with her mighty sorrow. With rare poetic insight Kalidas has declined to restore Sakuntala to Kanwa's hermitage. After the renunciation by Dushyanta it was impossible for her to live in harmony with that hermitage in the way she had done before. . . . She was no longer her former self; her relation with the universe had changed. Had she been placed again amidst her old surroundings, it would only have cruelly exhibited the utter inconsistency of the whole situation. A mighty silence was now needed, worthy of the mighty grief of the mourner. But the poet has not shown us the picture of Sakuntala in the new hermitage—parted from the friends of her girlhood, and nursing the grief of separation from her lover. The silence of the poet only deepens our sense of the silence and vacancy which here reigned round Sakuntala. Had the repudiated wife been taken back to Kanwa's home, that hermitage would have spoken. To our imagination its trees and creepers would have wept, the two girl friends would have mourned for Sakuntala, even if the poet had not said a word about it. But in the unfamiliar hermitage of Marichi, all is still and silent to us; only we have before our mind's eye a picture of the world-abandoned Sakuntala's infinite sorrow, disciplined by penance, sedate, and resigned—seated like a recluse rapt in meditation.

Dushyanta is now consumed by remorse. This remorse is *tapasya*. So long as Sakuntala was not won by means of this repentance, there was no glory in winning her . . . . One sudden gust of youthful impulse had in a moment given her up to Dushyanta, but that was not the true, the full winning of her. The best means of winning is by devotion, by *tapasya*. What is easily gained is as easily lost. Therefore, the poet has made the two lovers undergo a long and austere *tapasya* that they may gain each other truly eternally. If Dushyanta had accepted Sakuntala when she was first brought to his court, she would have only occupied a corner of the royal household, and passed the rest of her life in neglect, gloom, uselessness.

It was a blessing in disguise for Sakuntala that Dushyanta abjured her with cruel sternness. When afterwards this cruelty reacted on himself, it prevented him from remaining indifferent to Sakuntala. His unceasing and intense grief fused his heart and welded Sakuntala with it. Never before had the King met with such an experience. Never before had he had the occasion and means of truly loving. Kings are unlucky in this respect; their desires are so easily satisfied that they never get what is to be gained by devotion alone. Fate now plunged Dushyanta into deep grief and thus made him worthy of true love—made him renounce the role of a rake.

Thus has Kalidas burnt away vice in the eternal fire of the sinner's heart; he has not tried to conceal it from the outside. When the curtain drops in the last Act, we feel that all the evil has been destroyed as on a funeral pyre, and the peace born of a perfect and satisfactory fruition reigns in our hearts. Kalidas has internally cut right away the roots of the poison tree, which a sudden force from the outside had planted. He has made the physical union of Dushyanta and Sakuntala tread the path of sorrow, and thereby chastened and sublimated it into a moral union. Hence did Goethe rightly say that *Sakuntala* combines the blossoms of Spring with the fruits of Autumn, it combines Heaven and Earth. Truly in *Sakuntala* there is one Paradise Lost and another Paradise Regained.

The poet has shown how the union of Dushyanta and Sakuntala in the First Act as mere lovers is futile, while their union in the last Act as the parents of Bharata is a true union. The First Act is full of brilliancy and movement. We have there a hermit's daughter in the exuberance of youth, her two companions running over with playfulness, the newly flowering forest creeper, the bee intoxicated with perfume, the fascinated King peeping from behind the trees. From this Eden of bliss Sakuntala, the mere sweetheart of Dushyanta, is exiled in disgrace. But far different was the aspect of the other hermitage where Sakuntala, the mother of Bharata and the incarnation of goodness took refuge. There no hermit girls water the trees, nor bedew the creepers with their loving sister-like looks, nor feed the young fawn with handfuls of paddy. There a single boy fills the loving bosom of the entire forest-world; he absorbs all the liveliness of the trees, creepers, flowers, and foliage. The matrons of the hermitage, in their loving anxiety, are fully taken up with the unruly boy. When Sakuntala appears, we see her clad in a dusty robe, face pale with austerities, doing the penance of a lorn wife, pure-souled. Her long penances have purged her of the evil of her first union with Dushyanta: she is now invested with the dignity of a matron, she is the image of motherhood, tender and good. Who can repudiate her now?

The poet has shown here, as in *Kumara Sambhava*, that the Beauty that goes hand in hand with Moral Law is eternal, that the calm, controlled, and beneficent form of Love is its best form, that beauty is truly charming under restraint and decays quickly when it gets wild and unfettered. This ancient poet in India refuses to recognise Love as its own highest glory; he proclaims that Goodness is the final goal of Love. He teaches us that the Love of man and woman is not beautiful, not lasting, not fruitful, so long as it is self-centred, so long as it does not beget Goodness, so long as it does not diffuse itself into society over son and daughter, guests and neighbours.

The two peculiar principles of India are the beneficent *tie of home life* on the one hand, and the *liberty of the soul* abstracted from the world on the other. In the world India is variously connected with many races and many creeds; she cannot reject any of them. But on the altar of devotion (*tapasya*) India sits alone. Kalidas has shown, both in *Sakuntala* and *Kumara Sambhava*, that there is a harmony between these two principles, an easy transition from the one to the other. In his hermitage a human boy plays with lion cubs, and the hermit spirit is reconciled with the spirit of the householder.

On the foundation of the hermitage of recluses Kalidas has built the home of the householder. He has rescued the relation of the sexes from the sway of lust and enthroned it on the holy and pure seat of asceticism. In the sacred books of the Hindus the ordered relation of the sexes has been defined by strict injunctions and Laws. Kalidas has demonstrated *that* relation by means of the elements of Beauty. The Beauty that he adores is lit up by grace, modesty, and goodness; in its intensity it is true to one for ever; in its range it embraces the whole universe. It is fulfilled by renunciation, gratified by sorrow, and rendered eternal by religion. In the midst of this beauty, the impetuous unruly love of man and woman has restrained itself and attained to a profound peace, like a wild torrent merged in the ocean of goodness. Therefore is such love higher and more wonderful than wild and untrained Passion.

Tagore sees two unions in the play, one sensuous and earthy, and the other, spiritual and heavenly and the attempt to elevate love from mere physical beauty to the eternal heaven of moral beauty. In what seems to be a curiously Judaeo-Christian stance, Tagore argues that the poet has not concealed the gross earthiness of the fall/surrender of Śakuntalā; he has clearly shown, in the conduct of the hero and the heroine alike, the extent to which desire contributed to that fall. With equal ease he has shown the deeper purity of her character which, according to him, remained unimpaired in its innate chastity. Even with Tagore, it is the woman who is said to have been unable to remain unimpeachable; the insistence on Duṣyanta's responsibility, as stated in the epic, is hardly touched upon. In projecting the two Śakuntalās, Tagore, it is thought, may have been echoing an essay by Bankim Chandra Chatterjee published in 1887, comparing Śakuntalā to Miranda and Desdemona, arguing that the earlier immature Śakuntalā resembles Miranda and the later mature Śakuntalā, Desdemona.[152] Elsewhere, Tagore has considered the relationship between man and nature and contrasted the island of Prospero in *The Tempest*, where nature is an enemy, with the *āśrama* of Kaṇva which is at one with nature, and where life is a spiritual endeavour in search of harmony.

It is said that Kālidāsa was the poet to whom Tagore returned repeatedly,[153] and his reading of Śakuntalā is therefore significant. As he interprets her, the Śakuntalā of the earlier part of the play is contemplated neither in the earlier Indian tradition nor in German Romanticism. Tagore would seem to be reflecting some nineteenth century British Orientalist attitudes coupled with Victorian mores, and some perceptions inevitably influenced by nationalism. But where some may have seen the play as condoning an element of immorality, Tagore insisted that the intrinsic virtue of Śakuntalā lay in transmuting the dross into the luminous through penance.

The argument would run that Kālidāsa (or Indian tradition), does not concede transgression of the moral code (even if the transgression is doubtful), therefore penance is required. The fall/surrender of Śakuntalā is something of a contradiction since Tagore speaks of the *gāndharva* marriage as the wildness of nature joined to the social tie of wedlock. If such a marriage is socially accepted, then surely Śakuntalā has not "fallen", even by Victorian rules of the game, unless of course any expression of passion and sexual love constitutes a fall. Tagore adds that Kālidāsa has developed her as the model of a devoted wife with her reserve, endurance of sorrow and rigid discipline, and that at the end we see her true feminine being which is sober, patient in misfortune, intent on austerities and strictly regulated by the laws of piety.

There might be some hesitation in accepting the *gāndharva* form of marriage when, in the present, only the unqualified validity of *kanyā-dāna*, the gifting of the daughter, is acceptable. From this perspective, marriage by mutual consent may not be a sacrament, and requires the approval of the parents. Such approval is of course given by Kaṇva, although it is only in the last act of the play that the. marriage is blessed by Indra, Mārīca and Aditi. The question of Śakuntalā's identity as hovering between the two categories is thrown into sharp relief by the curse, which makes of her a wanton woman through Duṣyanta's rejection. The lifting of the curse elevates her to the status of a lawful wife. This rather prosaic interpretation however, seems to be contradicted by her being taken to the most elevated of abodes—the *āśrama* of Mārīca—precisely at the point when her rejection could assume the worst connotation.

Tagore argues that the desertion of Śakuntalā by Duṣyanta was a royal sin, therefore the curse of Durvāsas has its origin in human nature. It is interesting that he does not refer to it as the moral weakness of the seducer. Presumably, the curse and the ring are not irrational elements in the narrative, but take on an allegorical meaning. The focus is on human action and its consequences—the lovers have not observed the higher ethic and the curse is morally determined. Duṣyanta's remorse is his penance; Śakuntalā's separation from him, hers. Therefore penance is necessary to a true and eternal union. One may well ask: if penance is necessary, then is sin also a necessary precondition for penance? It is possible that in a reading of Śakuntalā as a *tapasvinī*, the meaning of the word as one who is ill-fated, rather than the one who is an ascetic or doing penance, was the more appropriate but gets marginalised. The long penance of Śakuntalā purged her of the evil of her first union with Duṣyanta and she emerged as the epitome of motherhood, tender and good. Kālidāsa has made the physical union of Duṣyanta and Śakuntalā partake of sorrow, and has thereby chastened and sublimated it into a moral union; the quality of love is thus heightened. This elaboration of the meaning of the play may also arise from embarrassment at the male assertion of authority in rejecting Śakuntalā, which Tagore then sought to explain through penance being necessary to moral union.

In Tagore's reading the empowerment of the woman through the birth of her son is unimportant, because now the question of morality has become central. This would seem to be at variance with both Kālidāsa and the epic, but since Tagore treats the play as an allegory, he is of course free to read it differently. What is of interest is the degree to which Tagore's reading reflects the social and moral concerns of his own time, and his response to both orientalism and nationalism.

Earlier, in 1892, Tagore had written a play, *Chitrangada*, which has some parallels with the problems he raises with reference to Śakuntalā. Interestingly his play, too, was criticised by some of his contemporaries as being immoral, and the *gāndharva* marriage as condoning sexual abandonment. Tagore defended the play by saying that it was sensuous as all good poetry should be, but not immoral.[154] In his reaction to the Kālidāsa play he could also have been reflecting one current view, whereby the sensuous in Indian art and literature was frequently justified as being symbolic of the spiritual.

There are many historical tangents to Ṭagore's reading of the play. That he focuses on the relationship between Śakuntalā and Duṣyanta may perhaps be due to the concept of romantic love beginning to be spoken of in middle-class society, and relationships between men and women in some circles were changing. That the woman was meant to typify the highest moral sensitivity was partly patriarchy attempting to place her on a pedestal to compensate for a different reality, and partly to encourage the notion that Indian women were the symbol of purity and strength. At some levels, then, this reading of Śakuntalā becomes the mediation between two cultures, the national and the colonial.

A few years later a controversial study of Tagore's works was published,[155] which some assessed as critical. Its intention was to dispel the myth of the mystical and exotic "other" Tagore, an image projected through William Butler Yeats' interpretation of his writing in the Introduction to *Gitanjali,* published in 1912.[156] Yeats was among the few major poets of twentieth century English literature who interested themselves in Indian thought, and particularly in Tagore. To some extent this interest was a continuation of the earlier enthusiasm of German Romanticism for Śakuntalā, now reduced to a much smaller literary circle. Yeats had been influenced by the same ideas as some of the earlier Romantic poets, which made him empathise with what was seen as mystical, but which its opponents decried as decadent. Yeats was not unacquainted with Indian philosophy and some translations of Sanskrit literature, and is likely to have read the Kālidāsa play. This interest grew out of the activities of the theosophists and Madame Blavatsky from about 1885 onwards, some of whom introduced Vedantic meditation and yoga to Dublin.[157] Yeats' interest in the occult included Hermetic writings and neo-Platonism. This alternative philosophy, which was a continuing undercurrent, surfaced again and echoed earlier Romanticism. Discussions on metempsychosis returned to the question of whether Pythagoras had visited India and been tutored by *brāhmaṇas* and Buddhists.[158] Neo-Platonists had drawn attention to common features among these philosophical ideas in their emphasis on vows of abstinence and silence; the denial of animal food; knowledge of previous incarnations; and non-dualist philosophy. For neo-Platonists, the *āśrama* of Kaṇva was evocative of many aspects of Indian thought: the soul searching for unity, forest retreats as places for meditation, and the breaking of ethical norms bringing sorrow and requiring the mediation of the gods.

This prepared the ground for Yeats' enthusiasm for Tagore, whom he met and introduced to various literary figures including Ezra Pound. The spontaneity of Tagore's poetry and his dedication to literature greatly attracted Yeats. He admired Tagore's attitude to nationalism, which was nationalist but remained on the cusp.[159] Tagore in turn was adulatory about Yeats, and referred to him as engaged in a war against modernism, a man who understood the world through his soul and not his intellect. The mutual admiration faded soon after, yielding place to occasional strident criticism from the English poet. Tagore's reading of the *Abhijñāna-śākuntalam*, in as much as it speaks of a higher spirituality, would doubtless have appealed to that western readership which was familiar with this aspect of Idealist thought.

Subsequent to Rabindranath Tagore's pronouncement, interpretations of the play tend to be rather flat by comparison. It is curious that later editors of the standard editions of the text—of which there were many, and from many parts of India—rarely refer to Tagore's views. A partial endorsement of his reading is the view that Kālidāsa disapproved of the *gāndharva* marriage and therefore projected śakuntalā as the *kula kanyā*, misguided by ardent passion.[160] However the same commentator disagrees with Tagore's statement that both śakuntalā and Duṣyanta had to do penance, in order that the marriage be acceptable: neither Śakuntalā in her loneliness in the *āśrama* of Mārīca, nor Duṣyanta, remorseful in his palace can be said to be doing penance. The play is therefore not a triumph of moral beauty over physical beauty, but a recognition that marriage is only acceptable when it is blessed by the elders. Such a statement echoes the prevalent view of marriage strengthening patriarchy.

Śakuntalā is sometimes projected as the ideal *gṛhinī*, the complete woman who serves her elders, is considerate to her co- wives, is not arrogant, ensures that her husband treads the moral path, and matures in motherhood.[161] In the final Act of the Bengali recension, the stage directions are that Duṣyanta fall at the feet of Śakuntalā when she appears—*iti pādayoḥ patati.* In the Maithila and Kashmir recensions, this has been changed to *praṇipātya*, which could mean his merely bowing down with respect. Commenting on this, D.K. Kanjilal states that according to Hindu custom, a husband is not expected to fall at the feet of his wife, although some commentaries on the *Nāṭyaśāstra* allow a shrewd lover to salute the feet of his lady as an amorous gesture! Such comments overlook the frequent depiction of Kṛṣṇa at the feet of Rādhā.

Yet another dimension is appended to that of the ideal *gṛhinī.* This follows from the obsession with Aryanism as a characteristic of early India, which grew out of the European theory of Aryan race and has embedded itself in the Indian middle-class consciousness. By the late nineteenth century the foundations of Indian culture were being referred to in some circles as Hindu Arya.[162] The pride in claiming an Aryan ancestry by the upper castes was that it also made such Hindus the kinsmen of the British, on the assumption that both were descended from a common Indo-European ancestry. The "Aryan woman" was assessed as spiritually superior to all others, capable of moulding the nation in the correct way. A Sanskritist, known for his editing of much in Sanskrit literature, has commented that on reading the play we breathe the pure air of Aryan India.[163] Śakuntalā illustrates the Aryan woman—when encountered by her lover she is the picture of womanly modesty. The fact that she continues to love Duṣyanta and regards herself as his wife even in separation, is said to be yet another characteristic of Hindu womanhood.

Commentaries from the translations into regional languages, if studied comparatively, are likely to indicate many new facets of interpretation. Introductions in English to the Sanskrit text seldom discuss the views of those writing in the regional languages—these are occasionally rather more vibrant discussions on the play. Thus in 1938, Akhtar Husain Raipuri translated the play directly from Sanskrit into Urdu for the first time.[164] His understanding is that Kālidāsa, being a man of his time and identifying with brahmanical high culture, has, through changes introduced into the original epic story, attempted to save the king from being seen for what he really was—a man who refused to accept responsibility for seducing an innocent woman. He sees this as an example of the age-old tradition of denying a voice to Indian women. It is therefore tragic that in his depiction of Śakuntalā, Kālidāsa cannot make her into anything but a woman without a voice. If this is any indication, introductions to the Indian language versions may well be found to express far more of a concern for the treatment of the woman than we are led to believe from comments in English editions.

9. Conclusion

Śakuntalā had by now changed many roles. The mother of a hero in an *ākhyāna* and the self-reliant woman of the *Mahābhārata* had been transmuted into the romantic ideal of upper caste high culture in the play by Kālidāsa, then cast as the child of nature in German Romanticism, and ended up as the ideal Hindu wife from the perspective of Indian nationalism and its perceptions of Hindu tradition. Such transmutations are closely linked to historical change which influenced the widely different forms and readings to which she had been subjected. The more recent projections of Śakuntalā proceeded essentially from a middle-class perspective—subaltern women remain outside this picture.

Of the two earlier versions of the story, clearly the Kālidāsa play has been more popular with the Indian middle class than the epic rendering. It was among the most popular stories performed as a school play, especially in girls' schools in the earlier part of this century, and the reason for this is obvious. It highlighted the qualities valued in a woman from the dominant social culture, and underlined what was seen as the triumph of morality. In part its popularity lay in the technical excellence of the play: well-structured with neatly intersecting symbols and tones, evocative imagery, striking metaphors, poetic language, a strong romanticism, but not undiluted in its projection of separation and its consequent suffering as necessary to the narrative. The extended learning of Sanskrit as a "classical" language in schools and colleges opened it up to wider circles, as did the translations into many Indian languages. Its availability as a text was accompanied by the hype that it was the work of the Indian Shakespeare, therefore if one were cultured one should be familiar with it. In addition to this it was known to have been appreciated widely in Europe, and Goethe's verse was quoted or at least mentioned in most publications of the play. That which Europe values should be valued by Indians even if, in this case, it had been valued by Indians much before it reached Europe. In the projection of the utopia of the past—a projection necessary to nationalist ideology—the idyllic elements of the play were viewed as descriptive of reality.

But the popularity of the play in modern times has to do with the process of what we select as representing our past. This involves a perspective from history. Although it was argued by scholars such as Monier-Williams that Orientalist scholarship wished to reveal the greatness of Indian culture to the West, there was also, as he expresses it, the intention of creating a "tradition" which would lead modern Indians to view their past from the perspective provided by its modern "rediscovery". The claim that the tradition was being resuscitated by modern scholarship reinforced the perspective. That high culture was specifically Hindu was evident from the notion propagated widely in Orientalist writings of the nineteenth century, that the arrival of the British had saved the Hindus from the tyranny of the Muhammadans. The tyranny itself was not explained, but the assumption seems to have been that Muslims were hostile to the earlier culture.

It is now a truism to say that traditions are invented. *Parampara*/tradition, is not a handing down, unchanged, of belief and practice. It may even be argued that the process of handing down implies not a passive transfer, but some contestation in defining what exactly is to be handed down. Every generation selects what it requires from the past and makes its innovations, some more than others. Where this process involved Orientalist scholars working on the Indian past, the selection was even more apparent and the inventing of a tradition that much more recognisable.[165]

The privileging of Sanskritic high culture and looking upon it as the sole depository of tradition was an outcome of the colonial discourse. But the demarcations within Sanskritic tradition between high and not-so-high culture—or indeed the segments within a text, some of which emanated from brahmanical culture and others from a popular source—received little recognition. Thus there is not only a difference between the courtly culture of the Kālidāsa play and that of the epic, but even within the *Mahābhārata* it is necessary to differentiate between the interpolated didactic segments, and the narratives which are likely to belong to the oral tradition of popular stories. Both the epic and the play were ultimately a part of high culture, but the epic had its origins in the kind of culture which was effectively superceded by courtly culture. Epic narratives became a source for courtly literature, but the narratives were so changed in the process as to become virtually unrecognisable, as with the Kālidāsa play. Epic narratives often had a much more integrated relationship with popular traditions, to the mutual enrichment of both, since the latter could also change the narrative to an unrecognisable degree. Courtly culture, too, incorporated elements of popular narratives (as for example in the sub-plot of the signet ring) but the forms in which they were integrated were conducive to the furtherance of courtly culture. The ignoring of the epic version therefore signified rejection of that culture, seen to have its roots in social patterns contrary to those now regarded as normative.

When "Golden Ages" were a requirement of historical interpretation, there was an age of classicism which was inevitably golden. The period of Gupta rule has for long been viewed as a "Golden Age", registering political unity, economic prosperity symbolised in the issuing of gold coins, the rise of Puranic Hinduism (which some would like to project as resurgent Hinduism), and high classicism in art and literature, of which Kālidāsa was one example. Hence the reference to it as the period of the Hindu Renaissance. It would therefore have to epitomise those features of Hindu tradition considered unique, essential and attractive; associated with this was the idyllic picture of the *āśrama* which fitted into a construction of life in "ancient India" as eternally peaceful, harmonious and non-aggressive, with people given to meditation and spirituality. In other words, the image conjured up by Max Müller. This was supposed to be the utopia of the past, now lost to us. Kaṇva's *āśrama* recreates that utopia and is believed to be a representation of reality rather than a figment of fantasy.

In the historical questioning of the notion of "Golden Ages" generally, and the Gupta period specifically, conventional descriptions are critically assessed; this involves, among other things, a reconsideration of the creative literature of the times. The assessment draws not on the uniqueness of this literature, but rather on its antecedents and cultural impact, and is likely to involve a departure from conventional historical treatment and the introduction of new interpretations.

I have tried to show that pre-modern Indian culture was not a monolith. Cultural items have their hierarchies, and placing them in their historical context encourages a richer perspective. In a colonial context, culture for the colonised involves an awareness of the colonial attempt to imprint the culture of the colonised, as well as attempts to counter this from a nationalist perspective. It thus requires that in a post-colonial situation there be a reconsideration of the culture of the past through questioning both colonial and nationalist constructs. This does not mean veering towards indigenism, chauvinism and that which is narrowly nationalist; but centrally, a constant critiquing and re-critiquing of the reconstructions. These are aspects of the multiple identities of our times. I have tried to suggest that every recreation is situated in its contemporary condition and conforms to contemporary vision. The contemporising of our cultural pasts to make them a part of the present is a process which requires both awareness and analysis.

Contemporising the icon is implicit in all the versions of Śakuntalā I have referred to, but its essentially contemporary quality has to be perceived, drawn out and underlined. The attempt is more evident in some recent visual versions of the narrative. Miniature paintings from Nalagarh, painted in the Pahari style, carry echoes of the Braj version, and the depiction parallels that of other narratives popular at the courts of the hill states. Raja Ravi Varma's oil paintings on themes from the play suggest a mingling of prevalent Orientalist taste with nationalist overtones. Paintings by artists of this century exhibit a different style. Films made on the story are another departure. Of these the earlier ones tended to stay close to the play, such as K. Subramaniam's *Sakuntalai* in Tamil (1940) or V. Shantaram's *Shakuntala* in Hindi (1943).[166] The latter does introduce innovations in the last Act, stemming from the self-perceptions of contemporary Indian women. Śakuntalā emerges as defiant, refusing to return with Duṣyanta and encouraging the independence of her son to the point where he implicitly challenges his father. A more deliberate attempt at contemporising is evident in one of the more thoughtful Hindi comedies, *Anantayātra*, made in 1985 by Nachiket Patwardhan.

The Śakuntalā of *Anantayātra* steps out of the past and spends a few days in the Bombay of today, with the business executive responsible for bringing her into contemporary times. Coming from Kaṇva's *āśrama*, her surprised reactions to twentieth century metropolitan ways are treated with wit and charm. The sub-text of the child of nature, trying to cope with modern society, and the business executive slowly harrassed by her questions and reactions, underlines the kind of queries that a contemporisation of the play would raise. The superimposition of the business executive on Duṣyanta opens up the question of just how divergent the two societies of the *āśrama* and the court may have been, and would be today. It is also an effective way of showing that our present-day appreciation of the play as a classic is, in part, a fantasy and an escape from our own hassles, the very ones which are a puzzle to Śakuntalā. Behind the humour of her reactions and the attempt of the "hero" to explain the world as it is now, there is an undercurrent of quiet irony which is a commentary on the present. The film comes halfway to doing an adaptation of the play for contemporary times; such an adaptation could more sharply bring views on gender in modern Indian society to the surface, since the implicit tensions would not be disguised as the fantasy of the author.

The characterisation of Śakuntalā through many historical moments, was eventually chiselled into an image of a woman appropriate to the ideals of the new middle class. Here the reading of Tagore becomes pertinent. The child of nature was an innocent girl who was led astray, but she remained submissive, long-suffering, patient and still devoted to her husband and was finally exonerated. We select from the past those images which endorse what we want from the present. These contribute to the construction of the self-image of our contemporary culture and its projection back into what is believed to be "tradition". In the last two centuries we have ignored the Śakuntalā of the *Mahābhārata*, the liberated woman demanding to be justly treated, and have endorsed the more submissive Śakuntalā of Kālidāsa, a woman waiting patiently for a recognition of her virtues.

Endnotes

1. Preliminaries

1. E.J. Hobsbawm and T. Ranger (eds.), *The Invention of Tradition*, Cambridge University Press, Cambridge: 1983.
2. R. Thapar, *Interpreting Early India*, Oxford University Press, New Delhi: 1992.
3. M. Winternitz, *History of Indian Literature*, I., University of Calcutta, Calcutta: 1927-33, 319 ff. denied the priority of the epic version but this is rejected in A.B. Keith, *Sanskrit Drama*, Clarendon Press, Oxford 1924, 157.
4. V. Propp, *The Morphology of the Folk Tale*, University of Texas, Austin: 1968.

2. The Narrative from the *Mahābhārata*

5. 13.5.4.11-14.
6. 8.23.1 ff.
7. *Ṛgveda* 1.158; *Bṛhaddevatā* 4. 11-25
8. *Mahābhārata* I. 62 ff.
9. His speech is flawed and his descent is said to be from the *asura rākṣasa Ṛgveda* 7.18.13.; *Śatapatha Brāhmaṇa* 6.8.1.14.
10. E.W. Hopkins, *The Great Epic of India*, Punthi Pustak, Calcutta: 1969 (reprint); V.S. Sukthankar, *On the Meaning of the Mahābhārata*, Asiatic Society of Bombay, Bombay: 1964.
11. R. Thapar, *From Lineage to State*, Oxford University Press, Delhi: 1984.
12. R. Thapar, "*Dāna* and *Dakṣiṇā* as Forms of Exchange," in *Ancient Indian Social History: Some Interpretations*, Orient Longman, Delhi: 1978.
13. R. Thapar, *From Lineage to State*, 155 op. cit.
14. B.B. Lal, "Exacavations at Hastinapur and Other Explorations in the Ganga Valley," in *Ancient India*, 1954-55, 10-11, 5-151.
15. Gouri Lad, *Mahābhārata and Archaeological Evidence*, Deccan College, Poona: 1983.

16. *Mahābhārata, Ādi parvan* 214 ff.
17. Otto Rank, *The Myth of the Birth of the Hero,* Dover, New York: 1959, makes a comparative analysis from various cultures of heroes born of high status but forsaken and brought up by lowly foster parents.
18. This kind of verbal duel, which is not uncommon in epic literature, is referred to as 'flyting'. Ward Parks, *Verbal Duelling: The Homeric and Old English Traditions,* Princeton University Press, New Jersey: 1990.
19. D.D. Kosambi, "Urvaśī and Purūravas", in *Myth and Reality,* Popular Prakashan, Bombay: 1962, 42-81.
20. 10.125.7.; 10.95; 10. 123.
21. 4.37.4 ff.; 4.38.
22. 3.82.136; 3.83.20; 9.36.8.
23. Gouri Lad, "*Mahābhārata:* A Mythology in the Making," *Bulletin of the Deccan College Research Institute,* 1985, 44, 83-93.
24. 10.129.
25. S. Settar and G.D. Sontheimer (eds.), *Memorial Stones,* Karnataka University, Dharwar: 1982. R. Thapar, "Death and the Hero", in S.C. Humphreys and H. King (eds.), *Mortality and Immortality,* Academic Press, London: 1981, 293-316.
26. V. Dehejia, *Discourse in Early Buddhist Art,* Munshiram Manoharlal, Delhi: 1997.
27. V.S. Agrawala, "Vasavadatta and Sakuntala Scenes in the Ranigumpha cave in Orissa," *Journal of the Indian Society of Oriental Art,* 1946, 14, 102-09.
28. C. Rapin, *Indian Art From Afghanistan,* Manohar, Delhi: 1996.
29. J.H. Marshall, "Excavations at Bhita", *ASIAR,* 1911-12, Calcutta: 1915, 29-94, Pls.XXIII-IV No. 17.

3. The *Abhijñāna-śākuntalam* of Kālidāsa

30. V. Raghavan, *Some Old Lost Rāma Plays,* University Press, Annamalai: 1961
31. B. Stoler Miller, "Kālidāsa's World and His Plays," in B.S. Miller (ed.), *Theater of Memory,* Columbia University Press, New York: 1984, 3-41.
32. Lama Chimpa and Alaka Chattopadhyaya (trans.), *History of Buddhism in India,* K.P. Bagchi & Co. Calcutta: 1980, (ed.) D.P. Chattopadhyaya, 114-16.
33. B. Stoler Miller, *op.cit.*

34. R. Thapar, "Renunciation: The Making of a Counter-culture?" in *Ancient Indian Social History*, Orient Longman, New Delhi: 1978, 63-104. "The Householder and renouncer in the Brahmanical and Buddhist Traditions", *Contributions to Indian Sociology*, n.s. 1981, 15, 1-2, 273-98.
35. D.H. Ingalls, "Kālidāsa and the Attitudes of the Golden Age," *JAOS*, 1976, 96, 15-26.
36. S.H. Deshpande, "The Hunted One," *Journal of the Asiatic Society of Bombay*, 1977-78, n.s. 52-53, 112-21.
37. G.V. Bapat, "Hunting, a Royal Sport in Ancient India," *Journal of the Asiatic Society of Bombay*, 1974-76, n.s. 49-51, 23-30.
38. *Abhijñāna-śākuntalam*, II.5.
39. Chandra Rajan, *Kālidāsa*, Penguin, Delhi: 1989, 90.
40. C. Malamoud, "Village et forêt dans l'ideologie de l'Inde Brahmanique", *Archives de Sociologie Europeene*, July 1976; *Cooking the World*, OUP, Delhi: 1996, 87-88.
41. *Mahābhārata*, 12.57.44 ff.
42. S.K. Belvalkar, "The Original Sakuntalā," 349-359; *The Abhijñāna-śākuntalam of Kālidāsa*, Sahitya Akademi, New Delhi: 1965.
43. H.D. Sankalia, *Rāmāyaṇa, Myth or Reality*, Peoples Publishing House, New Delhi: 1973
44. B. Stoler Miller, *op.cit.*
45. Ibid.
46. C. Malamoud, "By Heart: Notes on the Interplay Between Love and Memory in Ancient Indian Poetry," in *Cooking the World*, Oxford University Press, Delhi: 1996, 247-58.
47. W. Ruben, *Kālidāsa*, Akademic Verlag, Berlin 1957, 50.
48. M.R. Kale, *The Abhijñāna-śākuntalam of Kālidāsa*, Booksellers Publishing Co., Bombay: 1961. Introduction.
49. Ruben, *op.cit.*
50. E.B. Cowell (ed.), *The Jātaka*, Vol. I, No.7.; B. Stoler Miller, *op.cit.* 336.
51. *Ādi parvan* 113.31 ff.
52. Iravati Karve, *Yuganta*, Sangam Books, Poona: 1969, 65 ff.
53. Chandra Rajan, *op.cit.*, 93.
54. Belvalkar, *op.cit.*
55. The aerial chariot recalls the story of Vasu Uparicara, the Cedi *rājā* who receives the chariot from Indra and is also associated with the Pūru lineage, and of course the aerial chariot of Rāma.
56. B. Stoler Miller, *op.cit.*, 9.

57. *Ibid.*
58. Ingalls, *op.cit.*
59. R. Thapar, "Renunciation", op.cit.
60. Chandra Rajan, *op.cit.* 82 ff.
61. S. Ortner, "Is Female to Male as Nature is to Culture?" in M. Rosaldo and L. Lamphere (eds.), *Women, Culture and Society,* Stanford University Press, Palo Alto: 1974.
62. M. Strathern, "No Nature, No Culture: the Hagen Case," in C. MacCormack and M. Strathern (eds.), *Nature, Culture and Gender,* Cambridge University Press, Cambridge 1995 (reprint), 174-222.
63. Manu 3.32.
64. Manu 5.147-48; 9.2-3.
65. Minoru Hara, "*Tapasvinī*", *Annals of the Bhandarkar Oriental Research Institute,* 1977-78, 151-159.
66. Ingalls, *op.cit.*
67. Kumkum Roy, "La représentation des relations hommes-femmes dans l'Inde antique à travers les pieces de Kālidāsa" *Raconte Avec l'Inde,* 1997, XXVI, 2, 176-87.
68. B. Stoler Miller, *op.cit.*
69. Manu 10.11.17; *Viṣṇu Purāṇa* 1.13.51-64.
70. S. Levi, *Le Theatre Indien,* Paris: 1890
71. F.B.J. Kuiper, *Varuna and Vidūṣaka,* North Holland Publishing Co., Amsterdam: 1979, 221.
72. D.D. Shulman, *The King and the Clown in South Indian Myth and Poetry,* Princeton University Press, New Jersey: 1985, 163.
73. M. Coulson, *Three Sanskrit Plays,* Penguin Books, Harmondsworth 1981, 32.
74. In the *kūṭiyāṭṭam* theatre of Kerala, the *vidūṣaka* translates the verses of the main characters into Malayalam, and this can take the form of social satire as well. G.K. Bhat, *The Vidūṣaka,* New Order Book Co., Ahmedabad: 1959, 79.

4. Popular and high culture as historical parallels

75. *Matsya Purāṇa* 49. 11-15.
76. *Padma Purāṇa, Uttara-khaṇḍa,* 3.1-6.
77. 9.20.7-32.
78. Book 6, Chapter 32. See also Chapters 28, 33, and 34 for passing references to Śakuntalā.

79. *Epigraphia Indica* XII, 320 ff; VI. 4 ff.
80. *Harṣacarita*, 259 ff.
81. Ingalls, *op.cit.*
82. D.K. Kanjilal, *A Reconstruction of the Abhijñāna-śākuntalam*, Sanskrit College, Calcutta: 1980.
83. S. Levi, *op.cit.*; A.B. Keith, *The Sanskrit Drama in its Origin, Development, Theory and Practice*, Oxford University Press, London: 1924. P.V. Kane, *History of Sanskrit Poetics*, Motilal Banarsidass, Delhi: 1987 (reprint). S.K. De, *History of Sanskrit Poetics*, K.L. Mukhopadhyaya, Calcutta: 1960. E. Gerow, *Indian Poetics*, O. Harasswitz, Wiesbaden: 1977.
84. A.K. Warder, *Indian Kāvya Literature*, Motilal Banarsidass, Delhi: 1989, 97.
85. L. Bansat-Boudon, *Poetique du Theatre Indien: Lectures du Nāṭyaśāstra*, EFEO, 169, Paris: 1992.
86. *Kālidāsasya sarvasvam Abhijñāna-śākuntalam*
    tatrāpi ca caturthonko yatra yāti śakuntalā
    Quoted by S. Knonow, *Das Indische Drama*, de Gruyter, Berlin: 1920.
    Kāvyeṣu nāṭakaramyam tatra ramyā śakuntalā
    tatrāpi ca caturtho'nkaḥ tatra ślokacatuṣṭayam
    Quoted by E. Gerow, "Plot, structure and development of *rasa* in the Śākuntalā" *JAOS*, 1979, 99.4.1. p.564.
87. E. Gerow, "Plot, Structure and the Development of Rasa in the Śakuntalā," *JAOS*, 1979, 99, 4, 559-72; 1980, 100, 3, 267-82.
88. J. Tilakasiri, "Kālidāsa's Poetic Art and Erotic Traits," *ABORI*, 1978, 58-59, 365-74; C. Sivaramamurti, "Sanskrit Literature and Art," *MASI*, No. 73.
89. R. Pischel, *Kālidāsa's Çakuntalā: The Bengali Recension with Critical Notes*, Kiel: 1877; *Kālidāsa's Çakuntala, An Ancient Hindu Drama*, HOS, Vol.16, Cambridge Mass.: 1922.
90. L. Bausat-Boudon, "Le Texte Accompli par la Scene: Observations Sur Les Versions de Śakuntalā", *Journal Asiatique*, 1994, 282, 281-333.
91. N.B. Godbole and K.B. Parab (eds.), *Abhijñana-śākuntalam*, with the commentary of Rāghavabhaṭṭa, Bombay: 1883.
92. K. Kunjuṇni Raja, "Kūṭiyāṭṭam: the staging of Sanskrit plays in the Traditional Kerala Theatre", *Sanskrit Ranga Annual* (Madras), 1959-60, II,17-52.; C.R. Jones, 'Source material for thè Construction of the *Nāṭya Maṇḍapa*, *JAOS*, 1973,93, 286-96.

5. Adaptations: another popular traditon and its role in another court

93. George Steiner, *Antigones*, Clarendon Press, Oxford: 1984.
94. *Ibid.*
95. Jatindra Bimal Chaudhuri, *Muslim Patronage to Sanskrit Learning*, University of Calcutta, Calcutta: 1942.
96. I am grateful to my colleague, Professor Muzaffar Alàm, who drew my attention to the existence of these versions and discussed them with me. The background to how the story came to be composed in Braj-*bhāṣā* is given in the introduction to the later Urdu translation.
97. I have used the printed version from the University of Allahabad Library but have not been able to trace the publisher.
98. C. Vaudville, *Bārahmāsa in Indian Literature*, Motilal Banarsidass, Delhi: 1986.
99. C. Vaudville, "A Note on the *Ghataparkara* and the *Mẹghadūta,*" JOI(B), 1959, 9, 2, 129-34.
100. *Ibid.*
101. S.M. Pandey, *Lorikayan*, Allahabad: 1987.
102. Some of these have been discussed in the Introduction to the text by the editor, Mohammad Aslam Qureishi, published as *Sakuntala*, Lahore: 1963.

6. Translations: Orientalism & German romanticism

103. G. Canon, *The Life and Mind of Oriental Jones*, Columbo University Press, Cambridge: 1977.
104. M. Abrams, *Natural Supernaturalism*, Cambridge University Press, New York: 1971, 87-88.
105. P. Morgan, "From a Death to a View: The Hunt for the Welsh Past in the Romantic Period", in E. Hobsbawm and T. Ranger (eds.), *The Invention of Tradition*, Cambridge University Press, Cambridge: 1996 (rep.).
106. S.N. Mukherjee, *Sir William Jones*, Oxford University Press, Delhi: 1987 (2 ed.), 105. This label encouraged a variety of comparisons in the late nineteenth century between Śakuntalā and the heroines of Shakespeare, such as Miranda and Desdemona.
107. Curiously, he wanted the royalties from the translation to be offered to insolvent debtors! D. M. Figueira, *Translating the Orient*, State University of New York, New York: 1991, p. 26.

108. G. Canon and S. Pandey, "Sir William Jones Revisited: On His Translation of the Śakuntala," *JAOS*, 1976, 96, 4, 528-37.
109. Act III, v. 5.
110. Canon and Pandey, *op.cit.*
111. Quoted in W. Liefer, *India and the Germans*, Shakuntala Publishing House, Bombay: 1977.
112. A. Leslie Willson, *A Mythical Image: The Ideal of India in German Romanticism*, Duke University Press, Durham: 1964.
113. *Ibid.* 69. Translation and quotation.
114. M. Schuyler, "The Editions and Translations of Śakuntalā," *JAOS*, 1901, 22, 237-48.
115. G. Steiner, *Antigones*, Oxford: 1984.
116. *Fragments*, VI. 100.
117. A. Leslie Willson, *op.cit.*
118. *Ibid.*, 49 ff.
119. *Werke*, XVI, 85-91. Quoted in J. Sedlar, *India in the Mind of Germany*, Washington: 1982, 26 ff.
120. Leslie Willson, *op.cit.* 221 ff.
121. *Ibid.* 199 ff.
122. *Ibid.* 148 ff.
123. H. Drew, *India and the Romantic Imagination*, Oxford University Press, Delhi: 1987.
124. Drew, op.cit. M.J. Franklin, *Sir William Jones*, University of Wales Press, Cardiff: 1995, 9.
125. *The Edinburgh Review*, July 1858, Article X, 253 ff.
126. R. Schwab, *The Oriental Renaissance: Europe's Rediscovery of India and the East, 1680-1880* (trans.), Columbo University Press, New York: 1984.
127. *India, What Can it Teach Us?* Longman, Green & Co., London: 1883, 101.
128. T.B. Hanson, "Inside the Romanticist Episteme", *Thesis Eleven*, 1997, 48, 21-41.
129. *Ibid.*
130. H. Kohn, *The Idea of Nationalism: A Study of its Origins and Background*, Collier-Macmillan, New York: 1967 (2nd ed.).
131. Schwab, *op.cit.*
132. L. Binyon and K.N. Dasgupta (eds. and trans.), *Sakuntala*, Macmillan, London: 1920.
133. Figueira, op.cit, 25 ff.

134. M. Praz, *The Romantic Agony*, Oxford University Press, London: 1933.

7. Translation: colonial views

135. *History of British India*, II.2.111.
136. G. Visvanathan, *Masks of Conquest*, Columbia University Press, New York: 1989, 121 ff.
137. *Ibid.*
138. *Ibid.* 5-6; 27 ff.
139. Monier-Williams, *Sakoontala*, Routledge and Sons, London: 1898, vi, vii, xv.
140. K. Hansen, "Stri Bhumika: Female Impersonators and Actresses on the Parsi Stage," *Economic and Political Weekly*, 29 August 1998, 2291-300.
141. *Asiatic Researches*, III.65; I.223-4; II. 58-63.
142. D.K. Kanjilal, *op.cit.*

8. Śakuntalā and middle-class nationalism

143. R. Thapar, *Interpreting Early India*, Oxford University Press, Delhi: 1992.
144. P. Chatterjee, "The Nationalist Resolution of the Women's Question," in Kumkum Sangari and Sudesh Vaid (eds.), *Recasting Women*, Kali for Women, New Delhi: 1993 (reprint) 233 ff.
145. P. Chatterjee, "Colonialism, Nationalism and Coloured Women: The Contest in India", *American Ethnologist*, 1989, 16, 4, 622-33.
146. K. Jayawardena, *The White Woman's Other Burden*, Routledge, London: 1995, 102-35.
147. A. Stoler, "Making Empire Respectable: the politics of race and sexual morality in twentieth century colonial cultures", *American Ethnologist*, 1989, 16, 4, 634-60.
148. Sujata Patel, "Construction and Reconstruction of Woman in Gandhi", *Economic and Political Weekly*, 20 February 1988.
149. G.N. Devy, *After Amnesia*, Orient Longman, Bombay: 1992, 27-28.
150. This is a reading suggested by Sujit Mukherjee.
151. The English translation of the essay was published in the *Modern Review*, 1911, IX, p.171 ff. and a further discussion entitled, "Kālidāsa the Moralist" in the same journal in 1913, XIV, 7-12, p. 347 ff. See also the interpretation of Tagore's views in

M. Krishnamachariar, *History of Classical Sanskrit Literature*, Motilal Banarsidass, Delhi: 1937, who reads Tagore as maintaining that infatuation leads to failure and that goodness is the final goal of love.

152. W. Radice, *op.cit.*; "Tagore and Kālidāsa", *South Asian Research*, 1996, 16,1,45-60.

153. Rabindranath Tagore, *Selected Poems*, Penguin Books India, Delhi: 1985, pp. 50,180 ff.

154. E. Thompson, *Rabindranath Tagore: His Life and Works*, Oxford: 1921, 118.

155. E. Thompson, *Rabindranath Tagore: Poet and Dramatist*, Oxford University Press, London: 1926.

156. *Ibid.* Introduction by H. Trivedi, Oxford University Press, Delhi: 1989.

157. Quoted in R.F. Foster, *W.B. Yeats—A Life*, Clarendon Press, Oxford: 1997, 469-73.

158. H. Drew, *op.cit.* 128 ff.

159. Foster, *op.cit.*

160. R.D. Karmakar, *Kalidasa*, Karnataka University Press, Dharwar: 1960, 159.

161. S. Ramachandra Rao, *The Heroines of the Plays of Kālidāsa*, Bangalore: 1951 (Transaction No. 7, The Indian Institute of Culture).

162. V. Dalmia, *The Nationalisation of Hindu Traditions*, Oxford University Press, Delhi: 1997.

163. M.R. Kale, *The Abhijñāna-śākuntalam of Kālidāsa*, Bombay: 1961. (9th.ed.) 47.

164. Akhtar Husain Raipuri, *Sakuntala-az-Kalidasa*, Delhi: 1953 (reprint).

9. Conclusion

165. R. Thapar, *Cultural Transaction and Early India*, Oxford University Press, Delhi: 1988.

166. Nachiket Patwardhan was kind enough to take the trouble of arranging for me to see these films at the National Film Archive at Pune. I was not able to see Bhupen Hazarika's film or the second film by Shantaram on the same subject which he called, *Stree*.